Telling Our Lives

feminist
constructions

Series Editors: Hilde Lindemann, Sara Ruddick, and Margaret Urban Walker

Feminist Constructions publishes accessible books that send feminist ethics in promising new directions. Feminist ethics has excelled at critique, identifying masculinist bias in social practice and in the moral theory that is used to justify that practice. The series continues the work of critique, but its emphasis falls on construction. Moving beyond critique, the series aims to build a positive body of theory that extends feminist moral understandings.

Beth, Linda, and Frida, DePaul University, Chicago, IL, December 2002

Telling Our Lives

Conversations on Solidarity and Difference

Frida Kerner Furman
Elizabeth A. Kelly
Linda Williamson Nelson

ROWMAN & LITTLEFIELD PUBLISHERS, INC.
Lanham • Boulder • New York • Toronto • Oxford

ROWMAN & LITTLEFIELD PUBLISHERS, INC.

Published in the United States of America
by Rowman & Littlefield Publishers, Inc.
A wholly owned subsidiary of The Rowman & Littlefield Publishing Group, Inc.
4501 Forbes Boulevard, Suite 200, Lanham, Maryland 20706
www.rowmanlittlefield.com

PO Box 317
Oxford
OX2 9RU, UK

Front cover (clockwise from top): Frida's Argentinean passport that brought her from
Latin America to the U.S. Linda at age fourteen. Beth and her father at 55th and
Jefferson, Philadelphia, PA, 1952.

Back cover (clockwise from right): Beth's mother, Maude Kelly, in the Women's Army
Corps. Linda's mother's Jamaican passport, 1902. Frida's grandma Ella (then Elka), age
14, Ukraine, with unidentified cousin.

British Library Cataloguing in Publication Information Available

Library of Congress Cataloging-in-Publication Data

Furman, Frida Kerner, 1948-
  Telling our lives : conversations on solidarity and difference / Frida Kerner Furman,
Linda Williamson Nelson, Elizabeth Kelly.
     p. cm. — (Feminist constructions)
  Includes bibliographical references and index.
  ISBN 0-7425-4173-8 (cloth : alk. paper) — ISBN 0-7425-4174-6 (pbk. : alk. paper)
  1. Furman, Frida Kerner, 1948- 2. Kelly, Elizabeth A. 1950- 3. Nelson, Linda Williamson,
1947- 4. Women's studies—United States—Biographical methods. 5. Women college
teachers—United States—Biography. 6. Working-class women—United States—
Biography. 7. Minority women—United States—Biography. I. Kelly, Elizabeth A. 1950-
II. Nelson, Linda Williamson, 1947- III. Title. IV. Series.

HQ1186.U6F87 2005
305.43'37812'092273—dc22   2004029788

Printed in the United States of America

♾™ The paper used in this publication meets the minimum requirements of American
National Standard for Information Sciences—Permanence of Paper for Printed Library
Materials, ANSI/NISO Z39.48-1992.

Anything is an autobiography but this was a conversation.

Gertrude Stein, *Everybody's Autobiography*

To all those who come before
To all those who follow

Contents

Acknowledgments

This book is a testimony to three women's commitment to friendship, collegiality, and solidarity across differences. We acknowledge with gratitude the significance this project has had for each of us and the opportunity it has given us to connect in deep and sustaining ways for the past seven years. We are most appreciative for the financial support we received from our home institutions that made this work possible. Frida and Beth thank the College of Liberal Arts and Sciences and the University Research Council at DePaul University for research grants and leaves. Frida is also grateful for funds received during the year she occupied the Wicklander Chair in Professional and Business Ethics, which facilitated her return trip to Chile. Linda thanks The Richard Stockton College of New Jersey for a Distinguished Faculty Fellowship Grant for the summer of 2004, supporting her completion of this project. We also want to acknowledge Lynne Lavelle's cheerful welcome to her summer home, which we rented in Sea Isle City, New Jersey.

Each of us has many others to thank.

Frida: Several years ago, Donna Maeda and Thandeka urged me to write about my complex hybrid identity. Unbeknownst to them, that conversation led to the inception of this project. Many people have provided me with helpful, even enthusiastic feedback on this work since then, including various audiences at DePaul University, the American Academy of Religion, and The Society of Christian Ethics. I am grateful to Roy Furman and to my special friends Rosellen Brown, Mechthild Hart, and Marvin Hoffman for reading and responding to sections of this work, and to my dear friend Chana Zelig for her generous proofreading of the complete manuscript. I also extend thanks to my sister, Gina Kerner, for feedback on early writing, and to my mother, Sara Kerner, and my brother, Leo Kerner, for their assistance in clarifying aspects of my childhood and family history and for their ongoing support. Close friends have nurtured me in special and heartfelt ways through the years of this project; I thank, especially, Shani Beth-Halachmy, Jim Block, Ruth Fuerst, Juanita Goergen, Teresia Hinga, Ginger Hofman, Martha Holstein, Adina Kleiman, Jill Roth, and Naomi Steinberg. I gratefully acknowledge my husband, Roy Furman, and my daughter, Daniella Furman, for their sustaining love. Last, but not least, I thank Havurat Lomdim for providing me with an embracing spiritual home.

Beth: I am grateful to the teachers and mentors who have inspired me to think and write about class and education over the past two decades; Bill Daly, of course, heads the list—and the rest of you know who you are. Thanks are due to Michael Forman, Sandra Jackson, and Meredith Weiss for reading and commenting extensively on portions of the text (even though I didn't always do as they suggested). Perle Besserman and Manfred Steger's generous reading of and enthusiastic support for early chapters made a big difference at a difficult time. I have relied on Kate Kane and Barbara and Henry Schaffer for stimulating conversation, laughter, and good fellowship across the years. Alex Papadopoulos has given many gifts, none greater than abiding friendship. As always, Vicki and Norm Ervine have a special place in my heart, as do Ken Zavoskey and Mike Wilensky, more recent additions to my family of choice. Herb Fischer's great good humor has been a treat on many occasions. I have relied on Brian D. Maj's friendship and technical expertise for the past three years and bless the day he entered my life. My nieces and nephew in New Jersey—Alexa, Kira, Emma, and Max—light the horizon of my heart, alongside my mother, Maude Kelly, and my "other mother," Ila T. Burman—in whose garage apartment in Ocean City, New Jersey, this book was born.

Linda: I begin with thanks to Susan Gal, who first showed me how to discern the subtleties of language and its relationship to human connections. Thanks to friends Jane Retter and Judy Matsunobu for sharing their remarkable linguistic insights over the years. I am grateful to Pamela K. Cross, Margie Barnes, and Ricky Epps-Kearney for friendship as well as enthusiastic responses to sections of the book. I also thank a number of supportive audiences who heard parts of the work in progress: Naomi Miller and the Women's Studies Faculty of Sussex County College of New Jersey, as well as Mimi Schwartz and the students in her Creative Non-Fiction course in Spring 2004. I am grateful to Yvonne Brooks, Sharon Cohen, Orease Cohen, Sonia Gonsalves, Wenda Massey, Barbara O'Garrow, Angelia Tutt, and all the Women of Winslow for their ongoing support. Special thanks to my sister-friend, Marilyn Mobley McKenzie, for generously sharing her creative vision, always encouraging mine, and reminding me of our larger mission. I offer recognition and gratitude to the memory of my mother, my father, and my eldest sister, Marie, whose presence in spirit encourages all that I do. I am grateful to my dear sister, Jean Williamson Oliver Davidson, for her steadfast encouragement. In addition Jean, my cousin, Daphne Godphrey Linton and my aunt, Evadne (Cissy) Godfrey, ensured the accuracy of our family history. I am grateful to my brother, George Williamson, and my sister, Raquiyah Sharrief, for staying the course; to the second generation, Jeannie, Caroline, Charlene, Kimberly, and Shani, who give me reasons to imagine more; and finally, to my son, Sean Randall Anthony, and my daughter, Robin Gair Nelson, thanks over and again for your wisdom, your patience, and your sustaining love.

We are *all* grateful to the DePaul Women's and Gender Studies Program support staff, who, over several years, have provided first-rate secretarial assistance. Peter Zachocki deserves special thanks for his exemplary work during the early stages of this project, especially for developing a data management system that worked. Whitney Pedian, Susan Gartner, and Karyn Haney all provided good humor and good help after Peter moved on. Over the past three years, Brian D. Maj's work as a research assistant has been, simply and unambiguously, beyond compare. His technical skills, attention to detail, penetrating comments and questions, and patient good humor have made our work easier in countless ways; he has gone far beyond looking up citations and checking references. We are especially grateful to Kathy Martin for her wonderful transcriptions over the many years that we "talked difference," as well as her invariably insightful comments on our conversations. We thank Eve DeVaro Fowler, Tessa Fallon, Stephen Driver, and other members of the Rowman & Littlefield staff for their good-humored support and assistance throughout the production of this book. Finally, we are most grateful to Sara Ruddick, Hilde Lindemann Nelson, and Margaret Urban Walker for their enthusiastic advocacy and support of our work.

Introduction

In the Beginning, There Were Stories

In the beginning, there were stories. Stories of escapes and ocean crossings, stories of deprivation and survival, of pain and laughter. These stories had lived in our consciousness for decades, told again and again through the years to establish the baselines of our lives. But the telling was different this time; there was more candor, greater emotion, and deeper interest in marking similarities and differences in the memories, the histories that transected our three lives. We allowed ourselves to be more vulnerable than ever before. There were tears as we told our tales, as we read and reread the transcripts afterward, trying to make sense of what shapes a particular life or a moment of commonality. On occasion, we experienced that zestful insight, the "Eureka!" moment, when one of us came to see some part of herself in a new light, reflected in another's narrative or interpretation. These were poignant moments, colored by a delicate mixture of warmth and sadness.

Over several years, we have sat around kitchen tables, sharing life narratives. As children or young adults from working-class families, we each knew uncertainty, alienation, and deprivation. As inheritors of different diasporic traditions, we have all stood on the shifting ground of social marginality. Even today, as college professors, we often struggle to sustain a sense of stability and safety, forever negotiating complicated relationships to mainstream, middle-class culture. Our life narratives represent very different, but no less shared, struggles to legitimize our experiences and mark points of articulation—if not, necessarily, agreement—along the divergent paths of three individual lives.

Our perspectives have been shaped by distinctive social locations. Frida Kerner Furman is a Jewish social ethicist whose family emigrated from Chile to the United States when she was a young teen. A professor at DePaul University in Chicago, Frida has been married to Roy Furman, a rabbi and uni-

1

versity lecturer, for twenty-nine years. They have one daughter, who, as of this writing, has just graduated from Vassar College. Elizabeth (Beth) Kelly is a feminist political theorist who grew up on Strategic Air Command bases at the height of the Cold War. Beth's cultural background is largely Irish and Roman Catholic, although she lapsed from the church in the early 1960s. She is a single lesbian who has never been interested in becoming a parent. Throughout much of the time we worked on this project, she served as director of the Women's Studies Program at DePaul University, where she teaches. Linda Williamson Nelson is an African American linguistic anthropologist with a background in writing pedagogy and literary studies. For twenty-four years, she was a writing professor in the General Studies program at Richard Stockton College in New Jersey, but is about to assume a professorship in the Anthropology program. Linda is a divorced mother of two adult children who have both sought careers in higher education. Spiritually, she identifies as "a Baptist who also takes part in Buddhist chanting." While we have a great deal in common—as feminist scholars, as women who have built careers in higher education while meeting complex family responsibilities, and as working-class intellectuals—our differences remain profound.

YOU'VE GOT TO WRITE THESE DOWN

Two strands of storytelling and friendship coalesce in this collaboration. Linda and Beth met in 1982 at Stockton College, where for a time they were colleagues before becoming Ph.D. students at Rutgers University—Beth in political science, Linda in anthropology. Across many years, of sharing trials, tribulations, or moments of sheer joy as "sister-friends," their friendship grew, as did their passion for narrative. Telling and analyzing their family histories and life experiences became a powerful tool by which they could mutually make sense of their changing lives and aspirations.

Beth and Frida met ten years later, shortly after Beth joined the faculty at DePaul University in 1992. They developed a friendship, which deepened when, a few years later, they traveled to Central and Eastern Europe with a group of DePaul colleagues. On long bus and train rides, in outdoor cafés in Prague, or in coffee bars in Budapest, the two shared some of the stories recounted in these pages—powerful tales, of Frida's grandmother carrying a dead baby in her arms as she approached the Russo-Chinese border or of Beth's growing up in the shadow of B-52 bombers, and poignant ones as well, such as Frida's father's struggle to earn a living by selling crucifixes to Mexican farm workers in California. Beth's response to Frida's stories was consistent: "You've got to write these down," she would urge. "You've just *got* to write these down."

All projects have some definite moment of genesis and this one is no exception. In October 1996, Frida attended a meeting of the American Academy of Religion's Committee on the Status of Women in the Profession in Atlanta, where the Committee on Racial and Ethnic Minorities was also meeting. One evening, members of both groups mixed over dinner, and Frida found herself sitting with two women, one African American, the other Asian American. It was one of those moments when relative strangers can be, as Frida put it, not only "present to one another at levels that are uncommon at academic conferences," but also deeply engaged around difficult and complex issues. Somehow the conversation turned to the question of family origins.

Frida shared stories of her family's history—a series of diasporic migrations from Europe through China, Chile, and California. Her audience, fascinated, pressed her to tell more tales of "moving outside safe spaces, moving into other realms." Over a couple of hours, with a few tears shed, a profound exchange took place, and Frida's dinner companions soon urged her to write, emphasizing the extraordinary nature of her saga and how they had been deeply moved by hearing it. When Frida returned to Chicago, she felt both "thrilled and terrified—thrilled by the affirmation and encouragement, and terrified at the thought of putting my life out there on my own." Over coffee in the DePaul cafeteria, Frida told Beth of her Atlanta encounter, explaining that she had been interested in beginning a project exploring issues of difference. Frida outlined two models for such a project: a traditional memoir that would likely open up old wounds and vulnerabilities, or a collection of essays solicited from colleagues, which seemed safer, but far less engaging.

Then Beth asked, "How about a third model?" She and Linda had been thinking about "doing something" with their stories; given their shared passion for storytelling, the notion of bringing Frida into a three-way collaboration was intriguing. With that simple question, this project was born. A series of excited phone conversations and several face-to-face meetings in New Jersey and Chicago would follow, as would a challenging and at times difficult process of mutual adjustments and engagements involving personal styles, work habits, and complex personal and professional commitments and demands. But in that moment and beyond, just as at that Atlanta restaurant where Frida joined in deep conversation with her dinner companions, a spirit of solidarity across differences both drew us together and impelled us toward this book.

As Frida said, turning toward Beth, "If I had not had you to talk to, and had you not given me this model, I don't know that I would have followed through, because it would have felt too scary to tell the kinds of stories I've been telling, and to publish this."

To which Linda rejoined, "Absolutely! I know that I'm not in this alone—you two are coming with me! That's the feeling, you know—we're not in it alone."

And so our work began.

BORDER CROSSINGS AND BOUNDARY
TRANSGRESSIONS: COMMONALITY AND DIFFERENCE

This book explores how three women find points of commonality and understanding through the process of sharing life narratives. We share a great deal:
we are women, scholars, and feminists, facing mid-life, and we are daughters
of diaspora and the working class. In other ways we differ greatly: two are
white, one African American; two are heterosexual, one lesbian. We have diverse religious backgrounds. Two were born in the United States; one is an
immigrant. Two are mothers of now-adult children; one has never parented.
Each of us has crossed many borders, transgressed multiple boundaries, in her
day. In chapter one, we explore how our family traditions have left us rich
legacies of boundary transgression. Our shared narratives represent a further
act of border crossing, for the co-constructed life narrative is a moment of
bearing witness, of validation and unspoken mutual affirmation that can
bridge apparent gulfs of ignorance or misunderstanding. When the three of us
sat down, poised to speak into each other's lives, we could not know what we
would learn about ourselves, individually or collectively. When one of us began to speak, her narrative often spun in unexpected ways, reflecting unanticipated encounters with her own lived experiences as well as her listeners'
engagement with the tale. At such moments, we were often able to understand
ourselves and each other in new and compelling ways.

Over time, we came to see our work as a political act, in which our coming together to co-construct narratives not only created knowledge (of ourselves and each other), but did so in ways that would not have been available
to us had we been working individually within the frameworks of our respective disciplines. We believe that this says something quite powerful about
the politics of knowledge creation within and outside of the university. On
one level, we were engaged in doing something that generations of women
have done—we sat together around the kitchen table and told our stories. But
we were also engaged in a very different sort of undertaking. We could not
forget that generations of women before us, especially within our own families, were neither trained nor encouraged to engage in scholarship or public,
critical analysis. Sadly, given today's global gender politics, the same may be
said for generations of women around the world—and for generations to
come. Thus, we cannot divorce this book from that long (and for too long devalued or dismissed) kitchen-table tradition without doing both ourselves and
that tradition a disservice. We acknowledge continuity with how women have
related to one another through the centuries; moreover, our work illuminates
the moral significance of what has all too often been dismissed as merely
"girl talk."

One of the thorniest ethical problems in the United States today is the reality of diversity. Enormous difficulties in dealing with diversity in productive ways have emerged at all levels of society, including business, the professions, and academia. At worst, the hard work entailed in coping with the challenges of a multicultural, multi-vocal, and multifaceted social reality devolves into endless debates over "political correctness," fueling ideologues on the Left and Right alike—debates that most often seem to go around in circles. At times, even the best intentions seem to drown under the din of univocal demands that attention be paid to claims of "difference"—as if this were all that mattered. We believe that there is much more to be said and done.

One thing that we found striking, as we dug into our work, is how so little of the diversity and experiences that we exemplify had been explored in any thorough-going or rigorous manner in any of the literatures with which each of us was conversant—despite the often vast differences between our various fields. There is a paucity of scholarship on working-class women in higher education: collections edited by Janet Zandy and by Michelle Tokarczyk and Elizabeth Fay offer notable exceptions. However, their contributors remain focused on individual narratives without engaging in dialogue across boundaries of difference. Despite the extensive literature on feminist theories of knowledge and women in higher education, there is little work that speaks to the problematics of shaping a full life as both "outsider within" the college or university and "juggler" of professional and family responsibilities.[1]

Critical analysis of our own life narratives serves, in the chapters that follow, to bridge some of these gaps. Indeed, each of us can look back to, and draw on, family histories that offer a rich tradition of diasporic border crossings and boundary transgressions. What makes this book unique is its grounding in collaboration and mutuality that take place *across*, not in spite or in ignorance of, difference. Up until now, the issues we address in these pages have largely been approached from the perspective of the individual. Our three voices are distinct, yet their interactions produce an integrated, analytic, and collective whole.

The late political philosopher Hannah Arendt recognized the importance of narratives as a locus of theory construction in *The Human Condition*, where she commented that "[e]ven though stories are the inevitable results of actions, it is not the actor but the storyteller who perceives and 'makes' the story."[2] Over the past decade or so, narrative forms have been appropriated by a number of non-literary disciplines as constituting an authentic, indeed necessary, starting point for understanding human experience. Each of us has utilized narrative in her own scholarship.[3] What we do, in these pages, is forward a vision of human commonality that neither erases nor elides difference. We draw on our life narratives to affirm the validity of subjective interpretation by resisting positivist, "value-free" theorizing. We touch on many themes: experiences of marginal-ization—racial, ethnic, religious, sexual, economic—all of which reflect key moments in our lives. In addition, we examine how those experiences have shaped our respective moral sensibilities and commitments to social justice and social transformation in the classroom and beyond. We challenge the pervasive silence regarding social class across much of the United States today, including the university. We also explore, separately and together, how fluid identities emerge as we construct our selves and how these become manifest in a variety of "border crossings," calling into question the assumptions of an identity pol-itics founded on essentialist ideas of some unchanging, unidimensionally de-fined "selfhood."

We do this as feminists. Throughout our adult lives, feminist theory has been a rich source of lively and ongoing debates over questions of position-ality (the notion that one experiences the world as, for example, "a working-class woman"), essentialism (the notion that one might speak or feel "as a woman"), and the use of life experience as a springboard to critical analysis of social problems. As scholars and educators who participate actively in our institutions' Women's Studies Programs, we have been engaged with these debates throughout our careers. For Linda, this has been even more the case within Stockton's African American Studies Program, to which she is deeply committed. As women who came of age at the moment when the Women's Liberation Movement was a vital and affirming presence in everyday life, we share a deep and abiding commitment to feminist values, ideals, and prac-tices. These ideals, along with those of the Black Liberation Movement, vital in Linda's development, have literally made us who we are today; none of us grew up with aspirations of independence, autonomy, professional and per-sonal self-actualization, or the concomitant critical authority it takes to inter-rogate social injustice and imagine positive change. Feminism has given each of us the model—and the courage—to grow into ourselves in ways that we could never have imagined. (For Linda, the Civil Rights Movement as well as her immersion in the study and practice of African American traditions ac-tually preceded her feminist sensibilities.) We share a common belief in what bell hooks has described as "feminist advocacy," focusing on "feminism as political commitment" that requires "an act of will" while leaving open the possibility of supporting other political movements as well.[4]

CLASS, COMMONALITY, AND DIFFERENCE: SOME OVERARCHING THEMES

We have done well in our professional journeys. All of us are tenured by re-spectable institutions; one is a full professor. Our work has been published in prestigious journals and in top-flight presses and been recognized with awards from independent scholarly or professional associations. We have all been recognized for excellence in teaching in our own institutions; we are respected in our departments and colleges and are active contributors to their accomplishments. We enjoy the friendship and collegiality of many of our peers. In spite of this, some deep-seated uneasiness remains. We have never been able to see ourselves as fully naturalized citizens of academia. Despite their claims to inclusivity, academic institutions—colleges, universities, professional associations—often reproduce, in subtle and overt ways, the unequal power dynamics of society at large. It can be difficult for working-class individuals, or ethnic minorities, to embrace the academic ethos and its social practices, or to be embraced by them. As we discuss throughout this book, while each of us continues to struggle with other markers of identity in addition to class, we converge most powerfully at the point of our working-class origins, and thus this problematic is a central theme of this book.

Many, if not most, in the United States today deny the realities of class; traditionally, educators have found the idea downright distasteful. This tendency was perhaps best expressed by Mortimer Adler, who flatly stated in his best-selling *The Paideia Proposal* that the United States is "politically a classless society. Our citizenry as a whole is our ruling class." He concluded that we "should, therefore, be an educationally classless society."[5] Today, America is far from being a classless society; Adler simply substitutes myth for fact. The myth of the United States as an egalitarian society relies on the simplistic notion that merely declaring "All Americans Are Equal" will actually make it so.

The weight of history, as well as current statistics on polarization of wealth and increased emmiseration of those at the bottom of the "social ladder," show how far the United States is from achieving an egalitarian social order.[6] Furthermore, the notion of upward mobility does not in itself deny the possibility of class hierarchy. An individual may grow up poor and end up as an entrepreneurial capitalist, but someone else will have to take her or his place as a domestic worker. Upward mobility only signals the absence of a rigid caste system; it does not denote the absence of class structures. As the gulf between rich and poor has widened in the United States, our educational system has become increasingly stratified along racial, ethnic, and economic lines. On the one hand, we have rhetoric linking public education with civic culture and political democracy; on the other, we have a set of economic and social practices that have increasingly militated against empowering the masses while privileging an elite few.[7]

The rhetoric of the "American dream," predicated on individual opportunities and social mobility, further obscures the existence of workers, poor people, and others who stand outside the middle-class mainstream.[8] Yet the notion of class denotes more than just economics or wage standards; it also has to do with the range of choices available in one's life, along with the deeply enculturated meanings that attach to those choices and profoundly shape our lives. Mary McKenny summarized this powerful connection succinctly: "[E]ducation and a good job don't turn a black person white and they don't negate a white working-class person's background."[9]

Concrete discussions of class are also largely absent from academic discourse. Many working-class academics are, as Linda Frost has pointed out, happily complicit in this silence. Frost is critical of how "many (if not most) of my academic colleagues and cohorts who come from a background somehow marginalized by academic culture may not articulate [the] dilemma of class division as a dilemma at all." She notes that such individuals are "more than happy to lose" their working-class identities, having "struggled valiantly to discard or minimize the presence of their backgrounds in their daily academic lives."[10] Thus, even in college and university settings, where clear, honest, and critical thinking is presumed to shape the production of new knowledge, the myth of classlessness prevails. Those few scholars who do focus on class all too often do so on a high level of abstraction, describing class "as a social system and a function of institutions," while paying, as Susan Raffo notes, "little attention . . . to its actual effect on individual lives and individual methods of survival and interpretation."[11] It is precisely such abstractions from and inattention to the real lives of individuals that we seek to overcome, not only in this book, but in who we are and how we "compose our lives" as scholars and educators.[12]

For example, during one of many conversations about social class, Linda demonstrated the continuing impact of her early experiences on her current life. Frida asked how the prestige of Linda's educational accomplishments had affected her sense of self. "Class has been primal for me," Linda replied. "I can name all kinds of marginalizations that have had to do with color and gender, but they don't have the same awful, awful pain for me as class. I lived with Black people and women who validated me, but we knew no one at our level of poverty." For Linda, there is always a residual fear of losing everything—the persistent vulnerability of the economically marginal. She added, "It's such a mixed bag, because in many ways I feel that my history of poverty has given me a sensitivity and an awareness and actually a compassion—without romanticizing it."

Beth also refuses to adopt a romantic attitude. She spoke of resenting the rhetoric, frequently attached to class and often celebrated, that "has a lot to do with 'plucky victim of class surmounts all obstacles and makes it.' Well, I am neither plucky nor a victim." Linda and Frida teased Beth at this juncture, claiming some people might very well call her "plucky." "No, *not* plucky," she argued. "Stubborn and tenacious, I will accept. As a working-class woman, I have always been defined by middle-class experience, ethics, and values. I don't want that. I want the right to claim my own experiences, my own values, on my own terms." Here Beth alluded to the middle-class tendency to assume that anyone lower on the class scale must unquestioningly wish to join the middle class and entirely abandon their former class position. Beth's loyalty to her class of origin informs one of her important professional commitments—her deep well of empathy for students who are outsiders to the academy.

It is precisely the unexamined middle-class assumptions and commitments of our academic peers, and of many students, that we challenge in this book. Beth can recall the example of an uncomfortable dinner conversation, where she had to cope with a colleague's insistence that she buy a condominium after receiving tenure. Beth expressed her anger at her colleague's social class blinders, but also her own humiliation and sense of insufficiency at not being able to meet middle-class expectations:

> There are times when I see colleagues who are about my age who have established homes, families, lives. We socialize together. Yet I'm embarrassed to invite people to my apartment. I'm not so embarrassed that I won't do it, but I often feel that people are judging me and finding me inadequate because I don't measure up, my home doesn't look like theirs. Afterward, for a couple days, I just feel so bloody incompetent; and all I want is a washing machine and some counter space and some privacy.[13]

Linda affirmed her understanding by responding, "I'm still often feeling that way. It always comes back to some failure on the part of the have-nots, which is why I can flash on your feeling of embarrassment."

Frida's current economic situation is beyond her wildest dreams, when examined from the perspectives of her childhood and adolescence. She and her husband own a home, travel, and are able to enjoy entertainment and dining out on a frequent basis, whereas her parents only managed to go to the movies once in a while. Yet, remembering her own upbringing as well as empathizing with the economic marginalization so many experience today, she feels uncomfortable with displays of consumerism or affluence, which remind her that economic injustice has symbolic as well as actual dimensions.

Frida bristled while telling of dining out with departmental colleagues. Each academic term, Religious Studies faculty would meet at a restaurant near DePaul. When the bill arrived, no matter what people had consumed (and some of her colleagues are enthusiastic drinkers), the bill would be split equally among those present. Frida explained, "I didn't start with an appetizer as the others did. I had one glass of wine; they kept ordering bottles. I had to leave early, I don't remember why—I think it was *Shabbat* (the Sabbath).

They went on to order dessert and coffee, but the bill was split evenly. I was stuck with a huge bill and felt really ripped off."

Linda responded angrily: "That makes me furious, it makes me freaking furious."

"And so I said something about it to the chair later," Frida continued. "'I think it would be a good idea if next time we split the bill according to what people consume,' and he replied that *I* should be the one to raise it with the faculty if it was of concern to me. I felt terribly embarrassed; I felt humiliated even having to raise it with *him*."

At that point, Frida was new to class analysis, so Beth and Linda offered some practical strategies for addressing such situations—things like requesting separate checks at the start of dinner, or giving the server one's credit card and asking that one's charges be placed on it directly. While such strategies might be effective, they leave the ethical dimension of inequity unattended. In the sort of situation Frida experienced, people often feel pressured to conform to unexamined practices that privilege style ("It's easier to do it this way") over substance (the unfairness of their choices). Middle-class conventions remain silently yet powerfully operative in the academic environments in which we live. Frida's immediate solution was simply to skip the next department dinner, but she was able to come up with a long-term remedy when she took over as department chair a few years later. She proposed that department get-togethers take place on campus, ensuring modest and equitable costs for all. Her recommendation was unanimously approved. This incident, along with its long-range solution, certainly suggests the possibility of change once people's consciousness has been raised.

The experiences recounted here lead us to a set of larger questions that are fundamental to this book. Whose problem is the sort of cultural blindness just described? Is an inability to see beyond middle-class conventions endemic to academics—or Americans? Should the responsibility for positive change, whether in- or outside the academy, always fall on those from working-class backgrounds? And, perhaps most importantly, how do we open up an honest discourse about class and other forms of marginalization? We do not pretend to offer definitive answers to these questions; neither can we forget them, for they have shaped our lives and our work, implicitly as well as explicitly.

We begin to address questions of class, location, and identity in chapter one, "Daughters of Diaspora: Negotiating Family and Cultural Heritage," by tracing our family histories and their diasporic legacies. Each of us has been shaped by very different traditions, expressed through "family stories," geographical locations and displacements, and childhood memories, as well as by scholarly accounts of historical, cultural, and social trajectories of given cultural groups. We pay particular attention to how these legacies have influenced our own development and also foreshadow themes to be developed in subsequent chapters. In chapter two, "A Friend of My Mind: Co-Construction and Cooperation in Extended Conversations," we offer a close analysis of how our experiences of border crossing are made manifest in our co-constructed narratives. Here, the reader is witness to the complex, yet concrete negotiations that literally bespoke our efforts to bridge some of the cultural divides that might otherwise separate us. We also discuss how culturally constructed cues, idioms, and intonational patterns both shape our individuality and speak to our ethnic and cultural diversity.

Chapter three, "The House that Words Built: Education and Dissidence," focuses on connections between social class and our educational experiences, from elementary school on. We were raised in working-class households, yet each of us, early on, developed the high literacy skills associated with middle-class experience and academic success. Our roads to college and graduate schools were rocky; as first-generation college students, none of us could draw on family models as we moved into the new and often alienating realm of higher education. This chapter investigates the ways in which our shared experiences of class and nontraditional educational trajectories has sensitized us to social injustice and influenced our commitments to feminism, social solidarity, and critical, transformative pedagogies.

In chapter four, "For Every Border, a Bridge: Identity, Hybridity, and Moral Selves," we turn to questions of identity construction. Positioned as we are across standard boundaries of identity, we have often experienced identity as a form of hybridity. We argue that identity is best conceptualized as fluid, not static, more contingent than essentialist, and more inclusive than exclusive. We examine the development of our moral characters in terms of empathy and compassion, moral orientations rooted in religious visions, our own experiences of marginalization, and the will to reach across difference. We explore the nascent relationships between identity construction and one's links to larger circles of community and commitment, arguing that these provide openings for reconfiguring identity in ways that realize humanity, reciprocity, and inclusivity.

Chapter five, "Work as Prayer: The Spiritual Dynamics of Professional Lives within and against the Academy," extends the notion of links between religion and the moral self developed in the previous chapter by exploring our current religious commitments and spiritual orientations and how these influence our approaches to teaching, the construction of knowledge, and our engagement in transformative education and social change. We examine some of our successes and failures in the classroom, as well as the challenges and potential of multicultural education, paying particular attention to how resisting the values of the middle-class mainstream may, at times, leave us feeling

spiritually erased. Ultimately, we argue that these experiences allow us to em-
pathize more thoroughly with similarly positioned students. We are also able,
at times, to raise the consciousness of those who lack an organic understanding of working-class experience and other forms of marginalization.

Chapter six, "Interwoven Lives, Cosmopolitan Visions," begins with some
personal reflections on the impact this project has had on our individual lives,
using them as a springboard from which we discuss and sum up what we have
learned, over the years, as we "talked difference." We offer some conclusions
regarding this process and suggest ways in which similar efforts could be utilized by others. We argue that even with the best intentions, the border crossing and bridge building efforts central to our overall discussion will not come
about without hard work involving patience, dedication, and empathetic listening that is both critical and self-critical. We see this as a necessary effort,
aimed at realizing a vision of feminist practice where human dignity and justice prevail and true solidarity becomes possible.

A WORD ABOUT METHODOLOGY

Each of us came to this book and approached the generation and analysis of
our narratives from the perspective of her respective discipline as well as the
various forms of interdisciplinary work with which we were familiar. Yet the
process of creating and shaping this book quickly showed us that it would entail a good bit of methodological innovation, because we wanted to move beyond mere reportage of conversation to an integrated, analytic treatment of
the thematic content of life narrative discourse. We began, in the summer of
1997, with a week of intensive conversation. Frida and Beth traveled to
Ocean City, New Jersey, meeting up with Linda in a summer cottage belonging to a friend of Beth's. In subsequent years, we rented the Sea Isle City
home of Linda's friend Lynne Lavelle. We tape-recorded most of our conversations, from our first gathering through the subsequent meetings that took
place at roughly six-month intervals between 1997 and 2003 in Chicago or at
the Jersey shore. The tapes, now over fifty in number, were transcribed, eventually comprising a data book of over six-hundred typescript pages.

Once our raw data were assembled, a process of coding began, in which
each of us assigned sections of our narrative texts to various categories designed to evoke a number of thematic associations (i.e., "class," "borders and
marginalities," "ethnicity," "family," "professional identity," and so on). The
categories were not mutually exclusive; thus, a segment of narrative might be
coded as falling under one, two, or several different categorical designations.
We then generated lists of those segments of the narrative falling into each

category. There was a great deal of overlap between and among categories; since our data are qualitative, this was not problematic.

Each of us took responsibility for the initial analysis and interpretation of the categories we found most interesting. Here, our various experiences within and beyond our respective disciplines came to the fore.

Frida looked to our narratives for what they might say about the construction of self and the moral life; she then turned an ethical lens on the material, in a manner similar to that employed in her earlier book, *Facing the Mirror: Older Women and Beauty Shop Culture*.[14] There, as here, she argues for the relevance of an "ethics of everyday life" that focuses on and values the sorts of life experiences that have traditionally been ignored by more mainstream scholars in her field.

Linda, as a linguistic anthropologist, was concerned with the continuity of our individual narratives as well as the intersection of our shared stories. She analyzed these stories as cultural performances that derived their coherence from a range of specific language strategies that marked both agreement and mutual support, in addition to divergent experiences and points of view, which were also indicated by linguistic strategies. Moreover, her training in literature was evident in the distinctly metaphoric nuance of her extended family stories along with some of her analysis.

Beth brought her training and experience in political theory to bear on analysis of the ways in which these shared and individual narratives might evoke and/or contest claims that "the personal is political." She also offered insights into contemporary debates over such issues as essentialism and the relationship between the "public" and "private" spheres, paying particular attention to how our discourse illuminates the problematics of globalized, abstract theoretical frameworks. She also drew on her previous work on the relationship between class, education, and democracy in analyzing how these issues have played out in our three lives.[15]

In the end, our process of studying data and shaping our chapters became something akin to ethnographic analysis. We realized that although we had not set out to do so, in some senses we were, indeed, constructing a kind of ethnography of an intentional community—our own—that evolved as we shared and analyzed our narratives.[16]

Examination of our life narratives inherently calls forth questions about the subjectivity of selective memories, revisionist histories, and biased reconstructions of knowledge. However, as the postmodern critique of positivism has clearly demonstrated, no investigations are ever value free, and no investigator can claim to be unbiased in shaping her conclusions.[17] As Joan E. Hartman puts it, "We construct ourselves as agents by piecing together our stories, by emplotting the events of our lives." She goes on to suggest that,

"As we make our narratives our own, we apprehend ourselves as agents: we become conscious of ourselves as makers of our lives as well as makers of narratives about our lives."[18] Camilla Stivers further extends the linkages between the personal and the political in arguing that, "Personal narrative models a way of knowing . . . by blending the subjective with the system-wide."[19] Indeed, it is in this very spirit that this book was conceived.

Allan Bérubé raises a cogent methodological caution by noting that "the danger in describing a working-class life from the inside is the temptation to frame one's narrative within a 'rhetoric of hardship'—a storytelling strategy that tries to mitigate class oppression by appealing to the sympathy and generosity of the more fortunate." Bérubé describes the seductive nature of these rhetorical strategies; when working-class lives are shaped into stories of courageous struggle against daunting odds, class hierarchies are merely reinforced, not challenged. By reducing working-class people to either victims or heroes, turning our lives into "satisfying dramas of suffering that end in inspiring victory or poignant tragedy," the rhetoric of hardship depoliticizes them.[20] In telling our stories, the three of us have struggled to define ourselves and claim our places in the world. As co-constructed knowledge, our narratives are not "merely" stories told for entertainment; rather, they locate us in the larger context of learning to read both the word and the world, as Paulo Freire put it.[21] Telling our lives is a political act.

The inductive nature of our work differs from traditional normative approaches to doing social ethics and social science. Further, in its sociolinguistic approach to narrative analysis, it differs from structural analyses of narrative discourse. However, in recent years new methodologies have been embraced in a variety of disciplines, including women's and gender studies, an area of scholarship that we all embrace. Our approach is novel, but it falls well within the scope of contemporary efforts to understand human experience in new and creative ways—efforts that cut across a variety of fields and disciplines.

While each of us initially proceeded from the perspective of our respective disciplines and within the parameters of our particular interests, we have worked to produce a text that is thoroughly integrated. We have all contributed substantially to both the theoretical framework and the narrative discussion of each chapter. We chose not to divide the labor of producing chapters among individual authors, nor did we opt for the perhaps easier route of simply rendering our narratives as reported conversation. All of these commitments served to make the process of producing this book more complex and at times more challenging than it might otherwise have been, as our three individual stories, lives, and work habits intertwined, diverged, and reconnected.

The stories that shape the chapters following this introduction were all generated by our ongoing conversations. At times, however, each of us clarified or amplified parts of particular stories in writing, after the fact, so that they would be understandable to readers who were not parties to our talks. Because our conversations were often marked by mutual interrupting, overriding, or otherwise fragmenting one another's narratives, particularly the longer ones, we deemed it appropriate to edit these segments. Throughout the book, such narratives will be presented in italics. Where quotes from an individual speaker appear without italicization, the text was taken verbatim from the transcripts of our conversations. When absolutely necessary, such text was lightly edited to render the transcription clearer to the reader.

EMBODYING THE POLITICS OF LOCATION

We had a lot of fun over the years we worked on this book. Our summer weeks in Ocean City or Sea Isle are as precious to us in memory as they were often demanding, indeed, at times grueling. While we often worked intensely for long hours, we still carved out time to play. Shopping expeditions—whether to Boscov's department store in Cardiff or the Gourmet Garage in Somers Point—were diversions, but they were also times when we could bond in different ways. Sometimes we laughed ourselves silly while trying on clothes, or turned the intensity that had earlier been expressed in probing talk and analysis to hunting down the perfect pair of sandals on the half-off racks. One sultry August twilight in Ocean City saw us leaping on the furniture, swatting madly at a sudden infestation of flies, and laughing till the tears flowed—a moment that does not fully survive its translation to text but will live forever in our memories. We surely needed to let off steam; our diversions served as a necessary release of the tensions that built during the long hours of shared talk, border crossings, and boundary transgressions. But there were deeper meanings and issues at stake. In a reflective moment toward the end of the project, Beth suggested that "where we go to play and what we do is very much in the kitchen table tradition, but it's also more than that. Sea Isle is a very working-class resort; that legacy is evident in the confluence of working-class Irish and Italian traditions. So, just as we embody this project, the project embodies the locale."

Linda chimed in: "Mirrors, right?" She continued, "There's also the fact that Ocean City and Sea Isle are family resorts—and our work is focused on the devalued domestic sphere. We're foregrounding the kind of work that's been ignored and denied its significance; there's a parallel here."

Frida extended that metaphor: "We could say that the book grew up in Sea Isle. I had never heard of Sea Isle, but this says something about my wanting to share in your lives: it's become important for me to come here. See, this says something about us. We're not doing this work at a sophisticated, fancy place like Martha's Vineyard or Hawaii!"

"We're articulating things that have been devalued by the larger culture," Beth asserted, rounding off the exchange. "For me, this is an example of complicating the situation. Nothing's going to be clear, simple, unitary, or linear; we can only speak in terms of these complexities if we want to get to the point of making the new kinds of meaning that we want to make."

NOTES

1. Michelle M. Tokarczyk and Elizabeth A. Fay, eds., *Working-Class Women in the Academy: Laborers in the Knowledge Factory* (Amherst: University of Massachusetts Press, 1993); Janet Zandy, *Calling Home: Working-Class Women's Writings: An Anthology* (New Brunswick, NJ: Rutgers University Press, 1990); and *Liberating Memory: Our Work and Our Working-Class Consciousness* (New Brunswick, NJ: Rutgers University Press, 1995).

2. Hannah Arendt, *The Human Condition* (Chicago: University of Chicago Press, 1958), 171.

3. By Frida Kerner Furman: "The Long Road Home: Migrant Experience and the Construction of the Self," in Miriam Ben-Yoseph and Mechthild Hart, eds., *Psychological, Political, and Cultural Meanings of Home* (Binghampton, NY: The Haworth Press, forthcoming); "There Are No Old Venuses: Older Women's Responses to Their Aging Bodies," in Margaret Urban Walker, ed., *Mother Time: Women, Aging, and Ethics* (New York: Rowman & Littlefield, 1999), 7–22; *Facing the Mirror: Older Women and Beauty Shop Culture* (New York: Routledge, 1997); *Beyond Yiddishkeit: The Struggle for Jewish Identity in a Reform Synagogue* (Albany: State University of New York Press, 1987; reprinted by University Press of America, Lanham: MD, 1994); "Women, Aging, and Ethics: Reflections on Bodily Experience," *The Annual of the Society of Christian Ethics* (1994), 229–54. By Elizabeth A. Kelly: "A House Made of Words: Class, Education, and Dissidence in Three Lives," in John Freeman-Moir and Alan Scott, eds., *Yesterday's Dreams: International and Critical Perspectives on Education and Social Class* (Canterbury, NZ: University of Canterbury Press, 2003), 248–80; "You Could Throw Them Away without Breaking Your Heart: My Life in Magazines," in Ann Russo and Sandra Jackson, eds., *Talking Back and Acting Out: Women Negotiating the Media across Culture* (New York: Peter Lang, 2002), 71-83; "In Goldilocks' Footsteps: Exploring the Discursive Construction of Gay Masculinity in Bear Magazines" (with Kate Kane), in Eric Rofes and Sara Miles, eds., *Opposite Sex: Lesbians and Gay Men Writing about Each Other's Sexuality* (New York: New York University Press, 1998), 66–98. By Linda Williamson Nelson: "A Co-constructed Narrative: Shared Memory, Recognition and the Reconstruction of Community in *Beloved*" (presented at The Second Biennial Conference of the Toni Morrison Society: Toni Mor-

rison and the Meanings of Home, Lorain, Ohio, September 28–October 1, 2000); "Begging the Questions and Switching Codes: Insider and Outsider Discourse of African American Women," in Lois Benjamin, ed., *Black Women in the Academy* (Gainesville: University of Florida Press, 1997), 124–33; "Hands in the Chit'lins': Notes on Native Anthropological Research among African American Women," in Gwendolyn Etter-Lewis and Michéle Foster, eds., *Unrelated Kin: Ethnic Identity and Gender in Women's Personal Narratives* (New York: Routledge, 1995), 183–99; and "Codeswitching in the Oral Life Narratives of African American Women: Challenges to Linguistic Hegemony," in special issue, *Boston University Journal of Education*, 172, no. 3 (1990), 142–55.

4. bell hooks, *Feminist Theory: From Margins to Center* (Boston: South End Press, 1984), 28.

5. Mortimer J. Adler, *The Paideia Proposal: An Educational Manifesto* (New York: Macmillan Publishing, 1982), 5.

6. Kevin Phillips, *Wealth and Democracy: A Political History of the American Rich* (New York: Broadway Books, 2002).

7. See Elizabeth A. Kelly, *Education, Democracy, & Public Knowledge* (Boulder, CO: Westview Press, 1995) for a fuller treatment of the issues summarized here, particularly 17–19. Also see Paul Willis, *Learning to Labor: How Working-Class Kids Get Working-Class Jobs* (New York: Columbia University Press, 1977); Peter W. Cookson, Jr., and Caroline Hodges Persell, *Preparing for Power: America's Elite Boarding Schools* (New York: Basic Books, 1985); Jeannie Oakes, *Keeping Track: How Schools Structure Inequality* (New Haven, CT: Yale University Press, 1985); Michael Apple, *Teachers and Texts: A Political Economy of Class and Gender Relations in Education* (London: Routledge and Kegan Paul, 1986); and Steven Brint and Jerome Karabel, *The Diverted Dream: Community Colleges and the Promise of Educational Opportunity in America, 1980–1985* (New York: Oxford University Press, 1989).

8. Barbara Ehrenreich, *Nickled & Dimed: On (Not) Getting by in America* (New York: Henry Holt and Company, 2001).

9. Mary McKenney, "Class Attitudes & Professionalism," in Quest Book Committee, eds., *Building Feminist Theory: Essays from Quest* (New York: Longman, 1981), 147.

10. Linda Frost, "'Somewhere in Particular': Generations, Feminism, Class Conflict, and the Terms of Academic Success," in Devoney Looser and E. Ann Kaplan, eds., *Generations: Academic Feminists in Dialogue* (Minneapolis: University of Minnesota Press, 1997), 231.

11. Susan Raffo, "Introduction," in Susan Raffo, ed., *Queerly Classed: Gay Men and Lesbians Write about Class* (Boston: South End Press, 1997), 3.

12. See Mary Catherine Bateson, *Composing a Life* (New York: Plume, 1990), 1–10, for an extended discussion of the metaphor borrowed here.

13. Since that conversation, Beth has purchased a condominium with these longed-for amenities (for an elaboration, see chapter six).

14. Furman, *Facing the Mirror*.

15. Kelly, *Education, Democracy, & Public Knowledge*.

16. For a groundbreaking ethnographic study of a single woman's life, see Ruth Behar, *Translated Woman: Crossing the Border with Esperanza's Story* (Boston: Beacon Press, 2003).

17. This is not to endorse the postmodern project in its entirety. For a discussion of the dangerous apoliticism of postmodernism, see Kelly, *Education, Democracy, & Public Knowledge*, 92–94; Stephen Eric Bronner, *Socialism Unbound* (New York: Routledge, 1990), 169–172; Jürgen Habermas, *The Philosophical Discourse of Modernity: Twelve Lectures*, trans. Frederick Lawrence (Cambridge, MA: The MIT Press, 1987); and Peter Dews, *Logics of Disintegration: Post-Structuralist Thought and the Claims of Critical Theory* (London: Verso, 1987).

18. Joan E. Hartman, "Telling Stories: The Construction of Women's Agency," in Joan E. Hartman and Ellen Messer-Davidow, eds., *(En)Gendering Knowledge: Feminists in Academe* (Knoxville: University of Tennessee Press, 1991), 12.

19. Camilla Stivers, "Reflections on the Role of Personal Narrative in Social Science," *Signs* 18, no. 2 (Winter 1993), 410, 424.

20. Allan Bérubé, "Intellectual Desire" in Raffo, *Queerly Classed*.

21. Paulo Freire, Donaldo P. Macedo, and Ann E. Berthoff, *Literacy: Reading the Word and the World* (Westport, CT: Bergin & Garvey, 1987).

Chapter One

Daughters of Diaspora: Negotiating Family and Cultural Heritage

All autobiographical work is selective, part of a continuous process of identity making, of inventing ourselves anew through time. Among the array of stories in our individual repertoires, there were a few that we simply *knew* as central to our identities; they shaped the conception of self that Linda named "the me of me." There was power and risk in the telling of our family histories. On reflection, we saw that these stories were significant; they shaped us early on, yet they also anticipate many of the issues and passions that color our current lives. Our family histories were all marked by uprootings, transience, and frequent insecurities; these dislocations still resonate. Beth, for instance, had moved more than seventy times by the age of fifty. Linda's childhood was marked by frequent relocations: "The family home was always in flux, always temporary . . . always going somewhere. . . .We stayed a few months, sometimes longer, but it wasn't until I was about twelve that we achieved a sense of home." Until she left her parents' home at age twenty-one, Frida had lived in only five places, but they were located across three countries, two continents, and two different languages. All these dislocations, in memory as in fact, have left scars, but they have also endowed us with the capacity for imaginative entry into, and engagement with, lives and worlds very different from our own.

As variously as our heritages have been shaped, we are all daughters of diaspora—Jewish, Irish, and African.[1] While each of these traditions has its own extended and complicated history, too vast to recount here, themes of exile and uprootedness colored our parents' and grandparents' lives; the complex legacies of these diasporas—both historical and familial—resonate deeply within each of us today. Avtar Brah has argued that "the concept of diaspora offers a critique of discourses of fixed origins, while taking account of a homing desire which is not the same thing as desire for a 'homeland.'"[2] She goes on to suggest that "Diasporas are clearly not the same as casual travel. Nor do they normally refer to temporary situations. Paradoxically, diasporic journeys are essentially about settling down, about putting roots 'elsewhere.'"[3] The search for a home, a place of belonging out of exile, is a profound theme running throughout the family stories that have fundamentally shaped each of us, so it is here that we begin.

LEAVING HOME, STRETCHING OUT ON FAITH

Linda's parents, Ivylinne Rose Godfrey, known as "Rose," from Mandeville, Jamaica, and George Gerald Foote Williamson, or "Jerry," from New Albany, Mississippi, both left home prematurely. At nineteen, Rose boarded a "large vessel" and headed for Toronto and a chance to see beyond her Caribbean island home and the one-room school house where she sat as a pupil and later as a pupil-teacher to a mixed-grade elementary class. Jerry ran for his life, twice. First, Linda noted, he left New Albany, Mississippi, and an abusive home. Linda spoke of how he would say, "Dis heah scar on my head," pointing to a faded discoloration centered in the middle of his bald spot. "They burnt me, they burnt me. Tha's why I lef an na'er went back. Ran away and na'er turnt round." Some years later, during World War One, he stole away from the army, absent without leave. There was no story to embellish this flight, only an unsettling reminder that surfaced the first time Linda printed her name in uneven, block letters. She remembered: "We were not "Williamsons" at all, but "Footes," for it was Jerry Foote who, with a borrowed name—Williamson—had constructed an identity that promised protection from the pain of family violence and the military's disdain for the colored soldier."

Ivylinne Rose worked for about fourteen years as a domestic in Toronto. Then she sailed again, this time to New York City, seeking medical attention for a painful ulcer, intending only a brief visit. She planned to return to Toronto and work toward the goal shared by most West Indian immigrants—the accumulation of enough money to return to Jamaica, buy property, and build a house. A year in the Bronx mushroomed to many. There she met Linda's father, when he stopped her on the street one day, offering to carry her stack of library books. Their uncommonly romantic encounter could not anticipate the lacerating poverty that awaited Rose and Jerry in the marriage that followed this chance meeting outside a South Bronx public library. It is said that attendant in each union of two people is at least the preceding generation of forebears, if not more distant ancestors. Two great divides of race and geography separated Linda's grandparents, whose children found each other at a chance meeting.

Linda mused:

Of my grandparents I need first to say we were never to meet them, but, of course, they were always present. At least my mother's mother and father were, if not my father's parents. In fact, since I have no memory of my nuclear family even talking about my father's father, I should begin there, with the unknown. Where was he? Was he ever in my father's life? If my father was born sometime in the last decade of the nineteenth century, then his father must have been born between eight and twelve years outside of slavery. This means that the legend of my great-grandfather, the runaway slave, could well be true. And undoubtedly the empty pages that make up the story of my paternal grandfather's life must be read in the context of enslavement and the systematic destruction of familial connections that marked the day. Moreover, if my father, George Gerald Foote, was a sharecropper, then what must have been the occupation of the father who came before him? I cannot help but imagine that the immeasurable weight of racial injustice could have, by sheer force of its enormity, moved my grandfather frequently, unwillingly, and unexpectedly away from his family.

The obvious silence is most curious now since I remember that it is a silence that no one ever interrogated, a silence that in retrospect we did not, even in our innocence, wish to break. About my paternal grandmother, we knew just a little more. She was named Arkalee and corresponded with my mother for a short while after she and my father were married. Of Arkalee, as with my unnamed and undescribed grandfather, I can form no mental picture; I have no sense of her as short, tall, rotund, or lean. I do not know if she was sassy, defiant, or demure. There was little said and less remembered of which one of us grandchildren took after Arkalee, physically or temperamentally. We had a grandmother, but all we knew was her name and this had to suffice, then as now.

On an island in the Caribbean, there was another world to which I belonged. Through the eyes of my mother I could see Jane Pollack Godfrey, my Grandma Janie, whose picture greets all who enter my home today. She is a brown-skinned woman, with a head full of thick, wavy white hair and a haughty air, standing tall in her garden. I stare at her picture, looking for clues, bits of information that did not get translated in the stories I heard of her. She was a stern disciplinarian who dared not spare the rod. Her insistence on corporal punishment, the bane of my mother's existence, proved, ironically, to be good fortune for me and my siblings. Because she received such harsh discipline, Mother vowed to never strike her children; consequently, with the exception of a few remonstratory gestures of negligible significance, I cannot recall ever being spanked.

Grandma Janie had two daughters, my aunt Marie and my mother, Ivylinne. She had four sons, Eustace, Cleveland, Errol, and Vincent. I grew up with Eustace and Cleveland as my extended family. Uncle Cleveland was like a second father; his generosity and love sustained us materially and emotionally, particularly since he and my Aunt Paula had no children of their own. Uncle Bertie, my mother's beloved baby brother, was constantly present through letters or pictures and on a visit to Jamaica I was able to stay at his home and visit the country store in the hills of Mandeville that bore his name.

I try to imagine what it must have been like for Janie Pollack Godfrey to have borne six children before the turn of the century. She and my grandfather were a "colored" and white; the significance of that fact in Jamaica of a century ago was remarkably different from how we regard such unions today in Jamaica or in America. Jamaica's peculiar history of racial mixing—Arawak and Carib Indians, Africans, Chinese, Spanish, and British—made for an inherently hybrid island culture. They were small-scale farmers, who grew coffee, breadfruit, mangoes, cassava, and other root crops and fruit trees while they raised cows, chickens, and goats. I do not know what kind of resources my grandfather's family brought with them from England. His privilege in this British colony surely brought with it access to cheap labor and land, the remnants of which still remain. When I visited in 1971, I stood on the hill in Mandeville, looking down toward the coast from Uncle Bertie and Aunt Cissy's yard. A great sign stood in what seemed like a vast expanse of undeveloped land: "Godfrey Lands," the sign proclaimed—my mother's name; I had proof of a legacy of agrarian means and industry that structured mother's stories of a deep, rich family history.

Few stories were told of Grandfather Bean Godfrey, and not many more of his wife, Janie Pollack Godfrey, who, as some maintained, emigrated from Colombia to Jamaica. Of the untold stories, I cannot determine whether they were omitted because of insufficient information or because of the weight of my mother's loss in leaving home never to return. I don't suspect heavy secrets or even sorrows, save for the enduring pain my mother owned for having left her beloved Island home at the age of nineteen. In the cosmologies of many cultures, among them the West African, the individual must be buried in her homeland to go peacefully into the spirit world. I can only hope that my mother, Ivylinne Rose Godfrey, has made the journey home to Jamaica in death, as she could not do in life.

At the end of my visit to Jamaica in 1971, Uncle Bertie and Aunt Cissy took me to my grandparents' graveyard. I stood in awe at the foot of the gravestones, lying horizontally over their resting places. I strained to read the names and quietly feel my connection to the spirits that lingered there. I steadied my flash camera, which had served me well through four rolls of film. I focused carefully and I snapped; in that instant, a crisp, loud pop startled everyone as the flash bulb blew and fragments burst in the air. Auntie Cissy jumped back, threw up her hands in a peculiar mixture of fear and delight and exclaimed in patois, "Lawd Gawd 'a mercy, Granma Janie say, 'picnee Ivy dawta come ta greet me!'" In the absence of my mother, whom Aunt Cissy called "Ivy," the pickanniny's daughter, Linda, had, indeed, come home to greet her forebears; I thanked them for bidding me welcome.

It almost goes without saying that Linda's hybrid family legacy was socially, politically, and economically complicated by race—on her father's side, by the inheritances of slavery and apartheid in the post-Reconstruction

Mississippi Delta, and on her mother's, by the complex colonial and post-colonial traditions of Jamaica. These dual traditions would coalesce in New York City in the 1930s. Jerry and Rose came together in a time and place where, for all New York's progressive liberalism, race remained deeply implicated in daily life, when questions of social justice and social change along racial lines were barely being asked. The varied—yet "always already" racialized—strands of culture, language, politics, and tradition that are Linda's inheritance shaped *her* generation in very particular ways. As Linda put it:

> *I have said this more than once. I believe that my comfort and even curious delight with this perhaps unusual cultural exposure comes from my good fortune in having genetic attributes that land me squarely in the circle of the African American community. In contrast, those of my kin who have skin color and hair texture that mark them ambiguously, who have the white middle-class-sounding voice, without the clear vernacular markers, have not fared as well as I. In the absence of obvious physical markers, language can be one's passbook of membership. Without either, the African American is called upon eternally to reckon her kinship line, to be subject to interrogation, to prove that she belongs.*
>
> *The pain of this alienation is only intensified when the other world holds you suspect on different grounds, their perception of your sense of unwarranted entitlement based on skin color. If there is any larger gain to be had from this dubious melding of cultures in one family, it is the advantage to the development of our humanism that comes with the experience of growing up in a family where along the lines of extended kinship there were others who looked different from you, who sounded different from you, whom you knew to be kin, family, even when they shunned you. Such an experience allowed us on some level to imagine our unavoidable human connectedness.*

ACROSS OCEANS INTO THE GREAT UNKNOWN

One of the most salient metaphors of difference, change, and adaptation is the image of water crossings. It is fitting, as well, that water universally symbolizes life; in each of the many ocean crossings told in our family histories, survival would hang in a precarious balance of struggle against the unknown and unbidden, a common diasporic situation. No story speaks more plaintively of human fragility or strength than Frida's family saga. "My whole life is colored by this story; it announces my own concerns with difference," Frida asserted as she recounted her maternal grandparents' journeys across frontiers, continents, and languages from youth to old age. Born and raised in a *shtetl* (a small Jewish town found in Eastern Europe) near Kiev, Ukraine, Elka and Abrum Karlinsky were forced to escape during the turmoil of the Russian Revolution, when both White and Red Russians mounted pogroms against the

Jewish population. Along with other Jews, they boarded a Trans-Siberian train
that eventually took them into the Chinese city of Harbin, where Frida's
mother, Sara, was born some time later. But the crossing into China was traumatic for the young couple in more than one way. Besides the sudden separation from family the departure entailed (they would never see their families
again), Elka carried Reuben, her newborn baby, anticipating the crossing of
national frontiers as the child crossed from life to death. Elka's milk supply
had dried up in the absence of food and water; the baby starved to death, cra-
dled by his mother for several days until a proper burial place could be found.[4]

The family soon moved to Shanghai, where another child, Leah ("Lily"),
was born in 1925. By the late 1920s, Abrum grew desperate; unable to find
work as a tailor in the worldwide Great Depression, he earned a living any
way he could. Sara remembers her father making soap at home that he tried
to sell, mostly unsuccessfully, on street corners in the bitter winter. When
their situation became unbearable, Abrum left for six years, seeking work
wherever he could find it; the journey took him to the Philippines, Argentina,
Uruguay, and Peru, finally landing him in Chile. When the family was reunited in 1935, Sara was thirteen years old, Lily ten. Sara remembers embracing a father she barely remembered as their ship docked in the port of
Valparaíso, Chile, that long and skinny country seemingly at the end of the
world. Abrum was a complete stranger to Lily. That separation from their father was never fully bridged; although the family was permanently reunited,
Abrum would always remain rather distant to his daughters.

"My grandmother was a small, round woman, but she had huge muscles in
her arms, even as an old woman," Frida recalled, emphatically sketching a
large, imaginary arc around her own slender arm. On their own in Shanghai,
Elka and her daughters had been desperately poor; she worked, variously, as
seamstress, cook, or housecleaner in other people's homes. Frida remembers
her grandmother saying she developed her muscles while working as a ferry-
woman, rowing folks across a river. Sara believes that drawing water from
wells and carrying the water in buckets formed Elka's muscles. No matter
which memory is correct, in that day, such muscles in a woman were surely
the province of the working class. The current preoccupation with body building has always appeared to Frida to reveal a narcissistic cultural turn, reflective of affluence and blindness to the ways that the body is often sculpted by
necessity rather than by choice. Class issues thus begin early in this narrative,
in ways that run deeper than the surface of the family's poverty, itself quite
memorable. Sara remembers that though they had little to wear and lived in
tiny quarters, everything was always immaculately clean. Elka made magic in
the kitchen, turning delicious meals seemingly out of nothing, a memory
heard often enough in other stories told by Jews about their *bubbes'* (grand-

mothers') prodigious ability to make meals happen, even in the direst of circumstances. The family never went hungry.

Yiddish was the language of home, though Elka and Abrum had also spoken Russian in their early years in China. They used English publicly in China, since Shanghai was a British protectorate. Now transported to Latin America, the family had to learn Spanish as well. In Chile, Elka became Ela; Abrum became Abram. Their border crossings transcended geography, as names, languages, and identities transliterated and transformed. Sara was thirteen when she learned Spanish, the same age Frida would be when she struggled to conquer English after her nuclear family emigrated to California; today, Sara's English is inflected by the British accents of her Shanghai childhood, just as Frida's is by the soft inheritance of Chilean Spanish.

Frida's parents met as youngsters in the Jewish community of Valparaíso. Julio, who would become Sara's husband, was also an immigrant, but barely. He was a year old when his parents moved from Argentina to Chile; the family's peregrinations, however, had brought them from much farther. Ana and Arón Kerner had been born in Rumania in the last decade of the nineteenth century; each of their families moved to Mannheim, Germany, where the two would eventually meet as young adults. Sensing trouble, Arón decided to leave Germany for South America after serving in the German army during World War One.[5] He settled in La Plata and was soon joined by Ana; they married and Julio was born in 1922. German was the main language spoken in the Kerner household as Julio was growing up; his parents spoke a heavily accented Spanish. Frida remembers with loving amusement her grandmother's tendency to mix together her various languages much later in their lives, in North America, when Frida was an adult and Ana an old lady: German and Yiddish intermingled with Spanish and a bit of English to boot, emblematic of the intermixing of cultures and countries the family had experienced across the generations.

Frida's parents were married in 1944, a testament to Julio's perseverance in the face of opposition: first from Sara, who liked him well enough as a friend but needed to be won over by his charm and solicitude; then from his own parents, who wished him to move up in the world by marrying "well." Sara's father was a tailor, and her mother a seamstress; the family's financial straits had forced Sara to leave school at age fifteen and enter the workforce as a stenographer. Julio had been pressured by his parents to leave high school in order to dedicate his youthful energies to the family business. Julio and Sara would regret their foreshortened formal educations for the rest of their lives.

There is a word in Hebrew—*galut,* or exile—that Jews have used to refer to their dispersion from the land of Israel following the destruction of the

Temple in Jerusalem in 70 C.E. On the one hand, this exile suggests the diasporic condition of the Jews for all these centuries until the establishment of the State of Israel in 1948. In this regard, the exilic condition refers to the political, national, and territorial disenfranchisement of the Jews and the suffering and many hardships endured during this long period of collective vulnerability. *Galut* enjoys a more spiritualized meaning as well, however. It refers to the separation and sometimes alienation experienced by the Jewish people from God, or to the separation between God, the transcendent being, and the *Shechinah*, God's in-dwelling presence, under conditions of exile from Zion.

"I sometimes wonder," Frida asked one chilly December evening, "if my life, and that of my family, has been part of the master *galut*, that great metaphor of not-at-homeness, or passing through, of being disconnected from that primal center of security we humans seem to crave so much." Later, she reflected further on this:

> *Undoubtedly, my predecessors experienced this galut more keenly than myself. After all, my mother's parents moved from Ukraine to China to Chile to the U.S. (where they became Ella and Abraham)—not counting my grandfather's six years in the wilderness. My paternal grandparents are a close match: from Rumania to Germany to Argentina to Chile, and, in the case of Grandma Ana, to the U.S. as well. My mother went from China to Chile to the U.S., and my father from Argentina to Chile to the U.S. Actually, there is a year in Argentina prior to the U.S., but that story's time is not yet upon us. I moved internally within Chile—from Valparaíso to Santiago—at age eight, then at twelve to Argentina, and at thirteen to the U.S. Seems simple by comparison. That has been my galut, along with the experience—more muted and more episodic—of living as a Jew among those who don't know me, see me, or care to understand me by virtue of my Jewishness. Given education and other privileges, I have had tremendous opportunities in my life to seek and find heim (home). What pieces of identity, along with words, songs, landscapes, sensibilities, faces, names, friends, and other loved ones were lost by those who came before me? And what does it mean to be a survivor of these sorts of crossings? What responsibilities accrue to those like myself who have made the journey?*

This is a question to which we will return, repeatedly, throughout this book; it marks the very purpose we have taken from our shared family stories of diasporic experience. Out of legacies of dislocation, exclusion, and alienation, we have managed to draw not bitterness but strength, not selfishness but a sense of responsibility to others. Our shared sense of that responsibility does not elide our differences; on the contrary, it is drawn, variously and uniquely, from them.

FLOATING SIGNIFIERS, FLUIDITY, AND DENIAL:
BETH'S FAMILY LEGACY

Ethel Curley, Beth's maternal grandmother, worked in Philadelphia as a chambermaid for the Bromley family, who owned the Quaker Lace factory that churned out tablecloths and curtains for middle class homes as the twentieth century turned. Her parents had emigrated from Ireland to Newcastle-on-Tyne in the north of England, in the years when vast numbers of Irish fled famine, disease, poverty, and the iron hand of British colonial rule. They lacked the resources to make the longer and more dangerous journey across the Atlantic to North America; crossing the Irish Sea was all they could manage. Ethel's father, Jonathan, had found work in the collieries—hard, dirty, dangerous labor; her mother, Catherine Burn Curley, had borne seven children who lived past infancy (three others died). Catherine died when Ethel was twelve. At not quite sixteen, in 1906, Ethel had saved enough money from domestic service to emigrate to the States, joining two older sisters, Addie and Lizzie, who had earlier made the same journey.

In Philadelphia, just as in Newcastle, to be Irish was nearly on par with being Black. Indeed, in the United States, Irish immigrants had only recently (and unevenly) begun to "become white."[6] Ethel Curley sailed to the States in steerage, but on a British passport; her accent—no brogue, but an odd regional blend of British, Scottish, and Scandinavian heritage—identified her as a "Geordie," a Newcastle native.[7] In Philadelphia, she worked to reinvent herself as "English"; to the end of her days she would deny that she was Irish, just as she would erect sophisticated walls of denial about the other things that shamed her, such as not knowing how to read or write.[8]

Ethel, the "nice English girl," caught the eye of Jules Hatman, a handsome young trolley motorman, at Willow Grove Park, where the two sat on the lawn, enjoying a John Phillips Sousa concert. Jules hailed originally from Liverpool, England, where his parents had been shopkeepers; as a young teen, he had been sent to school in Germany to learn the confectioner's trade. He quickly went on the lam, running away to his first great love, the sea; this may have been when he changed his first name from "Julius" to "Jules." He had served as a cabin boy on the last of the great sailing ships, traveling around the world and ending up in Philadelphia, whose greenery and gentility reminded him of England—his other enduring passion. His children and grandchildren would tease him mercilessly about being "more English than the queen" in later years—yet he never seemed to think about returning to the England he loved so much, not even for a visit. He would pass through there after enlisting in the Canadian Horse Cavalry in 1914, unable to bear the thought of the Great War taking place without him. But besides this expansively romantic (and, given the carnage he must have somehow survived, courageous) moment, England and all things English would remain more potent as fantasy than fact until his death in 1957.[9]

Perhaps it was because his fantasies of England, and of "nice English girls" like Ethel—or, ten years later, the "nice English boy," Albert Illingsworth, who would come to dinner in 1922 and stay on within the family as a fictive "Uncle" for five decades—could better be realized in Philadelphia than in Liverpool that Jules Hatman stayed put. When he died in 1957, the family would learn that this paragon of late Victorian English propriety—the man whose favorite breakfast was leftover Yorkshire pudding, warmed up and drizzled with Lyle's Golden Syrup—was mostly a fiction.[10] His parents had been Jewish exiles from Minsk, hardly native Liverpudlians; indeed, Jules had been born in Russia. The very name Hatman was itself a fiction—a translation or transliteration, perhaps.[11] No one would ever know for sure—a detail lost in diaspora. Just as Ethel would deny her Irish roots, so Jules would deny his heritage—after all, both reasoned, "What's in a name?" Long before anyone would speak of "floating signifiers," Ethel and Jules embodied the concept.

What did it cost Ethel and Jules to cross the sea in separate efforts to build new lives in an unknown world? What further costs would ensue as they negotiated their marriage, became parents, and struggled to maintain a "respectable" working-class existence? In 1920, Beth's mother, Maude, would be born—along with hints that she was not Ethel's natural daughter—the middle child, with older and younger brothers. The family knew hard times; Jules was often unemployed during the 1920s, even before the upheavals of the Great Depression, and would not find sustained steady work until 1938 when he began working as a ship fitter at the Philadelphia Navy Yard. The family would move many times, from one working-class neighborhood to another, ultimately settling in a row house at 55th and Jefferson in West Philadelphia. "Uncle" Albie became a household fixture, along with other blood kin—widowed sisters and orphaned nieces and nephews. The details are sketchy; this is a tale Beth's mother does not wish to tell. There are long gaps and long silences—the silences of survival. Hard lives in hard times; the less said, the better.

Maude's adult experiences replicated the pattern of voluntary exile established by her immigrant parents and grandparents. In 1942, she enlisted in the Women's Army Corps—over the strong objections of her parents and older brother, who held the then-common belief that women in the military would be "nothing more than streetwalkers."[12] She'd had a role model of sorts—her aunt, Ethel's older sister, Addie, who had trained as a nurse at Saint Timothy's Hospital in Philadelphia and served in France as one of a contingent of Red Cross nurses attached to the Allied Expeditionary Forces in World War One (also disregarding family objections). In the process of defying her parents' wishes and transgressing the boundaries of propriety, Maude went further than anyone—even she—might have thought possible. She eventually lived with Beth's father for over a year before the two married in San Francisco in 1946.[13]

William Laurence Kelly was the same age as Maude, but he was born and raised in Sterling, a small town set amid black earth farms whose soy- and cornfields stretch on forever in northern Illinois. All of his grandparents had left New England in the wake of the Civil War, seeking a better life in what was then "the West." Grandfather Kelly was born in Bennington, Vermont, of a family long established (though Irish and Catholic) in the States. The Kelly family roots, it was said, predated the Revolutionary War. Laurence ("Larry") Kelly, a young farmer, married Helen Foulds, dairymaid, as the first decade of the twentieth century drew to a close. Their wedding photograph survives; both Larry and Helen look frightened, awkward, and embarrassed in unaccustomed finery. Helen wears a headpiece of ribbons, low on her forehead and tied in huge bows over her ears, with a veil hanging limply in back. Larry sports a too-tight, obviously new, suit. Helen had to convert to Roman Catholicism to marry; she retained a convert's zealotry of faith to the death. Just as Jules Hatman had been more English than the queen, so Helen Kelly became more Catholic than the pope. Her children went to parochial school; Bill and his twin sister Betty were the only ones to graduate from high school—just as Maude was the sole member of her family to do so, in 1938. By this time, Larry had lost his farm to the Depression; the Kelly family moved to town, and moved fairly often once there, from one flat or small frame house to another. Eventually, in the late 1930s, Larry would find steady work as a foreman at the Northwestern Iron and Steel Mill. Bill also worked there after high school, in the chrome-plating tanks, before enlisting in the army in 1939 to escape his dangerous, dead-end job.[14]

War clouds were gathering in Europe, but Pearl Harbor was still in the future. Out of a romantic dream of flying, Bill found his way into the newly formed Army Air Corps, but washed out of flight school at least twice, perhaps because he had already developed the alcoholism that marked his later life. He served throughout the Pacific in World War Two, as part of a team of air corps men assigned to "island hop" with the navy and marines, setting up temporary airstrips on each island as U.S. forces advanced ever closer to Japan. In a grotesque miscalculation, he was sent ashore without a rifle during the second wave of the Marine landing at Iwo Jima, an experience that left him with demons he would attempt to drown in bourbon and vodka for the rest of his days. He never spoke of what he had seen on "Iwo" and the other islands. He didn't need to. His one souvenir of the war was an album of photographs of bombed-out pillboxes and rows of cemetery markers.

Maude, stationed at the Presidio in San Francisco, processed Bill's reembarkation papers when he returned from the South Pacific. She left the service shortly after they met; Bill reenlisted. After marrying in a brief, civil ceremony, the couple moved to Torrington, Connecticut, where Bill ran an Air Force recruiting station. When his enlistment ended in 1948, they moved to Sterling, where he landed a white-collar job as regional sales manager at the steel mill. For Maude, this was a particularly difficult relocation; as an Easterner and an Episcopalian, she was unwelcome in the bosom of the resolutely Irish-Catholic Kelly family, who did not see their son's marriage as legitimate. When Maude became pregnant, Bill's older brother, Ned, started dropping by for breakfast after his shift at the mill ended. Once Bill had left for his office, Ned would proselytize Maude to convert to Catholicism so that when the baby arrived, it wouldn't grow up "a bastard." Maude refused to consider converting; the tensions on both sides escalated.

Maude saw Larry, Bill's father, as her only ally within the extended family, but Larry died of a massive heart attack shortly after Beth was born in 1950. Frustrated with her anticlerical, areligious husband for not standing up to his mother and brother, feeling alienated and alone, Maude left her marriage and Sterling, boarding a train for Philadelphia with her baby daughter. Bill's response was to volunteer for recall into the military. The Korean War had begun, so he was welcomed back into the air force. For the next five years, he volunteered for duty at stations like Baffin Island, where dependents could not follow. Although the details of Maude and Bill's marital dislocation remain a deep secret, there must have been some moments of reconciliation. Beth and her mother lived in the row house with Ethel, Jules, Uncle Albie, and a movable feast of uncles, aunts, and cousins, but Bill joined them while on leave, and Beth's brother was born in 1953. However, parents and children would not experience life as a normative nuclear family until 1956, when Bill was posted to a newly built Nike missile base in Missouri, and, this time, his wife and children followed.

THROUGH THE LABYRINTH TOWARD HOME

It would be inaccurate to claim that we emerged from identical socioeconomic locations; indeed, our childhoods followed distinctive paths marked not only by how our parents made their living, but also by conditions dictated by race, nationality, and educational opportunities. However, our families were all positioned outside the middle class, and thus outside the mainstream of cultural attitudes and common knowledge; this imbued each of us with a

kind of "local knowledge," which at many points furthered a poignant identification with one another's experiences. Richard N. Coe argues, persuasively, that narratives of childhood are based on snapshot memories of particular events or experiences, which are then developed and re-created to fit
into a continuous narrative in the full-fledged autobiography.[15] We deploy this
photographic metaphor in sharing particular moments, persons, or events that
have had a lasting and central place in the making of our lives—in recalling and
sharing our childhood memories.

Linda remembered that there was almost no place where she felt safe belonging. The family was always on the move. Perhaps this was due to the circumstances of their occupancy—never as rent-paying tenants, always as the
building's "supers." In those days, superintendents and their families received living space in New York tenements as their primary compensation
for maintaining the buildings. The family's so-called apartments were never
more than sets of subterranean rooms, adjacent to the coal bin and the furnace, which once a week yielded heavy cans of ashes. The ash cans had
somehow to be hoisted up the concrete stairs to the street. Linda recalled her
father, who was by then nearly sixty, struggling to roll them upstairs before
the sanitation truck's weekly arrival. She drew a clear connection between
the challenges of this work, the frequent likelihood of error, the resulting dis-
satisfaction with her father's job performance, and her family's frequent
moves. She described how,

> At a later time, when we prepared to move to an apartment in the New York
> City housing projects, my mother and father and older siblings spoke excitedly
> about being *tenants*. However, from the limited vantage point of my eleven
> years, I cried at the prospect of being "tenants," for *tenants* were the bad guys,
> aligned with the landlords, who made unreasonable demands on my father and
> mother and were never satisfied with the heat, the cleanliness of the hallways,
> or the repairs.

The family's living conditions reflected the boundaries of class hierarchy
in the starkest of terms. Those who lived securely in the apartments upstairs
enjoyed unquestioned entitlement. Their angry hammering on heat pipes
would signal that Jerry had better hurry to the basement boiler room and stoke
the coals to send up more heat. Often the banging pipes sent him rushing to
the coal bin, to tote a wheelbarrow full of glistening black rocks down a dimly
lit corridor to the glowing furnace. Those who slept upstairs in warmth, away
from the furnace's steady roar, would never know the constant, low-droning
fear that crept into Rose's heart as the family slept beside the boiler in the
basement, which Rose believed might at any time blow up and "reduce the
family to ashes."

Linda reflected on the dichotomy between the upper world of the tenants and the subterranean realm of the supers:

> *While those on the upper levels sent garbage down for disposal on the dumb-*
> *waiter, Father, at the lower end, hoisted it off and carried it out for trash day. I*
> *don't remember him complaining aloud, but even then I drew a vaguely defined*
> *connection between his bitter fights with mother over money for "just one quart*
> *of Schlitz," his periodic drunken tirades, and the constant company he kept with*
> *the dumbwaiter and its cargo of garbage from the upstairs tenants. We kept them*
> *warm and disposed of their garbage and when either task was not executed to*
> *their satisfaction, we stood at risk of eviction.*
>
> *The physical and spatial arrangement of our lives in relation to the tenants was*
> *a concrete manifestation of our social location, which assisted me, I believe, in my*
> *nascent formulations of the intellectual abstraction that I would one day come to*
> *understand as my own class consciousness and class conflict. "Us and them" was*
> *indelibly impressed upon me by the thick concrete stairs that led down to our*
> *rooms by the coal bin and the bleached marble hallway stairs, ritually washed by*
> *my father on Saturdays, that led up to what I imagined to be the splendor of the*
> *tenants' apartments. They lived in clean spaces, they were warmed by my father's*
> *labors, and they were White. We were unseen, unwelcomed, scrutinized, and Black,*
> *and if anything went wrong in the building, there was only one person held ac-*
> *countable: my father, the super. In this way, no place could be fully home until sev-*
> *eral years later, when ironically we went to live in the housing projects.*

Perhaps all childhoods are marked by traumatic events that leave permanent imprints on our consciousness. Such memories mold us, or haunt us, taunting us throughout our lives. As we shared these stories, our pain was often palpable; we wanted to reach across the table to each other, to comfort, to soothe. Usually we settled for soft words and kindly looks or gestures. More than once a narrator had to say, "I want to stop now. I do not want to go there now." Being present to the pain of these lived and relived experiences—our own and the others'—rekindled with each telling, honed our capacity for empathy and moved us to the work of compassion.[16]

THE HOUSE BEHIND THE SYNAGOGUE

On a warm summer afternoon in Ocean City, New Jersey, Linda spoke of life in the house behind the synagogue:

> As we prepared to move to the house behind the synagogue, we were hopeful:
> the landlords were religious men and they would not always be present to "bear
> down on us," as mother would say. We would open up the *shul* (Yiddish for syn-

agogue), turn lights on and off, and clean. In our caretaker's house, we would have an upstairs and a downstairs, only four rooms, but seemingly spacious despite the lack of central heating and hot water. We traded heat for space, but in doing so we met tragedy that would profoundly scar our lives.

She sighed. It was clear that she would need to digress a bit before picking up the narrative line.

"You know, my father had no education, no marketable skills; he would take out a pail and a rag, and go and walk the streets of the Bronx, just hoping for somebody's house or windows to clean. He'd come back with whatever he could come back with. Sometimes it was three dollars and there were five children, a family of seven." Linda's voice was tense. "I remember once," she continued, "he brought back orange juice and floured doughnuts and that may be why I absolutely hate floured doughnuts to this day; I really don't like floured doughnuts."

"What's a floured doughnut?" Beth broke in, her tone curious and excited. "A powdered sugar doughnut?"

"Yes, yes," Linda nodded emphatically. "We were starving, and we had floured doughnuts, sliced in the middle with a slice, I think, of American cheese, just a little bit. And I can remember him in that house, where there was no oil for the frying pan, or butter, or anything, putting the flour with water into the dry pan and making whatever would happen with the heat underneath it."

Linda went on to describe the one large room upstairs where she slept with her parents, one sister, and her brother, while her two older sisters, Marie and Jean, shared a smaller, adjacent room. She swept her arms out expressively to demonstrate the relationship between the spaces of her memory and the room in which we worked. "I remember," she continued, "how we got bathed in front of the same stove that heated the house." She knew that the next story would have to be told:

It is the story of grave trauma for all of us, but especially for Marie. It is the story that defined our lives in the house behind the synagogue and in many ways forced an emotional trajectory that would forever delimit our shared familial psyche. On this January day in 1952, the temperatures had dropped to the single digits, and the wood frame of our shack on Washington Avenue was creaking from the force of the wind. The three youngest children played busily on the floor close to the pot-bellied stove, our only source of heat.

Marie and Jean, my older sisters, thirteen and fourteen years old at the time, encircled the stove, which glowed red from the chopped wood my father had stuffed in the wide opening that morning, hoping to save his kids from chilblains, his relentless source of concern. Marie and Jean spoke animatedly as they held out their hands, rubbing briskly, shifting from side to side in their long pink nighties. Then, in a moment that marked eternity, the flames encircled Marie's legs, eating at her nightgown, burning through layers of skin from calves to thighs. The trauma sent her bounding upstairs, dropping burning cloth on the landing, while mother ran behind, swiping with a dish towel in an attempt to extinguish the flames. On the lower landing, we four younger ones howled in agony and fear for our big sister, our anguished mother, and our own uncomprehending innocence.

In some small and dubious miracle, the flames stopped at her legs. The ensuing nine months of hospitalization and multiple skin graft operations saved my sister's life. But what she retained in the form of physical survival was lost double-fold in the damage to her psyche, marked by a dauntless depression that remained with her until she died at age fifty-seven and by the unending grief that we continue to suffer for all of the reminders of her life, never fully graced with any sustaining joy.

A lengthy and ultimately unsuccessful court battle ensued, which ended with the synagogue officials' taking definitive retribution for our attempt to extract compensation for my sister's suffering. We were evicted. As each day brought us closer to the scheduled day of leaving, my mother grew more and more agitated and distraught. On the day of evacuation, the marshals came and deposited every box, three beds, one dresser, and a chifforobe in front of the Temple on Washington Avenue. From this place we had called home, my father set out, to some uncertain destination, hoping to secure shelter for his homeless family. My mother's eyes were encircled with pain and terror as she paced frantically, glancing periodically at her bewildered brood. As the four of us (minus Marie, who was still in the hospital) sat on the boxes, we watched the other children come home from school, passing us by on their way to warm suppers and homes.

Linda vividly recalled the encroaching nightfall, when her father returned to the hungry, tired children and their mother, spent from the elongation of despair. They were transported from the sidewalk to two rooms on the second floor of a rooming house, where five families shared one bathroom and neighbors periodically came knocking to borrow household items. She summed up, ruefully, "It was while we lived there that I began—even in those early years, ages seven to eight—to discern what I later came to understand as the fundamentals of class difference."

"MY REFRIGERATOR IS ALWAYS FULL"

When it was Frida's turn to tell her story of a class-shaped childhood, she perched delicately on the wooden kitchen chair. "I must have been ten years old when Auntie Lily left Chile for the U.S.," she began.

She was heading for Los Angeles, to meet a man she had corresponded with for some time but whom she had not seen since she was a child in China. The plan was that they would marry if they found each other suitable. They did. They have had a good and happy marriage for almost forty years now. Her departure was a painful one for me and for my family—separations and goodbyes seemed destined to go on and on. I remember going to the airport, crying as I clung to my aunt, who had been like a second mother to me. She looked so fine—red coat and matching hat—setting out courageously to find happiness in a land where a woman past thirty could still find a marriage partner.

Many letters passed back and forth between Frida's family and her beloved Auntie Lily, most of which have been forgotten, but there is one that stands out vividly in Frida's memory. Lily was enticing those who remained in Chile to consider emigrating. She said, in words that remain indelibly imprinted in Frida's mind, "My refrigerator is always full." This from the woman who, while still living with Frida's family, worked as a secretary and had an independent life. Once in a while she brought treats home for Frida and her brother Leo—for instance, a large candy bar, which Frida's mother would distribute to the children one square at a time. Frida's parents owned a small women's wear store at that time, and they could not always count on a steady flow of cash. Once in a long while, if cash was short, Auntie Lily would arrive home with bags of groceries, to tide the family over until normalcy could be reestablished.

Frida's memories of these days are poignant:

I cannot say we felt deprived, though by U.S. standards we certainly were. I used to steal stray pesos *from my mother's empty purses to join my friends at the candy store—there was no such thing as an allowance in my home, and I expected none. But today my eyes spout tears and my throat constricts when I think of Auntie Lily's words. For though I don't recall any particulars, I do know that the refrigerator and its promises became a vivid topic of conversation around the dinner table for quite some time to come.*

SNOW GLOBES, PATENT LEATHER SHOES, AND MAY DAY MEMORIES

From time to time, as we shared family stories and childhood memories, the narratives seemed to twine around one another—respecting the differences in our experiences, while reinforcing our nascent care and compassion for each other. On one of Linda's visits to Chicago, she brought a present for Frida— a small, smiling snowman encased in a plastic dome filled with water, which,

when shaken, created a miniature "snowstorm." Linda felt she should apolo-
gize for the gift's Christmassy imagery, but Frida was too deeply touched by
the gesture to bother with the Christian associations. This was a potent moment. Some months earlier, Frida had told of peering into shop windows as a
young child, lusting after lovely toys that she could never name in Spanish or
English. When she described these objects of her desire, Beth and Linda simultaneously exclaimed, "Snow globes!" Linda's memory of that moment
had prompted her gift.

"I never asked my mother to buy me one," Frida acknowledged. "I felt it
was unacceptable to ask. On second thought," she added,

> I don't remember asking for anything for myself. I desperately wanted a bicy-
> cle, too. But I grew to be satisfied with the occasional ride on my friend Reizel's
> sister's bike in the summertime. It makes sense, in retrospect, that I held my si-
> lence about a bicycle. After all, they were expensive and I knew, I always knew,
> that my parents were on the edge financially, that the going was often tough. But
> a snow globe?

Frida shook her head, acknowledging how it has taken decades for her to feel
comfortable spending money on herself. She challenged the therapeutic perspective that suggests this was related to issues of self-esteem. "It's not a matter of 'you deserve it!'" she sighed. "It has more to do with what was once,
undoubtedly, a functional accommodation to certain realities of my childhood, realities shaped by social class."

Linda immediately signed on to Frida's suggestion: "It's amazing to me
how there's usually some very, very solid item that represents the whole
range, that has such multivalence. It represents the whole range of things that
you knew you had to be quiet on, that you couldn't clamor for." In Linda's
childhood, the issue was shoes. Her recollections take her back to a time, "at
the height of our low period of poverty," when all her family's clothes came
from second-hand stores. Her parents would dig through the bins looking for
sturdy shoes, while Linda dreamed of shiny, patent leather Mary Janes. Her
memories took us back to a long-ago day in May:

> *May Day bore the promise of the idyllic. I was in kindergarten; we would dress*
> *in our prettiest dresses, grab a brightly colored ribbon, and dance around the*
> *maypole, erected in the center of the schoolyard. Mrs. Cole, our teacher, spent*
> *considerable time preparing with us for this joyous day of song and dance in*
> *celebration of spring. I wanted one of those dresses that came out of big stores,*
> *not the hard, red plaids, with the paper in their sleeves to give them shape as*
> *they were piled one on top of the other on the bargain tables that lined the streets*
> *on Bathgate Avenue, where vendors sold from boxes and tables, and buyers—*
> *housewives with whining kids in tow—would push through the Saturday crowds*

haggling for the best buys. It was from one of those storefront bargain tables that Mother bought the red plaid dress. Looking back, I can only imagine how special—and difficult—it was for her to buy that dress for a dollar, maybe a buck twenty-five. To complete my May Day outfit, she and my father took me to our more frequent shopping stop—the Salvation Army, where we fished through large cardboard boxes of shoes, searching for the right fit and the sturdy heel and sole.

"Sturdy" was the word my parents used most often, "strong as a rock." "These will last until she outgrows them," meant a sure guarantee of superior quality. As the youngest of five, I knew that nothing was ever discarded or outgrown. So I left the Salvation Army with my brown leather oxfords. They had hard, slippery leather soles that resembled wood—the mark, as I knew even then, of good shoes, the kind I named—after the only children I remembered wearing them—"Jewish shoes." I was delighted to have such shoes and even believed I could be taken for a tenant. Wearing them, I felt like I belonged to a family that didn't have to lie about what they had eaten for dinner the night before.

As I skipped in tune with the other children, holding my maypole ribbon and feeling utterly transformed by the fairy-like song, one little boy stopped, pointed, and exclaimed loudly, "You have on boy's shoes. Those are boy's shoes." Then I looked, and looked again, probably incredulous as I glanced down at my wing-tipped, mannish shoes—the ones my parents and I had seen as good, sturdy, even "Jewish shoes." I had felt so lucky and proud. Now a five-year-old boy in his wide-eyed, innocent dismay had revealed my thinly disguised secret, and the plaid dress and the sturdy shoes had failed to hide my real identity.

Of course, my parents heard my complaint as just another, this time minor, obstacle in their daily battle for the most basic subsistence. They could only offer fragmented reassurance to me in response to their five-year-old's overdeveloped fashion sense.

Forty-five years later, sharing this story, Linda wondered aloud about the connection between that May Day and her nearly obsessive passion for fine leather handbags or shoes and disdain for anything that lacks the smell and feel of real leather. She also confessed to Frida her embarrassment, long after the fact, at having called the shoes "Jewish," cognizant, as an adult, of the racial or ethnic dimension such a label adds to her narrative.

ON NOT NOTICING THE JET NOISE: BETH'S BRAVE NEW WORLD

Some of the cultural contexts and confrontations that shaped our childhood identity formations were surprising. The experience of being working class was something that all three of us shared, to varying degrees, ranging from bleak impoverishment to relative, if undependable, comfort. But unlike Linda, for whom the racial divide of the United States in the 1950s and early 1960s was a brutally compelling factor, or Frida, whose exile from Chile and relocation to Southern California meant crossing linguistic, ethnic, and national boundaries commonly described by the emergent field of "cultural studies," Beth's childhood entailed crossing cultural boundaries that have seldom been articulated by scholars. Until the age of six, she had mostly lived in the extended family created by her "English" grandparents—first in the Philadelphia row house, and later in a suburban semi-detached, two-flat house full of relatives on a tree-lined street. When Beth's parents reunited in 1956, the family of four relocated to Whiteman Air Force Base near Warrensburg, Missouri. Two years later, her father was transferred to Westover Field in western Massachusetts, not far from the cities of Springfield and Holyoke. Both of these moves would entail crossing well-defined boundaries between civilian life and military culture at the height of the Cold War.[17]

Westover, now closed, was then the headquarters for the Eighth Air Force of the Strategic Air Command, encompassing the first strike nuclear weaponry of the day. Westover was a B-52 base, huge and sprawling. On the long flight lines, "Christmas trees" of bombers sat waiting, loaded, fueled, and ready to take off at a moment's notice. The flight crews lived in reinforced concrete bunkers, or "mole holes," underground, spending eight days on continual alert and ten days off, except at times of international political crisis. These men—the fathers of Beth's schoolmates—never knew, when the klaxons sounded for a "scramble," whether they would be ordered to turn back over the North Atlantic and return to base or continue on, dropping lethal payloads, presumably over the Soviet Union. Beth acknowledged, one sultry afternoon, that "all of that is what I learned only after we had been living at Westover for some time." She continued:

I can date precisely the moment when my education began: it was a September evening in 1958; my father, mother, brother, and I had driven the three-hundred miles from Ocean City to Westover, our new home. The moving van had pulled up outside, and the late afternoon had passed in the welter of unpacking that accompanied our moves. I took pride in being able to help; I was, after all, a Big Girl of eight, about to enter third grade.

As twilight drew on, I wandered outside to the small patch of grass that served as a "front lawn." In an instant, all hell broke loose. The world was ending. The ground shook beneath my feet and I was caught up in a vortex of sound, a deafening, unearthly mechanical whine unlike anything I had ever heard. I knew, in that moment, the totality of terror. The noise consumed all my being and took my breath away. "Any minute now," I thought, "there will be the explosion, and then the mushroom cloud, and we will all disappear. The world will end, and I will end with it."

I stood, trembling with fear, screaming at the top of my lungs, and suddenly my father appeared. He knelt down and asked what was wrong. He had to shout to be heard over the noise. I thought he was crazy. What was wrong? EVERY-THING! The world was coming to an end! It took a few moments for him to sort things out. As the noise subsided, almost as suddenly as it had begun, my father laughed, belittling my terror. "It's just the planes," he said. "Just the B-52s, revving up. They have to do that, to stay ready to fly."

There was nothing for me to be afraid of, or so my father told me. In the morning, he'd take me over to the flight line and show me the planes, show me how silly I was. I'd get used to the noise; he didn't even hear it anymore. I should just put it out of my mind. There was nothing to be afraid of. Nothing at all. And you know, within six months, I never noticed engine noise—not the bombers revving, not the fighters screaming overhead.

We all learned not to notice the noise. We learned not to think of what it meant that "Benny" Benedict, my dad's best friend, was a tail-gunner on a B-52 crew or that my friend Natalie Lehman's father was one of the first African Americans to command a squadron of fighter planes. I learned to forget the terror of that moment in front of 8B Haines, when I thought the world would end—or, at least, to pretend that it was possible to forget such terror. "I am afraid," poet Adrienne Rich would remind me, many years later, as an adult. "(It's not the worst way to live.)"[18]

ABANDONING "LA PATRIA," OR FRIDA'S EXILE[19]

As we spoke of our childhoods, we learned that each of us was touched by an inexplicable sense of disillusionment when our parents—to our childish eyes, all-knowing and all-powerful—proved to be at the mercy of forces larger than themselves and unable to protect us from either the vicissitudes of class or the pain of being uprooted. Today, we can acknowledge that our parents and grandparents simply did the best they could with extremely limited means. Linda's parents, a generation older than Beth's and Frida's, embodied a particular set of diasporic experiences, marked mainly by the racial apartheid of the first half of the twentieth century. In remarkably symmetrical ways, Frida's and Beth's parents seemed to replicate many of the dislocations that had shaped the lives of earlier generations. As Jana Evans Braziel and Anita Mannur point out, while "it is true that not everyone can cross borders with ease, and while it is also true that not everyone necessarily wants to traverse borders, it is also true that for reasons of necessity and sometimes choice, people do cross borders and see their lives unfolding in diasporic settings."[20] Here, Frida's story takes on salience:

The house was quite small and rather dark. More memorable was the back-yard, which accommodated both a garden and a chicken coop. For a city kid, this place on the outskirts of Santiago was a kind of oasis. At the center of my summerly pleasure was my great-uncle, my tío Max, whom I adored for his sweetness and mild-mannered indulgences. I was to spend a week in his company, and that of his wife, my tía Palmenia. I don't think the week was half gone before my uncle took me by the hand—I still remember the warmth of his hand in mine—and we walked to the local postal office so he could answer my parents' urgent phone call. Emerging from the phone conversation quite downcast, he announced, "I have to take you back to Santiago right away." I tried to negotiate another day or two, to no avail. There was an emergency; he did not know its nature. To this day the pain of leaving my uncle's home in such an unexpected and precipitous manner is emotionally conflated with the more radical departure I was to undertake within days of my return home.

My parents owned a small women's wear store in Santiago. My father's business partner evidently deceived him, leaving him with no funds to meet his financial responsibilities. Creditors were unwilling to renegotiate payment, and there were no bankruptcy laws extant in Chile at the time. There was no option but to leave. So within a week I packed in silence, and I left with my father, mother, and younger sister Gina—but not my brother (who stayed in Chile with my grandmother for two more years)—in silence. Limousines taking travelers to Argentina, I have recently learned, left only in the evenings for their Trans-Andean journeys. I had always thought that a night departure was an extension of our clandestine effort to leave unnoticed.

The next scene consists of our life at the pensión *(rooming house) in Buenos Aires, where we lived for the next ten months: two double beds in a large room, one, of course, shared by my parents, the other by my sister and me; a communal bathroom where one often had to line up for one's turn; a dining room where families sat at their assigned tables, and where conversation was animated and jokes abounded, sometimes at the expense of the management (like my father wondering whether the chicken soup was made by pouring boiling water over the bird). There was also the tragic day when a young couple lost their infant, the mother's inconsolable wails resounding, seemingly for hours, throughout the various floors of the house.*

My father routinely took Gina and me to the park on Sundays, while my mother spent hours washing sheets and towels by hand on the pensión's *rooftop, her break from the week of long commutes to her secretarial job. Later in the day, when the pensión's kitchen was closed, we trekked to the bakery for hard rolls of black bread and to the deli for cold cuts, returning to our room for our weekly picnic.*

School in Argentina, though manageable, was, nonetheless, foreign: "Sarmiento" did not roll off my tongue as my national hero, my double "l's"— as in llorar *(to cry)—sounded much softer than the norm, I was made fun of when I referred to a baby using the Chilean* guagua *(baby), which to them sounded like the barking of a dog.*

My emotional memories of the time are mostly those of absence, repressed grief, and the effort to be good by not adding to my parents' distress and my sister's vulnerabilities. As children, we knew we had to accept the circumstances

*and not speak too much about those we left behind. Given all the changes in my
life and the intrapsychic battles I undoubtedly waged to deal with our drastically
changed situation, perhaps it is not surprising that I made a pledge to myself to
reach for some form of permanence. One evening I was sitting on the bed Gina
and I shared. I keenly recall saying to myself, again and again, "I will remember this moment forever. I will never forget it." I have kept that pledge.*

*When I think about that fateful Trans-Andean journey, our life at the Argen-
tinean pensión, and the years that followed in the United States, I have to conclude that in important ways that phone call to my tío Max dramatically transformed my childhood.*

ROOTS AND DISLOCATION: BETH SPEAKS OF BETRAYAL

Wrenching border crossings shaped Linda's and Frida's childhoods. Linda's
parents and Frida's grandparents and parents all traversed great distances;
Linda's family negotiated cultural boundaries of race and impoverishment,
while Frida's crossed borders of language, ethnicity, and religion. Beth's family faced a far less compelling, but still emotionally charged and class-
constructed set of dislocations. Sometimes Beth wonders if any scholarly attention has been paid to the cross-generational effects or legacies of
constantly uprooting military families. "I don't know of any specific studies,"
she acknowledged on the evening that she began her story, "but then I've
never really checked—perhaps because I'm a little afraid of what I might, or
might not, find out." The sun was setting over the bay at the end of a long
summer's day in Sea Isle City; we were comfortable in the soft breeze, sitting
on the screened sun porch of our rented beach house. As Beth spoke, the pain
in her voice afforded a sharp contrast to the idyllic summer scene:

Only once in my life have I allowed myself to put down real roots, to dig into a
place so deeply that I felt planted in the very ground I walked upon. This was
when I was in junior high school—we had moved off base, to Granby, a small
village near Westover that to this day retains its picture-postcard New England
ambiance. My parents had rented an old farmhouse that sat on about eighty acres
of land; half was rented as pasture, half wooded. The house was still owned by
descendants of the family to whom a colonial charter had been issued in the
early eighteenth century. The house was spacious; it had pine floorboards a foot
wide, with cracks through which light from downstairs shone at night. It was
like no place we'd ever lived, shabby and in need of modernization, but more
space than we'd ever had just to ourselves.

A few months later, early in 1964, my father received orders for a tour of
duty as an "advisor" in a far-off peninsula in Asia that our old atlas labeled
"Indo-China." He was forty-four years old and had seen brutal service in the

South Pacific during World War Two and on isolated radar stations north of the Arctic Circle during the Korean War. He believed that U.S. involvement in Vietnam was misguided; he had also seen enough of combat for one lifetime. When he asked for a different posting, the Air Force gave him a choice: serve in Vietnam, or retire several years short of the thirty years it took to earn a meaningful military pension. For perhaps the only time in his life, he chose to take the high road. He opted to retire.

This choice would have dramatic consequences, although they were not immediately apparent. At first, once Bill's retirement became inevitable, my parents promised that we would remain in Granby, a place the whole family adored. Bill would find a job and we'd stay in the big old house that had become the "home" I'd always dreamed of. I have never been happier in my life. In the short time that we lived in Granby, I had broken the Service Brat's First Rule. I had put down roots; for the first and only time in my life I was popular and thriving academically. I took third place in the regional Science Fair. I was the first girl asked to dance at the seventh grade "semi-formal." With the exception of that horrible weekend in November 1963, when, devastated by President Kennedy's assassination, everyone sat glued to the television, the months in Granby constituted a glorious pubescent idyll. For once, I belonged.

In late March 1964, less than three weeks before my father's scheduled retirement date of April 15, Maude and Bill took my brother and me aside after dinner. They told us that since Bill had been unsuccessful at finding a civilian job, there was no way we could afford to stay in Granby. We would be moving to New Jersey, to live in an apartment in my grandmother's house in Ocean City.

This news split my heart. Ever since I could remember, I had armored myself against the pain of loss and separation; for such a short time, I had reveled in rootedness and belonging. I felt shredded. I had trusted my mother and father and they had betrayed me by breaking the promise of home. I hated them, but I hated myself more. I was furious that I'd let down my guard and bought into the idyllic fantasy of Granby, anticipating continued academic success and popularity in junior high. I knew that, eventually, I would have to forgive my parents. I wasn't so sure that I would ever be able to forgive myself. I'm not sure I have, even today.

The weeks passed; Bill's retirement ceremony came and went; the day before we left Massachusetts, our beloved dog, Sarge, was hit by a car and died. There was a lot of melodrama that my parents tried to drown in alcohol and I tried to drown in bitter tears that no one saw. Eventually, I got over most of it—but I have never again trusted the security of place. I have never trusted myself to fully belong or feel at home. I have moved forty-three times since I turned eighteen; I expect to make many more moves before I die.

Our conversations often represented concerted efforts of articulating our experiences—whether painful or joyous—in order to find points of contact, understanding, and insight despite—or perhaps *because* of—our differences from one another and our unique socio-cultural locations. Our family legacies, backgrounds, and childhood experiences reveal various cultural hybridities. Each of our identities has been predicated on complex cultural blendings rather than presumptions of cultural purity; as we will see in forthcoming chapters, this reality has been fundamental for our development as human beings and as citizens. Such hybridity, for each of us, is a legacy of generations of dislocation, uprooting, and exile. Braziel and Mannur remind us that various forms of hybridity, such as ethnic or linguistic mixing, mark the culture of individuals who come from a family history of diasporic movement. Consequently, they find themselves betwixt and between as they continuously negotiate that identity.[21] Frida opened our eyes to the difficulty of such negotiation as she narrated her complex relationship to the culture and country of her birth.

FRIDA'S CHILE

"I am a small child," Frida began on a muggy summer afternoon in Sea Isle, "probably four or five." She continued:

Holding hands, my brother and I descend the hundreds of steps leading from our home in Cerro Mariposa, one of the many hills gracing Valparaíso's landscape. I don't know if we are walking or running that particular weekday morning on our way to school—I do remember, in general, the exhilaration that came from running all the way down, the wind on our faces, our clothes in disarray. (I was deeply touched when my mother told me recently that as newlyweds, she and my father used to run down the hill, too—her memory provides me with a curiously powerful sense of identification with her as a young woman.) Seemingly out of nowhere, several neighborhood boys appear, thrusting epithets at my brother, all containing the word "judío," Jew. I am afraid, but my older brother's presence and his firm grip comfort me.

In Valparaíso, I attend a Jewish day school, but when we move to Santiago, I am enrolled at the local public school, grade four. I am eight years old. My experience of being an outsider is much more pronounced now. I am still called rusia *by all kinds of folks, a recognition of my blond hair and the foreignness that it encodes. But there is now a weekly reminder of my difference at school: I am sent out of the classroom whenever the local priest arrives to teach catechism. There is no program planned for me during this time—I just remember sitting in the playground with another Jewish little girl, waiting to be called back in.*

A couple of years later, when I am ten or eleven and walking home from school, I regularly stand on street corners with one or another of my classmates, who accuses me, along with all my fellow Jews, of having killed Christ. I am confused and disturbed by these onslaughts. These girls are supposed to be my friends. I will not know for decades yet about European medieval courts in which Jewish delegations must defend themselves from similar charges leveled by high positioned representatives of the Roman Church. When passing a church, people make the sign of the cross, whether they are walking or riding a bus. I don't in either case. I know I am different. The public culture is embued with Catholic symbolism. A Jew sticks out like a sore thumb.[22] *But we have the* colonia, *the Jewish community, to offer a buffer. Most of the time I feel safe.*

When I come to the U.S., I spend the first few years learning English, internalizing the culture, becoming a successful high school student. I attend high school where, as a Jew, I am an outsider once again. My parents are still too unsettled and short on cash to join a synagogue. So we don't do too much that is religiously Jewish. In college I come to experience religious longings and search for my Jewish roots. My identity increasingly comes to be shaped by this Jewish journey.

For decades, Frida lived in a state of suspension between two often conflicting, but hardly dichotomous, identities: *chilena,* on the one hand, symbolized her Latin American heritage, while *judía,* on the other, captured her religious and cultural Jewish inheritance. The overarching framework of Frida's family traditions, however, was diaspora, which has also shaped, and continues to shape, her sense of self and location. As she put it:

I recently heard a lecture by the Chilean writer Ariel Dorfman. Following the talk, I stood in line to speak with him briefly, to reveal my plans to visit Chile for the first time since my departure in 1962. He was more than cordial, in fact, he was charming, warm, embracing. His parting words, in Spanish, no doubt were meant to communicate his understanding of my sense of displacement, a theme that shimmers through his own life and work: "¡Anda a tu hogar!" (Go to your home/your hearth!) The words touched me—there is something so Latin American about them; they tap into rivulets of nostalgia for a romantic language that readily captures the hungers of the heart. But almost immediately I also realized that these words rung false to my situation. Chile may be his hogar; *I don't think that it is mine. For the Chile of my consciousness is my Chile. I do not know if it quite exists apart from me. It is the Chile of my childhood, filled with idiosyncratic images and memories. It is a Chile that no longer exists, for it has been asleep, like Sleeping Beauty, for some thirty-six years. Yes, I have read about political events in the intervening years: the brief government of Salvador Allende, followed by the coup; the long years of dictatorship and repression; the more recent efforts toward redemocratization. Is this Chile of external realities the same Chile of my inner life? Not quite. The Chile that I lost and mourn for symbolizes what can never be again because it is so closely linked to my becoming a self. That self somehow managed to move into adulthood without the actual Chile, though undoubtedly in its shadow.*

OUR DIASPORIC LEGACIES

The willed act of telling our family stories—recounting, at times, both "worlds" and generations of pain—steeled us to seek new challenges, individually or collectively, as we will discuss in future chapters.[23] We believe that such moments—of contact, of challenge, of growth—took place both *despite* and *because of* our differences from one another and the unique sociocultural locations and positions we brought with us to this project—a "perfect postmodern moment."[24] All three of our backgrounds and experiences reveal forms of cultural hybridity; our identities and family legacies were molded by cultural blendings, not presumptions of cultural purity. Each of us, in her life and work, has struggled with and against both the hybridities that are our legacies and against falling into facile traps of cultural essentialism, which, as Uma Narayan notes, "depict as homogeneous groups of heterogeneous people whose values, interests, ways of life, and moral or political commitments are internally plural and divergent."[25] These efforts have been as fundamental to our development as human beings and as citizens as the stories we shared with each other, some of which are recounted in this chapter.

It is important to note that for all of the struggle, denial, alienation, and difficulties that shaped the generations before ours—and, indeed, our own in turn—we do not interpret these stories as only, or exclusively, "narratives of pain and hardship." While it is possible to read our family histories, as well as aspects of our own life stories, as case studies in "the hidden injuries of class, ethnicity, and/or race" (to paraphrase Sennett and Cobb[26]), our inheritances are in no way always or exclusively limited to this. It is true that when Frida first told the story of Grandmother Ella's clutching her baby's corpse to her breast near the Russo-Chinese border, fearing that discovery would end their flight to relative safety and return them to the peril of pogroms, all of our eyes filled with tears. Yet it is important to remember that this narrative of pain is also a narrative of great courage; we know that our individual and mutual inheritances have been shaped by great bravery and resourcefulness in response to seemingly impossible challenges. At the same time as we discern patterns of alienation or denial in the past, so, too, can we limn structures of family solidarity, the generous spirits of people with little but their hearts to offer, and sheer, magnificent joy in life and the marvelous connections it can entail: here, Linda's telling of the exploding flashbulb at her Jamaican grandmother's Mandeville grave comes to mind. Grandma Janie may never have imagined "picnee Ivy dawta's" life as a linguistic anthropologist today, but in the moment back in 1971, Linda's family's diasporic inheritances surely came full circle.

Chandra Mohanty has argued that, when telling stories such as ours, "the point is not just 'to record' one's history of struggle, or consciousness, but how they are recorded; the way we read, receive, and disseminate such imaginative records is immensely significant."[27] Her words have resonated as we have worked, not simply to share our family stories, but also to find the transcendent or resistant moments embedded within them and to use those moments to create new meanings. We have tried, throughout this chapter, to take Shari Stone-Mediatore's suggestion regarding the "responsible reading of stories of experience" to heart; Stone-Mediatore stresses that "we must not reduce these either to empirical evidence or to mere rhetorical constructions, but we must attend to the ways they can help us to discern contradictions in our own experience and can thereby facilitate our own further oppositional speaking and writing."[28]

Something emerged from our sharing of family stories of dispersions, dislocations, poverty, and pain. We heard it as we told our stories, the words winding and twining around and across each other and through time, at kitchen tables in wintry Chicago or the summer sunshine of the Jersey shore; we saw it in each other's faces and felt it in a comforting touch or the group hugs we surrendered to after hours of conversation. As daughters of diaspora, we reached each other with words that resonated deeply across the great divides of our various cultural legacies and hybridities; just as our parents and grandparents had crossed the waters, so had we bridged distances of a different sort. We believe that we have a small gift to give, born of our legacies of hope and survival—of immigrant border crossings, racial or religious marginalizations, and working-class denial. Out of our own early experiences of isolation and marginality has come an empathetic imperative that guides our lives and informs our work—an imperative to which we will turn in the chapters to come.

NOTES

1. For an overview of these various diasporas, see Gérard Chaliand and Jean-Pierre Rageau, *The Penguin Atlas of Diaspora*, translated from the French by A. M. Berrett (New York: Viking, 1995), 1–72, 113–122, 157–163.

2. Avtar Brah, *Cartographies of Diaspora: Contesting Identities* (New York and London: Routledge, 1996), 180.

3. Brah, *Cartographies of Diaspora*, 182.

4. Frida poignantly adds that, in 1945, after a quarter century had passed, Sara would give birth in Chile to her first child, Leonardo, and choose the name Reuben as his Hebrew name, in memory of that other infant who did not live. Elka would no longer be able, after so many years, to repress the trauma of that first border crossing and the death of her son; her pain would now wash over her in seemingly never-ending waves.

5. Frida's grandfather and Beth's, as we shall soon see, fought on opposite sides of this war.

6. Noel Ignatiev, *How the Irish Became White* (New York: Routledge, 1996).

7. Beth recalls an incident from 1958, shortly after her nuclear family had moved to western Massachusetts, where her father was stationed at the now-closed Westover Air Force Base. Ethel had come to visit, and the family spent a Sunday afternoon driv-

ing around the New England countryside. They stopped at a Scandinavian gift shop in the town of Granby. On hearing Ethel speak, the owner of the shop went up to her and began addressing Ethel in Swedish, speaking at some length and utterly mystifying Ethel and the rest of the family. Realizing his error, he explained that he had assumed from overhearing Ethel's conversation that she must to be a native speaker of Swedish. Since he seldom got the chance to speak his native tongue, he was excited to converse with someone in that language—a "multicultural moment" long before the term came into common use.

8. During World War One, and afterward, she proudly—and, depending on the neighborhood, often bravely—flew the Union Jack outside her window every Fourth of July.

9. Krishan Kumar offers a lucid analysis of the rise of English nationalism in the late nineteenth century (the time of Jules's childhood and youth), linking this sort of popular patriotism to Britain's imperial power and hegemony over the rest of the United Kingdom. See Krishan Kumar, " 'Englishness' and English National Identity," in David Morley and Kevin Robins, eds., *British Cultural Studies: Geography, Nationality, and Identity* (Oxford: Oxford University Press, 2002), 41–55.

10. "Yorkshire pudding" is not a dessert, but a savory baked batter of flour, milk, and eggs that resembles a popover on steroids and is served, with butter or gravy, as an accompaniment to roast meats; Lyle's Golden Syrup is an English staple. It is a cane syrup, akin to the "imitation maple pancake syrup" that graces many American tables, but without the maple flavor.

11. Just as this book was going to press, Beth learned from a previously unknown cousin in Australia that the family name appears in public records variously as "Hauptman(n)," "Hatman(n)," and "Hortman(n)."

12. For a historically grounded articulation of such sentiments, see Leisa D. Meyer, *Creating G.I. Jane: Sexuality and Power in the Women's Army Corps during World War II* (New York: Columbia University Press, 1996), 33, 39, and 41. Beth has the interesting distinction, among our generation, of having had not one, but two, parents who served in the military—an experience far more "normalized" today in the wake of the Gulf War and the Iraq invasion.

13. For discussions of San Francisco as a place where unconventional social and sexual mores were available to returning military personnel in the mid-1940s, see Nan Alamilla Boyd, *Wide Open Town: A History of Queer San Francisco to 1965* (Berkeley: University of California Press, 2003); Allan Bérubé, *Coming Out under Fire: The History of Gay Men and Women in World War Two* (New York: Plume, 1991).

14. In the larger mills of Gary and Chicago, Beth would eventually learn, the chrome-plating tanks were where the most expendable workers—in those days, African Americans who had migrated north from the Delta lands—were found. The molten, hot metal, toxic chemical fumes, and constant spills meant short life spans for such workers in the days before OSHA. See David Montgomery, *The Fall of the House of Labor: The Workplace, the State, and American Labor Activism, 1865–1925* (Cambridge: Cambridge University Press, 1987).

15. Richard Coe, *When the Grass Was Taller: Autobiography and the Experience of Childhood* (New Haven: Yale University Press, 1984).

16. These themes will be discussed in detail in chapters four and five. For a discussion of compassion, see Laurent A. Daloz et al., *Common Fire: Leading Lives of Commitment in a Complex World* (Boston: Beacon Press, 1996), especially chapter three.

17. Cynthia Enloe's work affords a unique feminist interpretation of the vicissitudes of militarization and military culture. See, especially, *Maneuvers: The International Politics of Militarizing Women's Lives* (Berkeley: University of California Press, 2000).

18. Adrienne Rich, "Tear Gas," in *Poems: Selected and New 1950–1974* (New York: Norton, 1975), 141.

19. "La patria" is the Spanish for "fatherland" or "motherland," typically used in Latin American countries.

20. Jana Evans Braziel and Anita Mannur, "Nation, Migration, Globalization: Points of Contention in Diaspora Studies," in Jana Evans Braziel and Anita Mannur, eds., *Theorizing Diaspora: A Reader* (Oxford: Blackwell Publishers, 2003), 14.

21. Braziel and Mannur, eds., *Theorizing Diaspora*, 5.

22. On her visit to Chile in 1999, Frida noted that virtually no one any longer engages in this ritual gesture during bus rides or when walking by a church, perhaps a reflection of increased secularization and/or the decline of Catholicism in favor of evangelical Christianity, which has won many converts in the recent past. Given Frida's outsider status in Catholic Chile, it is ironic that she has spent most of her professional life teaching at a Catholic university.

23. We here refer to Lillian A. Rubin's path-breaking study of working-class experience, *Worlds of Pain: Life in the Working-Class Family* (New York: Basic Books, Reprint 1992).

24. Beth thanks Uma Narayan for coining this phrase in private conversation, about 1995.

25. Uma Narayan, "Essence of Culture and a Sense of History: A Feminist Critique of Cultural Essentialism," in Uma Narayan and Sandra Harding, eds., *Decentering the Center: Philosophy for a Multicultural, Postcolonial, and Feminist World* (Bloomington: Indiana University Press, 2000), 82.

26. Richard Sennett and Jonathan Cobb, *The Hidden Injuries of Class* (Reprint, New York: Norton, 1993).

27. Chandra Mohanty, "Cartographies of Struggle: Third World Women and the Politics of Feminism," in Chandra Mohanty, Ann Russo, and Lourdes Torres, eds., *Third World Women and the Politics of Feminism* (Bloomington: Indiana University Press, 1991), 34.

28. Shari Stone-Mediatore, "Chandra Mohanty and the Revaluing of 'Experience,'" in Narayan and Harding, eds., *Decentering the Center*, 124–125.

Chapter Two

A Friend of My Mind: Co-Construction and Cooperation in Extended Conversations[1]

We usually arrived in Sea Isle City in June, when the sun blankets streets and houses with a seamless shield of white heat. One morning we skipped our usual chat over coffee on the sun porch for a leisurely stroll on the boardwalk. We chose to go out early, while the seagulls lent a background chorus to our voices. We were an odd trio; the most casual observer would easily see this from a distance of two hundred yards. Beth, although of average height, stood taller than Frida and Linda and commanded a large physical space. And when we were in South Jersey, she often led these excursions near the ocean, for this is where she came of age in the early seventies. It is the closest she has come to feeling a sense of home. As Linda has observed aloud more than once, Beth seems to be more fully herself at the shore than in any of the many other places where she has lived over a span of twenty years that the two have been friends. Perhaps someone would say the same for Linda on Flatbush Avenue in Brooklyn.

As we walked, Beth served as an informal tour guide, offering notes on coves and inlets, flora and fauna, interspersed with personal narratives that situated aspects of her life within the geography of our excursions. She was unmistakable as her short, full salt-and-pepper hair waved against her square face, falling just short of dense dark eyebrows. Hazel eyes, heavily lashed, blinked, strategically, for pause after each narrative segment. On this morning, Beth's soft denim trousers, mauve t-shirt and Land's End sandals to match clearly reflected the casual professorial style she assumes behind her desk at DePaul. Linda was in the middle, at just five feet, the shortest of the three and stocky-round (although less so now than when we started the project). Her maple brown skin stood in distinct contrast to her fair-skinned companions, who had to fend off the morning sun's rays with SPF 40. Linda's dark braids framed an apple-cheeked face that smiles easily. Every few minutes she would break out in an infectious, hearty laugh. Here, too, the eyes dominated, with a wide-open smile vying for center focus. Her mustard t-shirt and navy shorts revealed strong calves, molded by years of clocking miles on footpaths. Frida, to Linda's right, was small and delicate, seemingly perfectly proportioned. On this day, her tapered slacks and smooth fitting polo complemented a silk scarf that fell rakishly around her neck, at least until the sun burned off a faint morning mist and chill. Frida's hair was reddish blond and fine, cut stylishly, pixie-like, accenting her warm brown eyes that readily convey the deep empathy that marks her disposition.

So began Day Two of our fourth summertime session, bringing us together for a week's work on this project. We started slowly, for we had spent the previous day narrating stories into the tape recorder from early morning until late evening. As we meandered through discovery, recovery, and creation, the process emptied us of energy and insights, even as it invigorated us and engendered renewed enthusiasm for and commitment to the project. Within that protracted engagement, over the course of a long day, we had traversed multiple categories of lived experience, ranging from our early education to our current professional lives, covering great swaths of ground in between. Our triadic life narration ultimately provided the texts on which this book is based, tracing the various and sometimes uncertain paths we three have traveled as we constructed our midlife identities. Rooted within the trajectories of our lives as straight or lesbian; as African American, Irish American, or Chilean-born, Jewish American; as originating in the working class or in deep poverty, we discovered how we came to claim our work as teachers and scholars, work that has been centered on a profound and abiding commitment to the interrogation of social inequities associated with class, race, gender, and sexual orientation.

TELLING EACH OTHER

In Toni Morrison's *Beloved*, Sethe is reunited with a fellow slave, Paul D., whom she has not seen in the eighteen years since she stole away from the place, ironically called Sweet Home, where the two and others were in bondage. In the safe presence of another who shared the same awful fate, Sethe and Paul D. begin to bid hidden memory into consciousness. Morrison's narrator tells us, "Her story was bearable because it was his as well to tell, to refine, and tell again."[2] Readers thereafter encounter the co-construction of their narrative, a process that takes place regularly between kin and fictive kin alike. Requisite to such co-construction is the sharing of cultural knowledge between those whose paths have either crossed decidedly or whose life experiences are significantly parallel to erode the boundaries separating them.

The co-constructed life narrative is a moment of bearing witness, of validation and unspoken mutual affirmation. When we sat down, poised to speak into each other's lives, we could not know what we would learn about ourselves, individually, or about the others. Such is the way with life story narration, which is necessarily revelatory and subject to yielding uncertainties. As we set out to tell an aspect of our story, we embarked on what seemed like a charted course. However, depending on the cultural identity of the other interlocutors, the setting of the narration, and all aspects of the speech event, the narrative unraveled in new ways. While the baseline remained the same, the speaker meandered over new and unanticipated encounters with the lived experiences, understood at the moment in new and compelling ways. The narrative, in effect, did not exist prior to the speech event of the telling.

This observation conforms to the findings of anthropologist Victor Turner, who suggested that the telling of the life narrative can be viewed as a cultural performance, in which the values of the participant are ordered as they are brought to consciousness. In this way, the event of the narration is "transformative," as it reveals the way in which the teller "scrutinizes" and comes to understand herself (or himself) in relation to others and to the material that has shaped that self-perception. This transformation, as Turner seems to suggest, results from the reflexive quality of life story narration, wherein the participant becomes conscious of both the interrelationship of events and her own consciousness of them.[3] This is the "processural" aspect of narration, according to Turner, when life story narrators would be periodically stilled by this realization and would metaphorically step aside themselves to marvel at their newly discovered awareness. The drama then closes, as it were, on this moment of discovery and resolution of the events. But the resolution or conclusive understanding is only temporary, as continued narration always promises to bring new knowledge, new realization, prompting the narrator to revise his or her understanding of the meaning of lived experience. Narrative is thus, as Charlotte Linde tells us, a temporally discontinuous discourse type that is capable of being told indefinitely and through the course of one's life.[4] In addition, each retelling is subject to revision as we reclaim memory, or *rememory*, as Morrison's Sethe knows it.

Aside from this revelatory potential of narratives in general, we are indebted to social scientists and linguists whose disciplines converge in the theoretical framework known as sociolinguistics for our understanding of relationship construction through talk. Overall, sociolinguists interested in a broad range of phenomena associated with talk generate a vast range of data from which they must construct a complex understanding of spoken communication. This methodology, known as ethnography of communication, was described in its rich complexity by Dell Hymes in his seminal study, *Foundations in Sociolinguistics*, in 1974.[5] A nuanced interpretation of talk within the context of its production demands that attention be paid to a complex set of issues. Among these are the initial relationship among speakers, the setting, the code or language choice, the actual words spoken, patterns of turn taking (i.e., different speakers taking turns), including pauses and interruptions, and a number of other variables that contribute to an in-depth interpretation of the meaning of the interaction.

Following Hymes's ethnographic model, this chapter considers the meaning of pauses, overlapping voices, simultaneous talk, as well as silences, in order to describe the processes and outcomes of our shared storytelling. Overlapping voices often stand as evidence of cooperation in conversation; however, we can only conclude that the overlapping is cooperative rather than competitive if we closely observe both the speakers' verbal and nonverbal responses to the apparent overlapping, which appears as a series of interruptions. We focus on two broad issues here: First, as we examine the progression of our talk, we identify the ability of our three-way process to engage us in productive negotiations across social and cultural differences. Second, we suggest that this very process of mutual negotiations helps us to challenge privileged ways of being in the world and analyze how, through the intersubjective, face-to-face sharing of our stories, we have become better able to understand ourselves and one another.

TRANSGRESSIVE TALK

We began with the expectation that we would narrate our stories in parallel fashion, by centering our talk on themes of mutual significance. We thought that our individual narratives would intersect one another and return again and again to earlier points. Indeed, the natural discontinuity of life narrative discourse, as noted by a number of observers,[6] describes how we would, repeatedly, return to specific subjects and ideas until we had exhausted our understanding of a particular topic. Our list of topics ranged from work, family, and elementary through university education, to our husbands and children (or lack of these), friendships, sexuality, spirituality, social class, feminist commitments, and beyond. While addressing one topic, we would inevitably branch off into tangential discussions of other topics before returning to the one at hand. One of us would begin to talk as the other two listened, most often issuing encouraging verbal cues such as, "Yeah," "uh huh," or "OK."

Some observers have interpreted such cues as essentially "contentless" fillers that further the conversation[7] without adding substantively to the talk, however, sociolinguist John Gumperz recognizes them as "effective and immediate way[s] of noting the listener understands during the course of conversation."[8] Moreover, in *our* storytelling, we all shared some familiarity with a range of common experiences, so these cues often acted as markers, highlighting cultural knowledge or presuppositions that we shared. The placement of such cues suggests that the unarticulated, but shared, cultural foreknowledge may actually contribute to the coherence of the talk.[9] Evidence for this can be seen in the progression of turn taking when one listener issues a cue, "noting her understanding," and the next speaker picks up the story, building on a range of unarticulated background knowledge.[10]

In the case of each of our specific categories for discussion, we sought more than just an understanding of the trajectories of our individual lives; we were looking for evidence that would argue for the choices we made. Were there tangible events in our own lives that could help us identify the causal threads connecting those events to the choices we have made in our teaching philosophies and in our research commitments? In chapter three, we will discuss in detail how, although we were each born into differentially marginal social locations, we nonetheless overcame impediments to academic success. Perhaps there is some relationship between the lessons of our lived experiences and the particularities of our subsequent philosophical choices in teaching and in scholarship. The very methods by which we produced this text demanded that we share a deep commitment to empathetic listening, questioning, and negotiating through differences, which we ultimately identify as the mandate directing our professional lives. These questions and issues set us in motion, but the unfolding talk, itself, stands as concrete evidence of the effort—the success, uncertainty, and challenge—of negotiating across boundaries. After all, we entered into this project with the shared belief that any potential obstacles to our mutual understanding could be dismantled or leveled as a result of our efforts.

LANGUAGE AND THE CONSTRUCTION OF RELATIONSHIPS

Given that the outcome of any interpersonal communication is dependent on the speakers' interpretation of a range of verbal and nonverbal signals, discussions of conversations in context can be enhanced by a description of elements that take us beyond words and idiomatic expressions. Patterns of intonation, rhythm, volume, and stress, along with facial expressions and gestures, cooperate with words and idioms to construct each message. Thus, our discussion begins with an intimate portrait of each speaker, as revealed through aspects of our distinctive communicative styles, including a complex assortment of both obvious and subtle features.[11] In what follows, we offer a brief description of the unique markers, sounds, and sensibilities that distinguish each of our communicative styles, suggesting how these reflect the various communities in which we have been enculturated. This description will also provide a framework for understanding how our talk reinforces our relationships and reflects the progress of our negotiations.

OUR INDIVIDUAL STYLES

Beth's encyclopedic recollection of literary works, historical facts, and social science literature affords her a dense archive from which to mine a stream of context appropriate explanations, aphorisms, and allusions. When Beth spoke, Frida and Linda heard her characteristic attention to detail. Specific names of places and brand names associated with a myriad of cultural products (particularly as these serve to indicate class background or location) carried listeners directly to her social context, which she was able to recall in detail even after decades had elapsed. This is demonstrated by her description of her father's efforts to belie his working-class status by dressing well. As Beth recalled: "After he retired from the Air Force, he took great delight in buying good suits. He was a small man; he was only 5 feet 6 inches tall and slender. He weighed about 128 pounds. He just loved being able to shop in the teenage boys' department and get Hart, Schaffner, and Marx suits for $150, when the same clothing displayed across the hall in the men's shop would be, say, $500. To him, wearing a Hart, Schaffner, and Marx suit meant that you had arrived, OK?" Beth habitually offered this subtle "OK?" as she spoke, perhaps in an unconscious expression of her self-authorization, if not as a bid for the listeners' acknowledgment or agreement. More often than not, this utterance punctuated a sober remark and underscored the irony of her statement, even though it may have been followed by a perfunctory chortle.

When Beth described her mother's best effort to send her daughter off to graduate school at Harvard with a new wardrobe, her wry humor revealed her ambivalent relationship to the Ivy League. Linda and Frida, sitting across the kitchen table in Ocean City, were listening intently as Beth began the story. Her speech was routinely marked by a characteristic mix of humor and cynicism, aided in delivery by an intensity of eye contact. Beth peered over her glasses as she leaned forward, resting on her elbows. Her glance moved from left to right, focusing first on Frida, then on Linda, assessing their readiness for the next installment of her narrative. A slow smile preceded her words as she raised her hands parallel to each other, as much to bring others in as to enclose and focus her talk. After this initial gesture, her hands swept upward, where she held them high, palms turned outward, in front of her chest, with the fingertips nearly touching. Within minutes, her hands in the same position, she gracefully turned them over, palms now nearly touching her chest. In this seeming act of testimony, Beth's hand movements served as a prelude to words that were marked by intensity and commitment.

Beth assessed her audience's readiness and then opened with an anticipatory laugh, full of mirth and irony in recalling how Maude had recently spoken of "sending Beth off to Harvard." The irony was marked by Beth's melding of wry humor, sympathy, and remorse: "When I was going off to graduate school at Harvard, my mother told me conspiratorially that I could order any clothes I wanted from the Sears catalog, but that we 'wouldn't tell Dad.' This broke my heart because encapsulated in that is just so much—you know—she wanted to give me *something,* but what she could offer was so far off the scale, in terms of class, given where I was headed."

Beth's smile was warm, but weary. Regret and dismay were evident in the upward contours of her tone and register, making a rhetorical question of her closing pronouncement. This was a moment of considerable emotional weight, when adequate words were not available to describe the satisfaction derived from success in clarifying a sober reality. After sitting silently, attempting to digest her words, Beth offered a succinct coda to her story, reciting lines from a poem by Adrienne Rich, words to which Beth returned at weighty emotional moments or, occasionally, in lighthearted self-mockery. By now, Frida and Linda could almost recite these words along with her: "My heart is moved by all I cannot save:/ So much has been destroyed/ I have to cast my lot with those/ who age after age, perversely,/ with no extraordinary power,/ reconstitute the world."[12]

Linda's quick retort lightened the mood as she jokingly lamented Beth's discovery of the Rich canon. In doing so, she freely code switched from Standard English to the emphatic multiple negatives of African American Vernacular English. "You know, there's another piece to this. You should have *never;* no one should have *never* given you Adrienne Rich's poems. We need to keep that woman's poems away from you!"

Nonetheless, Linda and Frida continued to remark on Beth's facility at the deft delivery of novel, even obscure words, phrases, and extended segments of poetry. After years of close association with Beth, the two readily anticipated her impromptu recitations. Frida remarked on this one morning. "There are people who collect jokes so that they can sound clever and later repeat them, but you are very eloquent," she said, turning toward Beth. "You use language unusually well."

After a moment's pause, Beth offered an explanation:

> I can't tell a joke to save my soul, so that's a good analogy because I *do* collect
> words; I collect sayings and oddities of language; it's unconscious. There are
> words that, because of their texture or sound, simply intrigue me. I use language
> to wake my students up. I use language to make people who are not disposed to
> like me decide that I'm funny or interesting. I use language as a foil against be-
> ing fat; people who look at me and want to write me off because I'm just an-
> other fat lady often listen to me speak, and then they *don't* write me off.

At another point, we began to broach the inherent significance of discussions of our differences. Linda entered the discussion, beginning slowly, as
she almost always did. Her pauses often landed where they would not be anticipated, as if she were silently constructing a first draft of her comments before sharing them. Once she began, she articulated the distinctive back vow-
els of the native New Yorker, turning coffee into "cauwfee," while
characteristic Black stylistic contours signaled irony, doubt, and contempt,
even before such sentiments were put into words. As she slowly articulated
her words, she raised intonations in the middle of her statements, as if they
were questions, making sure that listeners were following each word. This laborious pace was at times further halted by her habit of starting a new thought
before she had completed the last. It seemed as if she had relented to the ideas
grown impatient as they queued up, awaiting expression. In fact, such sentence truncation and overlap suggested a kind of cognitive relay as she was
speaking. This came to the fore in an exchange where Linda approached the
difficult topic of tensions among us as we considered addressing issues related to our ethnic differences:

> What comes to my mind is another aspect of the work. . . . This is connected. . . .
> I think that we said that we were going to talk a little bit about any tensions or
> concerns or thoughts any of us has had in the process, because of the process of
> confronting the way in which we meet each other across boundaries, but also the
> way in which we depart from one another and diverge from one another.

The areas of difficulty that Linda suggested were not unanticipated, as they
reflected concerns that have evolved over time in the larger society. They were
related to ongoing, intergroup misunderstandings, antagonisms, and misjudg-
ments, emanating as frequently from attempts at collaboration and cooperation
as from deep set hostilities. Here we had the opportunity to observe Linda's
speech style and habits more closely. In contrast to the seeming laborious
speech above, she often appeared animated and restless; it was as if she wanted
to rein ideas that had taken off running. We knew this by her shifts and turns
as she sat and by the expressive, energetic nonverbal responses she frequently
offered to others. This was not a restlessness of disengagement; indeed, her

kinesthetic responses, marked by subtle swaying and shifting in her seat, revealed Linda's most intense moments of emotional engagement. She spoke of discovering that she moves sensuously to the rhythm of her words when she writes. "I write with more than my mind and my hand. When I'm writing something that's moving me enormously, my body moves as I sit at my desk." Linda went on to recall a related habit; when our talk increased in intensity, she felt she had to put on her eyeglasses so that she could "see to hear more acutely." Linda's sensitivity is exquisite and her empathy abundant. She recognized each as a dubious gift and a potential source of unmooring.

At this point, Frida interjected, returning to an earlier question of when best to address the issue of our cultural differences. Frida asked, "Is this something we should be doing now?" We were reminded, not only of how important it was that we stay on track, but also of Frida's consistent commitment to engaging with difficult topics, when she continued:

> I mean, there are a couple of things we need to come back to, and, Linda, you and I have talked about maybe addressing issues that have emerged in passing in the text, but I would like to be able to discuss them with you as the whole African American/Jewish thing. We talked about how maybe that piece needs to be brought up so we can discuss where we're at with any of that stuff. What I have said to you is the whole tension is very painful to me, and I see this as an opportunity to talk about some of this with you, because it's not easy to talk about with folks that I don't know well.

At this particular moment, we could do no more than promise to return to the Black/Jewish relations issue at a later date. However, Frida's words here and throughout this book demonstrate the courage and gentle honesty undergirding her intentions, no matter how sensitive the issue at hand. Frida's style in this exchange was particularly compelling for its curious balance of both the boldness of assertion and the subtle blunting effect of hedging. Nancy Bonvillain explains that hedge words usually suggest that the speaker is questioning the validity of her statement. She also asserts, "Because females are socialized to defer to others and avoid conflict, they choose to state opinions interspersed with hedges to minimize confrontation with an addressee who may hold a different view."[13] We can hear such hedging in Frida's use of the word "maybe" as well as the passive voice, "needs to be brought up." The frequency of these moves in women's speech is well documented.[14] While linguists often identify hedges with women's deference, we argue that within the context of our discourse, hedging is a powerful strategy that facilitates the speaker's effort to raise delicate or difficult issues that touch on the most intimate and guarded aspects of our identities. Although Frida's hedges act to soften the impact of her statement, they are equally reflective of her insight and sensitivity.

The timbre of Frida's voice marked her authority. She sat not far from Linda, opposite Beth, slightly on an angle in order to offer equal amounts of eye contact. Before she paused to collect her thoughts, her hands moved in sweeping arcs, embellishing each pronouncement. They rested at each pause, the right hand stilled on her lips. These contrasting movements paralleled Frida's balanced alternation between reflection and high energy. With attention to her speech, we noted that Frida's pronunciation revealed a distinct blend of at least two linguistic communities, which together produced a rich musicality. Frida's careful and precise enunciation delivered these contrasting sounds with great clarity. She expressed her awareness of this, remarking, "I don't speak like a native. I enunciate much more than the native speakers do." A frequently alternating rise and fall in the rhythm of her words revealed a "long e" sound where others hear an "i," as in "ice," indicative of Spanish, her first language—despite Frida's having achieved, since adolescence, total fluency in English. Frida's words moved slowly at first as she shaped her thoughts. However, once she began, the words rushed forward, undulating musically, one word assimilating with the next, reminiscent of the blends heard in Spanish. "I see this as an opportunity," gently blends into "Iseethisasan—oppor-tun-ity," with the slight syllabic elongation in "opportunity" lifting the word upward through the emphasis on the middle syllable and convincing Beth and Linda that such a discussion would, indeed, be a worthwhile enterprise.

STEPPING OUT ON FAITH

The following exchange marked a pivotal moment in the early conceptualization of our project. We were ready to begin sharing our narratives, hoping that they would lead us to a better understanding of marginalization, empowerment, and social class. Besides contributing to these goals, the conversation recounted below also served as a prelude to the linguistic construction of what would become, for all of us, a mutual, emotionally supportive, and intellectually affirming relationship. We see evidence of this in our agreement and acceptance of one another's words, even when they were accompanied by elements of critique.

The following excerpt from our conversation illustrates how our work was both generated and sustained by a painful restlessness to break the silences that too often accompany the exercise of unearned privilege. It came early in our project; we were informally identifying events characterizing the sources of our alienation as well as describing our potential to act as agents of change. Linda shared her experiences of enlightenment and empowerment while attending the uniquely powerful and provocative academic conference, "Black Women in the Academy, Defending Our Name 1894–1994," held at the Massachusetts Institute of Technology in January 1994. The keynote speaker, Johnetta Cole, then president of Spelman College, conducted an open microphone, audience participation session, in an auditorium filled to bursting with nearly two thousand African American women and a small minority of men of varied races and non-Black women. Linda began by attempting to convey the headiness of the moment to Frida and Beth:

> In that auditorium, when Johnetta Cole spoke, she had this refrain, "When we are in charge." People were coming to the microphone to speak and out of this mass of Black women comes this young white man. There were some sounds from the audience that were unfavorable, so Johnetta looked around and said, "When *we* are in charge, it will be different," emphasizing that *we* don't have to reciprocate oppression. It was such a wonderfully healing moment, suggesting that if we do get a voice, then we don't have to say the same kind of things that have hurt us, that we can construct a new or healing way of communicating. I think that's what our gathering here begins to construct, begins to address.

Frida immediately "signed on," saying, "I was just flashing on what's happening in South Africa, the unwillingness to reciprocate oppression, which is so unusual because I think historically, the tendency is to do just that— vengeance and all that."

Beth added, "OK, but you know this notion of constructing new ways of communicating points to just how subversive such work is, and what 'we' really means." Beth went on to relate an incident, described in detail in chapter three, involving a professor's cavalier revelation of indifference to class matters, while joking around during a graduate seminar. She concluded:

> What such moments do is teach people that their elitism is OK, that laughing at this is acceptable, regardless of how fundamentally oppressive that communication may be. And the task of turning this over—not just over on its head, but spading up the ground with the rototiller so that you can plant anew in new ways—is a big one.

Frida, looking skeptical, responded,

> Well, it takes a tremendous amount of self-consciousness and I think what you're describing is the opposite of that. The students who laughed at the professor's "joke" were simply operating out of a taken-for-granted set of assumptions, as opposed to debunking and deconstructing that discourse. So, yes, at first there has to be a willingness and a desire to deconstruct—which, of course, people who feel entitled to privilege are not about to do.

Beth shot back, "But what do *I* do when *I'm* the only person in the room not laughing?" She went on to describe the risks associated with speaking up in the face of erasure or dismissal. On the one hand, it is hard not to join into the laughter when one has been granted entrée, however tentative, into the relatively exclusive corridors of graduate education. On the other hand, however, we do not enter institutions (or communities) with the intention of leaving them as we found them. We do not wish to collude silently. In the end, we returned to Johnetta Cole's promise, vowing that "when we are inside," even if *not* in charge, we will contribute to constructing new paradigms of cultural inclusion.

Our conversations thus far demonstrated considerable common ground. The following segments illustrate how class and other commonalities contribute to coherence in our conjoined narratives. At times, our conversations reflected supportive overlapping and the construction of individual stories around a common theme that Susan Kalčik treats when describing the structure of talk in women's rap groups.[15] The apparent eclipse of the typical pause between turns from one speaker to the next, known as "latching," is one indication of the way our talk concretely demonstrates cohesion powered by recognition of shared experience and a mutual need to mark this.[16]

A conversation that focused on our financial struggles while in graduate school generated a number of examples of continuous latching and overlapping that were clearly cooperative. We were sitting around the dining table in our rented beach house in Sea Isle; Beth and Linda recalled that difficult time when they were both working on Ph.D.s at Rutgers, when, at times, it seemed as though the two were competing to see who could survive on fewer resources. Beth remembered feeling frustrated and embarrassed by the economic challenges she was facing:

> Fellowships were awarded on the basis of merit and they were limited. One year, one of the four awards went to a very young woman who was subsidized by her parents. They bought her a car, paid for trips abroad. Two fellowships went to married men, whose wives were schoolteachers—now they weren't making huge salaries, but the wives earned enough to live on, and the men used their fellowship money to pay income taxes on an inheritance, or buy a new car.

Beth took a deep breath before continuing.

> I was surviving on $460, cash money, a month, nine months out of the year. Once my half of the $500 a month rent got paid, there wasn't a lot to spread around for food, books, car insurance, and gas. I spent two winters heating the house by carrying in five-gallon cans of kerosene three times a week, keeping the thermostat set at 45 degrees, and lighting the kerosene heater in one room, wherever I was working.

Linda interrupted, sighing, as she was painfully reminded of her nearly identical experience. "I'm sorry, but I remember that so well."

As if their sentences were one uninterrupted exclamation, Beth's words eclipsed Linda's in a typical example of latching: "And the reading that I was doing—the papers I was writing, and the books that I was reading, were not being read or written under anywhere near the same kind of conditions—"

Beth could not quite finish her sentence before Linda continued, "See, that's the kind of measurement that I can't help but make and I've tried not to make it, but it just astounds me. I remember those winters—"

Beth broke in, "So do I!"

Her words summoned Linda to continue with her parallel account of the "kerosene heater" story. Linda sighed again, then went on to say, "I feel like this is old homecoming week, because that was one of three years that I heated my house with kerosene, the third consecutive year of kerosene heat, when they turned off the gas heat." She shook her head emphatically.

I mean, when you are in that situation and you begin to measure the mental as well as physical energy that it takes to lift a five-gallon can, put it in the trunk of your car, carry it in the house, the tension, the stress in lighting a kerosene heater in the middle of your house, in trying to go to another room but it's not warm enough in there and trying to move the heater without turning it off, and my thinking that the whole house was going to go up in flames. Then I asked myself, "Now I'm supposed to read two hundred pages of Saussure?"

Beth cosigned—spontaneously signaling agreement—and continued with references to her own discipline, offering, "Phenomenology, or Hegelian political theory!"[17]

"Or ecological systems!" Linda added, "Whereas somebody else was sitting in a nice cozy house—or so we imagined—not worrying about these things, and meanwhile my kids are walking around saying, 'I can't stand this place; it smells like kerosene!'"

Until this moment, Frida had been listening supportively; she joined in with no small amount of indignation, asking,

Why is it that the rhetorical question is a stupid question? I know the answer, but I'm going to ask it anyway. Why is it that more of this category of class is not addressed in the academy? I mean, the immediate answer is because most folks are middle class and they don't want to be bothered, but beyond that, I would think there would be more, more of this stuff being written and heard by people like us.[18]

Beth wagered an answer.

It gets back to the great erasure; working-class people have only entered the academy in anything other than incredibly token representation within the last twenty years, maximum. At the time that most of my professors were graduate students, graduate fellowships were considered, and this is a direct quote from an advisor I love and respect, "Fellowships are only intended as pin money. You have to understand that these aren't supposed to be sole sources of support."

The context for this response was Beth's calling her advisor to tell him that she had accepted a full-time offer of employment at Livingston College before even beginning her dissertation; at this news, the advisor had "hit the ceiling."

This discussion of the stress associated with trying to fill the resource gaps and to work well and productively in graduate school illustrates how candid discussion can engender trust and further an exploration of the larger implications of painful personal experiences. In this way, our conversations often continued to build on rapport that had already put down deep roots. John Gumperz's discussion of the relational and ideational aspects of conversation illuminates this by clarifying the relationship between a topic of conversation and the participants' shared experience in substantiating rapport. He notes that talk constructs both a relational and an ideational context.[19] The latter is evident in our ability to cosign each other's words, obviously in agreement, and seamlessly weave one story into the next. The relational aspect in Gumperz's observation follows logically from the ideational, at least in the case of the exchange just described, which relies on a series of closely paralleled experiences to engender solidarity. Ironically, the graduate school experiences that seemed so debilitating at the time have become transformed, through the act of open discussion, into a potent source of insight, motivation, and agency.

The discussion continued with each of us remarking on our difficulty in managing the social expectations associated with being a graduate student, on the threshold, as it were, of the academy. To a significant degree, while in graduate school, each of us kept our working-class origins "closeted." In response to pressures to fit in, we tried to go unnoticed. Beth recalled the gulf she perceived existing between herself and her dissertation advisor, saying, "I might as well have been from Mars, and it wasn't just the gulf between me, out of Sterling, Illinois, by way of Granby, Massachusetts, by way of South Jersey, and him coming out of a much more middle-class family." She sighed, remembering difficult times, before going on. "It wasn't just the fact that he came out of a Jewish tradition that valued intellectual endeavor and I come out of a tradition that does not value intellectual endeavor; it wasn't just that he was a man and I was a woman; it was *class* and it was the Great Wall of China."

Frida joined in, remarking on the intransigence of these circumstances over several generations. "The fact is that it remains so to this day, when an increasing number of people are coming from the margins into the academy — and still this stuff gets hidden!"

This exchange gave rise to a moment of unanticipated clarity for Frida, who had not, prior to this point, been able to locate clearly her own experiences of class, especially in terms of her adjustment to U.S. culture. Our discussion provided a context within which she could begin to understand her own class background, a process that is described in chapter three. We see here how our co-constructed narration, in addition to contributing to coalition formation, may further each participant's understanding of her own experiences. When one of us looked outward at her awareness of herself as a cultural actor and marked this verbally, it appeared that she could see herself in new ways and perhaps assume greater agency based on that awareness. These moments were potent. An intersubjectivity emerged among us as a by-product of sharing a particular experience and receiving, in return, positive, enabling acknowledgment. This process of personal validation, supported and augmented by a co-narrator who intimately recognizes the "other's" experience, serves as the foundation for an epistemological shift.

Where there are multiple voices, each speaker moves potentially from the inner sensation of one individual to a larger framework of knowledge, which reflects neither one's private purview nor an aggregate of data, often divorced from individual experience. Instead, the co-constructed narrative allows us to see how shared, embodied knowledge informs our larger construction of qualitative meaning. Sidonie Smith helps us see the profound difference between individual and triadic narrating. The singular telling, she suggests, constructs a coherent, culturally located self, while the triadic acts to destabilize the homogeneous, in favor of a messy "*heteroglossic*" self.[20]

The destabilizing propensity of autobiographical storytelling can challenge the mythical notion of a culturally static and coherent self. This post-Enlightenment concept arose at a time when the presumption of such a regulated and disciplined being necessitated the idea of identity as unchanging, rather than fluid and open to redefinition within the autobiographical act.[21] By contrast, the multiplicity of voices enables the transgression of a limited sphere of the culturally coherent self.

In this book, we understand *heteroglossia* to refer to multiple voices coexisting in a conversation, expressing the multiple points of view and social locations they represent. Mikhail Bakhtin observes that novelists bring together socially and politically competing voices in their works, without submerging any of them but, instead, engaging them in dialogue with one another. In our conversations for this book, we pursued a similar objective as we determined to negotiate through our differences. Our voices often converged; they sometimes collided, but they never knowingly erased the others.[22]

The notion of shared causality, where different speakers identify similar causes or reasons for the choices that they have made, is woven throughout our conversations. There is considerable evidence that such causality may be shaped or influenced differentially by social class. As we shall explore in chapter three, the sense of shared causality that emerges from our narratives consistently highlights our having made pragmatic choices, guided by necessity. This appears to challenge the causal factors that Charlotte Linde described in her study of the life narrative discourse of middle-class white women, who shared a common belief that "one is not subject to external limits of opportunity imposed by gender, social class, race or ethnicity" and generally located culturally appropriate causality within an individual's character or personality.[23] Our narratives point to a shared causality structured around available opportunities for scholarships or other funding, proximity to family and the furtherance of familial responsibilities, and other factors structured by class, race, gender, religion, or ethnicity, such constraints, according to Linde, were markedly absent from the narratives of middle-class Americans of the postwar generation.[24] For the three of us, this shared recognition of structural constraints added to the dense body of foreknowledge that brought coherence to our intersecting narratives. For the middle-class individuals Linde studied, social class and familial affiliations are not only absent but also virtually erased; "character" substitutes for "privilege" in an elision of collective hierarchy by individual personality. As Linde observes:

> This choice of character over opportunity as a coherence structure is extremely interesting. It seems likely that an explanation rooted within the self and the self's agency, as character traits must be, is preferable to one rooted outside, since an externally based account invites attribution to either accident or determinism. . . . The opposite principle—citation of lack of opportunity as an account for one's career—is notably absent from the narratives of these middle-class professional speakers. As we have seen, speakers may indicate the presence of certain opportunities, even though they do not use these to structure their accounts. But none mentions restricted opportunities as a reason for professional choice.[25]

NEGOTIATION—A PERSONAL CHOICE

While we entered this project with many commonalities, we could not presume that we would share, or share equally, at all points in any conversation. Ultimately, the degree to which our talk could develop on shared presuppositions would depend on the conscious choices that we each had to make in entering the discourse or responding to one another's stories. We had to choose when and how to mark our commonalities or negotiate our way through our differences. As we discuss in detail in subsequent chapters, each of us acknowledges that cultural or ethnic insulation has been neither desirable nor useful, given our cosmopolitan commitments, even as we respect the historical and contemporary cultural constructions of our distinctive identities and the communities they reflect. Traveling through the many tributaries of our separate lives required a degree of magnanimity and patience.

While our mutual commitment to crossing borders to reach understanding engendered this project, the actual process of negotiation this entails was sometimes complicated and occasionally problematic. Despite our notable successes, there were times when we failed in our efforts to truly understand the other, perhaps because we fell short of stepping beyond our own standpoint or fully appreciating the complexity of the other person's world. These were painful moments all around; depending on one's own position in these conversations, we might have felt misunderstood, frustrated, or vulnerable as we expressed disappointment in and sometimes anger at our colleagues' limitations. One of these moments emerged in the midst of a lively, candid, wide-ranging discussion about sexuality—both our own and our views of its cultural role and its problematics.

Beth raised the issue of exclusivity, saying, "I'm not a separatist; I have never wanted to be one, although in some lesbian communities there's a real privileging around being a Kinsey Six. I've been asked, 'Oh, I'm a Kinsey Six, are you?'"

Frida, interested, asked, "Would you translate that?"

Beth replied, "A Kinsey Six is a score on the Kinsey scale, indicating that the respondent has only ever had same-sex relations."

To this, Frida replied, "Thank you," while Linda said, "Oh."

"It's been used as a sort of litmus test," Beth went on, "or, if not necessarily a litmus test, as a way of establishing a certain sort of lesbian superiority. The 'best' lesbians have never, ever slept with men; it's exclusive. I've always been as uncomfortable with exclusivity in same-sex relations as I am with compulsory heterosexuality."

Frida interrupted, pointing out, "Well, they're *both* compulsory."

Beth shifted her discussion to a somewhat broader focus. "I think sexuality is a continuum; if you're talking about fluidity of identity, many of us move back and forth, and up and down, and over, under, around—" Here, laughter broke the train of thought, but she didn't miss a beat: "and so on, through time, as we move through life. It saddens me that we lack a sexual vocabulary. It saddens me that we have difficulty in conversations like this.

We're uncomfortable, I think, each of us in some measure is uncomfortable
with this—"

Linda interrupted, offering an explanation she thought would be helpful.

> Sex is private! I think there are some boundaries in place that may have to do with
> inhibitions and conflict, but they're also there because there's a human propensity
> for privacy. People don't have sex in public, for the most part. The very fact that
> our genitals and our naked bodies are deemed private—we don't walk around our
> houses naked, most people don't, especially in families, with a lot of people in the
> house. So it's things that we do in private. We go to the bathroom in private.

She turned to address Beth directly. "Everything that you said is true, but sex
is in the realm of the private, so I think there's a certain taken-for-grantedness
about a degree of discomfort, you know?

"*My* sex isn't private!" Beth exclaimed, anger flaring in her tone. Ignoring
Linda's perfunctory "OK," she went on, the tension evident in her voice,
enunciating forcefully, "*My* sex is a matter of federal and state law, OK? It's
the visceral response that I have, OK? *Some* sex can safely be kept in private;
not mine."[26]

Linda tried to interject with "I understand what you are saying—"

But Beth continued, "OK? Lesbian and gay sex *can't be private*. That's why
I have to say I'm not so sure that I don't know—if 'behind closed doors' was
not a mandate, I don't know what I would choose to do, if certain forms of sexual expression were not prescribed as they are, and proscribed as they are."

Linda started to reply, "But, what's—"

Again, Beth kept going, "I have a very hard time seeing sex and privacy as
necessarily or inherently linked. Sex is not private if you are, always already,
an outlaw."

The conversation continued for some time in this vein, and it became clear
that there were real, and painful, disagreements on the table regarding the role
of sex in society, triggered by Beth's adamant assertion that "sex and sexuality are everywhere. I don't think it's private." Indeed, at the point, above,
where Linda said, "But what's—" we see an example of linguistic overlapping that is competitive, rather than supportive, something largely absent
from our other conversations. Our divergent positions, to some extent, reflected very different approaches to intellectual exploration of sexuality. We
had reached an impasse, and the conversation moved in new directions, not
because we had reached any closure, but because there was no place to go.
We tacitly agreed that we had come to a border we could not cross, at least
not in the moment. Acknowledging this would not lead us to give up our quest
for understanding across difference, but it did alert us to responses of justifiable anger and vulnerability around issues that have hurt us.

We left the table that evening feeling uncomfortable because we had experienced a failure to communicate. It was some time later that Frida was able to suggest that the unbridgeable difference that surfaced for us that evening, especially between Beth and Linda, was not one about conclusions, but rather about the types of questions that were raised and one that revealed our individual positionalities. She saw that Linda had been pursuing questions of privacy from a psychocultural perspective. She had been asking something like, "Don't people generally desire privacy in sexual encounters, given their needs for intimacy?" For Beth, the critical question was political: "Who gets to define privacy? Or whose sexuality is privileged, and whose is not?" Beth spoke from the standpoint of a lesbian, who, faced with a relentlessly homophobic society, was intent on interrogating and resisting political power she saw as illegitimate, yet that had, historically, been repeatedly turned against lesbians and gay men. She was really angry at the Supreme Court's stance on sodomy law; this anger spilled over into our conversation, understandably but clearly, at that point, unproductively.[27] She also felt hurt and vulnerable, because it seemed to her at that moment that neither Linda nor Frida was willing to set aside heterosexual privilege and enter her world. She later came to understand that her perceptions were mistaken and, in the wake of Frida's analysis, clearly based on misunderstanding what Linda and Frida were saying.

The next morning, a different set of tensions emerged shortly after we sat down to work. Linda and Beth were late in arriving at Frida's house. Linda had forgotten to pack her curling iron in the rush to get on the plane to Chicago, so Beth had to drive her to several stores in search of a replacement, teasing her all the while by recalling a conference they'd attended together a few years earlier. Watching Linda unpack her suitcase in the hotel room they had shared, Beth had been amazed to learn that Linda felt it necessary to bring two curling irons to the meeting. Soon after we began our conversation, Beth described her mother's impending visit to Chicago for the Christmas holidays and how she was feeling frustrated by Maude's "obsession with having the appropriate coat to wear to the art museum next weekend."

Frida responded supportively: "I can identify with that; I think my mother came out of a similar situation, where you have to 'look right' in order to be seen as acceptable and not be marginalized."

"That has such potency for me, such resonance, such force." Linda joined in enthusiastically. "I can't even say how much and in what ways. I'll mention what I was thinking about, in spite of the fact that it sounds like I'm dredging up silly stuff."

Beth attempted a light note: "Silly stuff, in this company, is entirely appropriate."

Linda addressed Beth:

> But you remember how we went on about that curling iron? That was an ab-
> solute emblem of what we're talking about in terms of your mother with the
> coat. Because I became angry with you when you seemed to be impatient with
> me. The words in my head were, "Your relationship to your hair is not the same
> as mine. Grant me my cultural space to do the things that Black women ab-
> solutely take for granted and don't think time-consuming or anything."

Linda's voice rose somewhat, and she continued,

> Because I remember those words, I need you to understand that when people are
> on the margins, like your mother moving in and out on this boundary of middle
> class and working class, they have to make sure their "uniform" is correct in or-
> der to go out into that world. You can say, "Oh my God, all the fuss, what's all
> the fuss about?" You know. But appearance has always, always had to be cir-
> cumspect, no matter what you're wearing. And your hair has to be "just right,"
> and *"just right" for me is not necessarily "just right" for you.*

Ever the conciliator, Frida added, "Another way I'm conceiving this is that,
for me, these things are tickets to respectability in a culture that judges people from the vantage point of appearance."

Linda agreed, "Exactly."

Frida went on, turning to Beth, "And I think that's your mother's preoccupation with her coat."

Beth tried to articulate her understanding of the tensions that were on the
table. "Oh, yeah," she began.

> I do understand it; I've felt this. But *my* commenting on the remarkability of two
> curling irons at the conference had nothing to do with cultural hierarchy, OK? I
> was amazed that someone would bring two curling irons—that was how I read
> it. And I remember it because it was unlike you to be so anal—and I know I am
> one who would express her anality in other ways—never with two curling irons,
> but certainly with equal magnitude.

She turned toward Linda, continuing, "It's entirely understandable, though,
that *you* would read it differently, as cultural hierarchy."

At this juncture, with Beth's less-than-clear attempt at an apology, we
backed off the topic and our talk meandered hither and yon, from issues of
self-presentation to how self-expression may be culturally shaped or individually constructed as a measure of our individual authenticity. But there was
more to be said. Linda eventually added a bookend to the conversation, asking Beth directly to "Hear me out." She began by alluding to Beth's charac-
terization of her concern with her hair as anal—or, in Linda's words, as a

"kind of compulsion"—and ended by referencing her own difficulties the previous day with understanding Beth's conceptions of sexuality and privacy.

Linda was intent on making herself understood: "It sounds like you don't know what I mean. There's a range of normalcy in every culture, with boundaries, in that what you do goes unnoticed because it's what everybody does. It's not remarkable, and it doesn't necessarily say anything about individual psychology; it's socially constructed and taken for granted." Both Beth and Frida were listening intently, attempting, with body language and deep silence, to understand Linda's words. She went on,

> Because it's important to me, I'm asking you to indulge me this minute to just say this. I can't think of any African American woman who I've ever known or been in touch with for whom there isn't some kind of ritual attached to hair. And I mention this because it's something that, as African American women, we talk about within our group, in comparison to white women. We say something like, "Are you ready to go out?" and "Yeah. I just have to bump my ends."

Linda explained her last statement: "That means turn them under with the curling iron." When Beth and Frida nodded their understanding, Linda continued,

> Or, "I don't have to do anything with my hair. I've got it braided, or locked [dreadlocked], and I can just go." Or, "she got hair like white folks." I don't necessarily mean texture—it can mean the way hair is cut, styled, whatever. So, in terms of preparation rituals, throwing on clothes, getting out of the house, "doing your hair" means blocking in twenty minutes, maybe longer, depending on what you have going on. This is part of the whole ritual thing, and there are essays about the hair braiding ritual, the straightening comb ritual.

Linda paused to take a deep breath.

> When you've got a Black kid who doesn't have naturally straight hair—unless you've had it locked or she has had an afro or something from an early age—when she reaches the age of ten or eleven, it is not uncommon for her to want a hair relaxer. That's a given. That's not abnormal. That's not self-hatred. At this point, it's so much of a ritual or a taken-for-granted option that it doesn't necessarily have the deep negative connotation that it earlier had. As Black women, we have given ourselves permission to do pretty much anything we want with our hair!

Again, Frida and Beth could only nod in affirmation, not wanting to get in the way of what Linda had to say. She sighed deeply, then summed up:

> So, anyway, I just wanted to say that. In this work, we happen upon the different places where we've come from—we have to join in our stories in ways that

have shaped us differently. To me this is an example of what you were, I think, wanting me to understand last night, but I couldn't understand sexuality the way that you understand it, Beth—that one's sexuality cannot be private if it is leg-islated against, you know. I tried to find the common denominator to get below all of that, and it's hard, if not virtually impossible; it's what I was hearing from you and trying to take in. OK. That's it.

When Linda finished, the three of us shared a long silence.

Linda's sensitivity to Beth's view of hair and curling irons devolved from her feelings of having been misunderstood. She felt that Beth had trivialized her rituals surrounding hair care by placing Linda's need for them in the psychological realm—"anality" in Beth's words, "compulsion" in Linda's. She needed Beth and Frida to understand that her response to her hair is cultural and strategic. It is within the ambit of Black women's culture that Linda has learned about self-presentation and survival. The need to look "just right" is something that she learned, even as a child, from her mother. Rose instilled in her daughters the belief that however impoverished you were, you always had to look right, especially in public, "because you're already suspect." In the conversation described above, Linda recognized the difficulties implicit in our efforts at crossing borders or building bridges. Still, she attempted to find the "common denominator" that would allow her to understand Beth's con-nection between sexuality and privacy. Recognizing that this may not have been possible at that time, she nonetheless seemed to be signaling to Beth to do likewise in regard to her own concerns about hair and its significance in her world.

In these conversations, however fraught, Beth and Linda have each planted seeds for the other's potential growth in understanding across difference. They both attempted to translate, for the sake of the others, insider knowledge gained within their principal communities of identification: Beth explained the implication of a "Kinsey Six" and the legal sanctions on LGBT sexuality. Linda, in turn, told of the significance of hair care rituals among African American women. Both sets of explanation rely on the kind of embodied knowledge that Beth earlier referred to as "visceral." The significance of Linda's hair rituals or Beth's anger at institutionalized injustice may be com-prehended intellectually by sympathetic others who do not share their re-spective cultural givens. Bridging the gap between such culturally specific, viscerally embodied knowledge and intellectual understanding demands more than good listening skills. At times, we believe, the gaps may simply not be crossed—but that does not obviate the mandate to keep reaching out or open-ing oneself to the possibility of eventual understanding.

For us, there were other arenas in which conflict over difference more read-ily yielded to negotiation. Many cultural groups around the world identify food sharing—even if supplies are scarce—as a demonstration of good will or a way to welcome a newcomer into the community. Food practices differ from other aspects of cultural study, in that they are eminently accessible and readily demonstrated to outsiders. This might explain the relative ease with which we worked our way through another moment of discord, although at the outset, Linda felt a great deal of frustration. She was feeling increasingly isolated with regard to our communal practice of food preparation during our group work sessions, which usually lasted a week and entailed Linda's traveling to Chicago or the three of us meeting up at the Jersey Shore. Linda's discomfort stemmed from her sense of a presumed homogeneity in food preparation styles and tastes.

Linda felt that our habit of communally prepared meals took for granted a particular set of practices that Frida and Beth seemed to share, but she did not. On our first day of working together, we had routinely gone to the market and stocked up on groceries. Especially in the spacious and well-appointed kitchen in the Sea Isle beach house, either Beth or Frida usually took charge, suggesting a menu and supervising the food's preparation. In retrospect, Linda acknowledged that she had generally acceded to this method, casually going along with what the other two took for granted about cooking. One of us would take on the assignment of peeling and slicing onions; another would garnish the fish with rosemary or dill. Someone would start the grill and get ready to broil chicken, or occasionally, at Linda's suggestion, lamb; before long, dinner was on the table.

At first, Linda cooperated cheerfully, in the spirit of community, but eventually she couldn't ignore her growing annoyance. Beth and Frida had simply assumed that this step-by-step preparation was satisfying to everyone, especially since Linda had never complained, even though she acknowledged, long afterward, that she felt the food prepared in this way lacked the seasonings she was used to and preferred. Linda also grew impatient with how the others planned and cooked meals in their step-by-step process. She was accustomed to

> what we call in Black vernacular culture "vibration cooking," where I would go to a pot, eye measure the water, throw in the rice, season with low fat margarine, and, at the very least, garlic powder, onion power, maybe even a little cayenne. No measuring cup measurements. In the time I was taking to methodically cut and slice—the way you do—I believed I could have had the food almost cooked and on the table.

She went on to share her increasing feelings of alienation from food preparation, wishing that she could "just throw something together," as she did at home.

Contrasting her more serendipitous method to the carefully planned and executed feasts that Beth is famous for, which always involve closely followed recipes, Linda explained that even when she prepared food for parties she still followed what she perceives as a much freer and more vibrant method. As she put it, "I also have had big parties where I have laid out spreads and had the same response. But, I also delight in getting other kinds of cultural influences. This gets to the vibration piece; I delight in going to an Indian restaurant, or the Chinese restaurant—" Here, Linda interrupted herself to demonstrate, moving her mouth in a tasting motion before continuing, "This is me, tasting the amount of yogurt or curry! I'll taste something and think 'If I can just get the ginger—yes, I see the ginger in this.' I'm filing the information away as I'm checking my taste buds. When I get home, I don't want to look up a recipe to re-create it. I just go to the stove to re-create it. I cook with a lot of ginger, generally, and I cook with soy sauce; I use the light Kikkoman, which is less salty."

With obvious support and enthusiasm, Frida interrupted Linda's explanation at this point, suggesting, "Try Tamari. They also make a low-salt version—"

For a time, Linda and Frida were involved in an energetic exchange, as each shared alternatives to the regimented method of food preparation that made Linda so uncomfortable and both grew increasingly enthusiastic about the prospect of trading off cooking styles from meal to meal. Then Beth, who had been relatively quiet throughout their discussion, interjected, "See, I never even think of inventing things."

Beth has a well-deserved reputation as a gourmet cook, so it was no surprise when Frida and Linda simultaneously exclaimed, "Really?"

Beth shrugged.

> No, I never do that. Linda, I've been with you at restaurants when you're asking "What is this, what's in this?" and I'm always impressed. But—well, I had sesame noodles for the first time about twenty years ago in Boston. I worked with a real sesame noodle maven, and we would go to the different Chinese restaurants just to try their sesame noodles. Finally I just decided, OK, I want to make these myself. Unlike you, I went through about two dozen sesame noodle recipes before I found the one that worked best.

Beth went on, describing her trials and errors in seeking out the best recipe. Linda was obviously supportive and genuinely interested; this was apparent in her running response, marked by energetic cues of "Yeah, yeah, yeah," delivered as Beth spoke. Frida joined in, and the discussion trailed off into a shared discussion of how we cooked rice, each consciously taking note of the practices of the other, and everyone voicing a commitment to make room in our joint food preparation for solo vibration efforts along with measuring, peeling, and mixing in response to recipes. In the end, not only did Frida and Beth respond supportively, but in the process of sharing, the distances between us surrounding culinary practices seemed to diminish markedly. Linda even remembered that one of the few recipes she has used over the years is Beth's own tried and true sesame noodle recipe!

As bell hooks reminds us, experiences of alienation are often far more threatening than our kitchen conflict described above and more frequently result in our vulnerability in public arenas. In her discussion of attendance in women's studies classes at Stanford, hooks describes despair and remorse on discovering that these classes left her feeling just as alienated in the university, after taking the courses, as she had been initially. She recalled, "I knew from gut level, everyday life experience that to be a black woman in this culture was to have a social reality that differed from that of white men, white women, and even black men, but I did not know how to explain that difference."[28]

"Black and female" is just one of the three (or more) divergent social realities that have given rise to the markedness and marginality explored in our life stories and throughout this chapter. Our various identifications and ethnic, cultural, and religious legacies were defined in the introduction and chapter one of this book and amplified early on in this discussion. Many differences attended our common purpose; our distinct positionalities had the potential to sediment boundaries between us. However, we believed that if, when sharing our life narratives, we made the effort to listen empathetically, we would learn to hear and understand difference in new ways. Moreover, we hope, our process could serve as a model, so that others might find the faith to take the risks of engaging in this kind of effort. The danger is that this can lead to the kind of disappointment described by hooks in the passage just cited. Unlike hooks, who described her undergraduate experience, by now we are seasoned academic professionals, committed to using language to explain, analyze, and, so far as possible, bridge the differences that shape our social realities.

However uncertain we may have been regarding ultimate success in bridging the divides, we saw our effort as urgent. All too often, simply "sharing" is not enough. Taking the risk of talk, persisting even in the moments when we might have preferred to give it all up and go home, led us to discover that traversing through some of our most significant and intimate life experiences would precipitate personal and collective transformations for us all. We found new insights into our individual life trajectories, even as we encountered unanticipated commonalities that encouraged the steady, if not necessarily linear or easy, erosion of the boundaries that would divide us. We hope that our work, with all its obvious, supportive engagement as well as its self-conscious vulnerability, argues for wider participation and faith in the experiment of resisting cultural isolation through committed conversations, such as those reported here.

NOTES

1. The words of the first part of this title, "A Friend of My Mind," are borrowed from the novel *Beloved*, by Toni Morrison. The protagonist, Sethe, is reunited with the former slave, Paul D. He reflects on their relationships from their place of enslavement and he remembers the love of two of the formerly enslaved. We are told, "Suddenly he remembers Sixo trying to describe what he felt about the Thirty-Mile woman, 'she is a friend of my mind.' She gather me, man. The pieces I am, she gather them and give them back to me in all the right order" (New York: Signet/Penguin Books, 1991), 335.

2. Morrison, *Beloved*, 121.

3. Victor Turner, "Social Dramas and Stories about Them," in W. J. T. Mitchell, ed., *On Narrative* (Chicago: University of Chicago Press, 1981), 152.

4. Charlotte Linde, *Life Stories, the Creation of Coherence* (New York: Oxford University Press, 1993), 4.

5. Dell Hymes, *Foundations in Sociolinguistics: An Ethnographic Approach* (Philadelphia: University of Pennsylvania Press, 1974). A number of additional works besides this one further enhanced our understanding of the interconnection of speaker, setting, hierarchical relationships, code choice, etc., in assessing the meaning of communicative acts. See also notes 7 and 8 below.

6. Sidonie Smith speaks of the "fragmentary nature of subjectivity," telling us, "there are many stories to be told and many different and divergent storytelling occasions that call forth contextually marked and sometimes radically divergent narratives of identity." "Performativity, Autobiographical Practice, Resistance," in Sidonie Smith and Julia Watson, eds., *Women, Autobiography, Theory: A Reader* (Madison: University of Wisconsin Press, 1998), 109. Charlotte Linde argues that the life story is necessarily discontinuous; that is, parts of it are told on different occasions to different audiences. And since we have defined it as the total of all stories of a particular kind that were told in the course of the teller's lifetime, it would be impossible to tell the entire life story even on one's deathbed (Linde, *Life Stories*, 27).

7. See Gillian Brown and George Yule, *Discourse Analysis* (Cambridge: Cambridge University Press, 1983), 92.

8. J. J. Gumperz, ed., *Language and Social Identity* (Cambridge: Cambridge University Press, 1982), 140.

9. The notion of foreknowledge derives from studies of pragmatics, which identify that body of knowledge that participants in a speech situation can take for granted as mutually understood. For an in-depth analysis of the many ways in which conversational interaction makes use of cultural presuppositions or foreknowledge, see

Stephen C. Levinson, *Pragmatics* (Cambridge: Cambridge University Press, 1983). Gillian Brown and George Yule offer an intriguing discussion of the ways in which speakers signal new information and known information in conversation. They identify "phonological realisation," that is, intonation, as one way that speakers signal known information. See *Discourse Analysis*, 154.

10. Gumperz, *Language and Social Identity*, 140.

11. Alan Cruttenden differentiates among three categories of communication—words and idioms, prosodic features, and paralinguistic and extralinguistic features. Prosodic features are those generally categorized as intonation, stress, pitch, "vocal effects which are used to convey meaning." Paralinguistic features, on the other hand, are not actual words, but vocalizations such as "uh huh," etc. While not actually words, such sounds communicate a great deal about the way the speakers are receiving each other's messages. Finally, extralinguistic features usually refer to immutable characteristics, such as the speaker's sex, body type, age, and perhaps voice volume, which is largely unconscious and habitual. See Cruttenden, *Intonation* (Cambridge: Cambridge University Press, 1986), 177.

12. Adrienne Rich, "Natural Resources" in Adrienne Rich, ed., *The Fact of a Doorframe: Poems Selected and New 1950–1984* (New York: Norton, 1984), 264.

13. Nancy Bonvillain, *Language, Culture and Communication*, 3rd ed. (Upper Saddle River, NJ: Prentice Hall, 2000), 188.

14. Jennifer Coates notes, "Research on the use of minimal responses [including hedges] is unanimous in showing that women use them more and at appropriate moments, that is, at points in conversation which indicate the listener's support for the current speaker." See Coates, *Women and Men and Language* (New York: Longman, 1986), 102.

15. See Susan Kalčik " '. . . Like Ann's Gynecologist or the Time I Almost Got Raped': Personal Narratives in Women's Rap Groups," *Journal of American Folklore* 88, 1975.

16. See Deborah Tannen, *Gender and Discourse* (New edition, New York: Oxford University Press, 1990), 64.

17. In her widely acclaimed study of Black Vernacular English, Geneva Smitherman distinguishes among a number of supportive cues recognizable in the call-response tradition of Black stylistics. Cosigning, a voiced agreement such as, "Go 'head now! or That's right!" would be classic examples. See Smitherman, *Talkin and Testifyin* (Boston: Houghton Mifflin Company, 1977), 107.

18. Janet Zandy's preface to her edited collection of essays from working-class writers announces that the book contains "narratives [that] are about the usefulness of private memory to democratic political struggle"; see Zandy, *Liberating Memory*, xii.

19. John J. Gumperz, *Discourse Strategies* (Cambridge: Cambridge University Press, 1982), 160.

20. Smith, "Performativity," 108–115.

21. Smith, "Performativity," 109.

22. For an in-depth analysis of the articulation of multiple voices in the novel, consult Mikhail M. Bakhtin, *The Dialogic Imagination: Four Essays* (Austin: University of Texas Press, 1981). See, especially, the essay "Discourse in the Novel," 257–422.

23. See Linde, *Life Stories*, 132. See particularly chapter five for an in-depth discussion of the relationship between cultural beliefs and notions of adequate causality.

24. Linde, *Life Stories*, 132.

25. Linde, *Life Stories*, 131–132.

26. As Larry Gross makes clear, a common claim of both LGBT advocates and their detractors is "that *sexuality is a private matter*. Each side means something different: *Let us live our lives in peace*, and *Get back in the closet*." It is to the latter position that Beth was responding, although neither Linda nor Frida was articulating that position. See Gross, *Contested Closets: The Politics and Ethics of Outing* (Minneapolis: University of Minnesota Press, 1993), 148.

27. See William N. Eskridge, Jr., *Gaylaw: Challenging the Apartheid of the Closet* (Cambridge, MA: Harvard University Press, 1999), for a comprehensive survey of the legal history referenced here.

28. bell hooks, *Talking Back: Thinking Feminist, Thinking Black* (Boston: South End Press, 1989), 150.

Chapter Three

The House that Words Built:
Education and Dissidence

"What is it," Beth asked Linda wearily, "that makes us do this, that brought us to Rutgers, that keeps us hanging on? What is it? Why *us*?"

In 1984, Beth and Linda were doctoral students. They sat in Beth's kitchen that afternoon, a tape recorder between them on the kitchen table. For a seminar assignment, Linda had been tape-recording their conversation. For hours, the talk ranged around issues they have shared as working-class women who came late to graduate school. Sometimes it was hard to tell laughter from tears, as the tales poured forth: stories of lugging five-gallon cans full of kerosene to heat the house when there wasn't enough money to pay the gas bill or fill the oil tank, of keeping rusted-out jalopies running on spit and prayers, of fears that they were leaving loved ones behind while not-quite-fitting-in at the university.

Beth's question came at the end of a long session. She and Linda had been talking about painful estrangements from parents, sisters, brothers, and other family members. As we have seen, they were the only ones in their families to attempt graduate study. In asking "why," Beth wondered how it was that she and Linda now found themselves doing what neither could ever have imagined. What had motivated them to undertake this journey that no one else in their families could envision? Linda was animated as she replied. "It was *words*," she said, her face set. "Beth, it *had* to be words. We were given that gift, at least. Yes. *It was words*."

Fifteen years later, our three voices intertwined around other kitchen tables as we co-constructed life narratives. As different as our stories are, we all grew up in economically marginalized—or, in Linda's early years, excruciatingly impoverished—families. Our narratives show that despite our differences, this commonality of class has shaped our life experiences. They have inspired us to explore how class, despite being perhaps the most ignored category in academic, social, and political discourse today, has had a powerful influence on our lives since childhood and to examine how our narratives confront the myth that the United States is "an educationally classless society." This chapter focuses on how we have come to name and understand the profound impact of class on our educational experiences. Despite the historical and cultural amnesia surrounding class in the United States discussed in the introduction to this book, this sort of interrogation can open up opportunities for a praxis of resistance and transformation.

One consistently emergent theme is our early access to the public literacy and learning skills that would, ultimately, move us away from our working-class roots. Some working-class academics have characterized access to higher education and graduate degrees as entailing inevitable separation and alienation from their families of origin. They describe this passage as a sort of Rubicon, which, once crossed, means there is no turning back.[1] For the three of us, the leap from family of origin to our present positions has not been quite so wrenching. Indeed, following bell hooks, we quite consciously "did not intend to forget [our] class background or alter [our] class allegiance."[2] What we have tried to do is more along the lines of Linda Frost's suggestion that for her, "the problem was not how to leave my family behind but how to bring them along."[3] None of us wants fully to discard our histories. Ultimately, our lives as professional academics have taken us far from where we began, as we have engaged in building, and finally inhabiting, our houses built of words. As adults, we have a different understanding of what class means; as children, we simply took our families—and ourselves—for granted.

EDUCATIONAL JOURNEYS: SETTING OUT

By elementary school, each of us had acquired the basic language of the classroom as our primary discourse. Linda and Beth spoke Standard English at home, and Frida the Spanish of the Chilean classroom. Nonetheless, there were other aspects of the classroom discourse that contributed to our individual struggles to stand out in a positive way, or even to fit in. James Gee's recognition of the broad range of skills and propensities associated with discourse is useful in clarifying codes operating outside of written or spoken language that hinder one's ability to fit into a particular cultural context. Gee, a social linguist, identifies the process of learning the rules of the classroom as the learning of a secondary discourse that incorporates knowledge of how to behave and speak appropriately.[4] As Gee describes it, a discourse is an "identity kit" that goes beyond language, providing individuals with a set of behaviors that, to a certain extent, bestow native status on them.[5] The person who has mastered the secondary discourse of a particular community knows how to behave in such a way as to go unnoticed among the natives.

While this process of enculturation grants a learner access to another community, membership is often accompanied by estrangement from one's family of origin. This alienation forever sets the high achiever outside the focal circle of her home community. It is not that the child and the home community openly or consciously reject each other. Rather, they coexist within a peculiar mix of admiration, distrust, and resentment. The scholar has seemingly abandoned one way of life for another that appears to offer greater rewards, enabling access to the larger community and all the accoutrements of mainstream existence. Here we see both the complexity and the paradox inherent in our achievements.

While for different reasons we were all marginalized early on, this did little to quiet our uncommon intellectual appetites. We were, in a number of ways, like Richard Rodriguez's "scholarship boy,"[6] whom the author deploys to describe his own propensity to absorb all he could of the formal word. Rodriguez recounts his practice of holing up in a quiet corner of a crowded home, tuning out busy family talk, the radio, or TV. He was intent on acquiring the literacy of the classroom, so he read avidly and thrived on the praise of teachers. In his urgency to become a part of the community of the educated, Rodriguez became more and more alienated from his family as the separation continued to deepen. Eventually, it would forever sever these most intimate ties, as he literally moved into another world.[7]

As young girls, we were not equally conscious of the role class would play in shaping our lives and our worlds. Linda was acutely aware of class, perhaps because her environment was so wrenchingly poor. She can remember her family's going two or three days with little or no food; she speaks of her mother saying "with utter, utter horror and despair, 'My children are going to starve to death, my children are going to starve to death.'"

"Even from the very beginning—it really was when I was a very, very little child—my earliest memories were of being different, and the difference having to do with class," Linda recalled. She speaks of learning, early in childhood, that words were a currency she could obtain and use; she largely attributes her ultimate arrival in the academy to her mother's insistence on early literacy. Rose believed that reading and writing, especially the language of the powerful, could mitigate the family's poverty and the experiences of racism. It was as if she anticipated what literacy theorists would argue much later—that the earlier the habits of reading and writing were learned, the more intrinsic they would be to the child's concept of herself and the range of her possibilities. Rose taught her children to read when they were little more than toddlers. Linda explained,

> My mother valued literacy and she was an extremely bright woman; she also did not want us to be distinguished by what we did not know. If anything, we would be distinguished for what we knew, so, in her words, "You don't send your kids to school at age four or five" (when we all started), "without their knowing how to read and write." So we learned to read and write from when we were like, around three. We grew up reading and reading and reading, and we didn't have television, like most of our friends had.

This set Linda firmly on the path to subsequent academic achievement.

Beth's earlier experiences were somewhat similar to, but also markedly different from, Linda's. There was no one in the Kelly family who could consciously mark the acquisition of literacy with the values attached to it by Linda's mother. As Beth remembered, in response to Linda's story,

> We had the literacy, but we didn't have the conscious appreciation of it. And that's the conundrum. I find it fascinating that both of my parents were highly, highly literate people—my mother still is—and like you, I grew up largely without television. We went to the library every Saturday and I always walked away with a pile of books. We were read to, we adored stories, but that's where it stopped. It remained tacit. It was never explicit.

Her parents placed a higher value on good behavior than on literacy, partly because they took the latter for granted, but also because they shared an entrenched respect for any form of institutional authority. As we have seen, Beth's father was in the Air Force and her mother also served in the military during World War Two. They came by their authoritarianism honestly.

Beth read early and voraciously, having taught herself literacy through a process educators have identified as "invented spelling."[8] Unlike Linda, she was never overtly praised for acquiring literacy skills, nor was she encouraged to achieve academic success. By contrast, Linda's mother wanted to hear *all* of her ideas. She valued them and offered what Linda now identifies as hyperbolic praise in response to everything her daughter wrote. What was explicit in Linda's experience remained implicit in Beth's. However, Beth's parents may have had more in common with Linda's mother than might appear at first glance. As Linda would remark, "These two apparently disparate attitudes—the explicit and implicit identification of the value of public literacy—share an inherent self-consciousness and a certain timidity in the face of the 'authoritative' institutional context of schooling." In Beth's case, the goal was good behavior. Linda learned that she would be able to speak and that her words would grant her a certain entrée into the public arena, where she knew well that Blacks were expected to remain silent. Consciously or not, young Beth and Linda both resisted the systematic stigmas and silences imposed on them by class. Overtly, in Linda's case, and covertly, in Beth's, both families' attitudes toward literacy served to reinforce the stigma of class, and perhaps to encourage their daughters' tendencies to assert themselves in school. This is consistent with Pierre Bourdieu's description of the sedimentation of linguistic hegemony: as a consequence of the ideology transmission that takes place primarily in schools, even those who are not "natural" inheritors of the language of public power still internalize beliefs about linguistic and cultural hierarchy.[9]

Both Linda and Beth learned to be good citizens; that is, both determined to be overachievers in school, exemplary when it came to public presentations of self. For Frida, gender initially combined with class in what would become a dance of silencing and resistance. Although Frida and her brother were both stellar students, it was *his* brilliance that was encouraged and rewarded within the family. In the face of this, she simply felt invisible:

> As a child, I was aware of this sense of invisibility that I experienced within my own home, because my intellect was not acknowledged. And I always felt that my brother's brilliance was constantly talked about. My parents said he should go to the Sorbonne. Where were they going to get the money for that? I remember that as a litany. It was like I wasn't there; the Sorbonne was never for me.

Frida nonetheless demonstrated extraordinary effort and achievement. She suggested that perhaps she pushed herself to be perfect in the hopes that this would earn her a share of the parental attention that was consistently directed toward her brother. Her mother had a hand in this; for example, she worked for an entire summer with Frida to help her daughter improve in spelling. Frida recalls that by the fourth or fifth grade, she was conscious of a sharp competitive edge, one that kept her at the top of her class and in overt competition with anyone who appeared similarly driven.

Frida implicitly acknowledged the impact of class and cultural context on her parents' inability to see her as she wished they would:

> My parents were survivors. They were barely making a living; I think they fell back onto the gender stereotypes and expectations then extant in Chile. I don't think my father ever took an interest in what I was learning in school, though he did expect me to get high marks. It was a "reading" of my worth that haunted me for years: If I wanted to get any attention I'd better be perfect. I cleaned the bathroom nicely, as instructed, and was praised for it. What I really longed for was to be affirmed for my intellect. It felt like a betrayal, not being seen for who I was.

Frida's early experiences marked her as developing a remarkable tendency toward overachievement. For all three of us, public presentations of self, enacted within and through the discursive regimes of the school, would became extremely important. At the same time, however, outstanding academic performances indicative of high levels of public literacy do not tell the whole story. The flip side of our overachievement (and, to some extent, its motivation) was marginalization—primarily class based, although other factors contributed. The houses we built of words always had shaky foundations.

We all recall aspects of our early schooling that distinguished us as individuals from the majority of our schoolmates, even from our friends. Beth carries painful memories of being ostracized by other students, and their parents, as the only child in an accelerated third-grade class whose father was not an Air Force officer, culminating in an ugly scene in the base commissary where a colonel's wife overtly berated her mother for not removing Beth from the class.[10] Despite her mother's ardent emphasis on reading and writing, Linda learned very early on that, in the early 1950s especially, "Blacks were expected to remain silent." In Chile, Frida was marginalized as a Jew in a Catholic classroom.

HIGH SCHOOL: THE GREENHORN, THE GEEK, AND THE DINGBAT

The tensions between our variously enacted scholastic overachievements and mitigating marginalizations of class, race, religion, and gender continued to color our educational experiences through high school. They would eventually shape more complicated issues as we sought out higher education—first college, then graduate training. There were few family models available to us. While both Frida and Beth had brothers who preceded them to college, Linda became the first—and only—of her siblings to graduate. The model of the "outsider within," developed by Patricia Hill Collins, characterizes many of our experiences in high school, college, and beyond. Outsiders within no longer belong to any one social group; they live in "social locations or border spaces occupied by groups of unequal power." We gain or lose identities as outsiders within according to how we are ranked in these locales; such spaces, Collins notes, are "riddled with contradictions." Significantly, she adds, "Under conditions of social injustice, the outsider-within location describes a particular knowledge/power relationship, one of gaining knowledge about or of a dominant group without gaining the full power accorded to members of that group."[11]

Frida the Greenhorn

Frida's high school experiences clearly illuminate the concept of the outsider within. Her entry into high school was preceded by an intensive five-month period of language study in an English as a Second Language (ESL) program. During those early weeks and months, her sense of displacement as a new-comer was acute. Virtually everything save her family was foreign—from landscape to language to dress. However, she found comfort in the ESL experience, for many students, as well as the teacher, were Spanish speaking. The teacher affectionately communicated understanding for the students' situation even while sternly admonishing them to resist the strong temptation to speak Spanish during class time. The first few months of high school were particularly challenging for Frida. Her strongest recollection is of long hours daily spent on homework, with a dictionary at her side, looking up one word after the other as she read. Her mother's assistance in learning English was essential to this process. In significant ways, Sara became her daughter's informal tutor, an advantage most immigrants cannot enjoy on the home front. Frida was thus spared the role that often falls to immigrant children—that of serving as translator and mediator between the family and the adopted society and culture.

Within a matter of months, Frida was on par with her native English-speaking classmates where syntax, grammar, and vocabulary were concerned. (To this day, she has a slight accent, although many people claim not to hear it.) With encouragement from home and teachers, and through her own well-honed work ethic, she studied hard and gained recognition through placement in honors classes and honor societies, as well as participation in school clubs and activities. She soon came to develop good friendships among her peers, becoming part of the "egghead" clique on campus. Thus, she came to experience some aspects of high school culture, American style. While for the most part she felt comfortable in her new situation, adaptable person that she is, there were areas of cultural unease that were particularly painful and, at least in her internalized experience, set her apart as an outsider. In retrospect, she says, "It is not surprising to me that my best girlfriends during my high school years were also immigrants, Elisa de León from Mexico, and Gloria Ibañez from the Philippines."

Frida's success in high school was influenced by the external demands of assimilation to a new culture, her inner drive to do well, and the support she received from others—parents, teachers, friends. The fact that she was an immigrant from a family with traditional values contributed to her inner tensions. The battles between the "old country" and the new are often played out around the children's efforts to fit in and find safety in their new surroundings. Being a Jew in a lower-middle-class, middle-American high school in

Alhambra, California, only added to the tensions. Her religion and ethnicity were ongoing reminders of difference, often provoking a sense of mild alienation from her peers.

Frida shared her high school experiences with Linda and Beth in bits and pieces throughout many conversations; her memories captured, by and large, in a series of flashbacks:

> *It is 1962. In my first semester of high school I respond to situations in ways that had been culturally appropriate for Chile. I arrive late to gym class one morning, join the class, and proceed to weep quietly for the rest of the hour. My teacher is shocked and chagrined—she reassures me after class that all is OK. Likewise, I have forgotten the meaning of some words during a vocabulary test in English class—the same emotional response follows on my part, the same perplexity on the teacher's. In the Latin American context of my past experience, it was standard to hear little girls crying during tests or when they did not meet expectations, and teachers did nothing to change it. I learn pretty quickly in my new environment that I must find other ways to deal with perceived failure. Here I must keep those feelings to myself, or not have them at all.*

> *It is 1963. I'm taking a test in my sophomore English class. I encounter a sentence I am to analyze that I don't understand, so I consult the teacher about it. It pertains to Babe Ruth, and I don't understand the allusion. I may have asked, who is this "Baby" Ruth? I remember the teacher laughing and laughing, out loud, long after I return to my seat. I may have passed the English test, but I surely failed the test of ordinariness.*

> *It is 1964, and at the open house at Alhambra High, my mother dutifully goes around visiting all my classrooms and meeting my teachers, with me in tow. My only memory of that day is intensely charged. She is speaking with my biology teacher. He is a good sort of man, concerned about his students, invested in his work, a bit cranky at times, as when he scolded my friend Gloria and me because we crack our knuckles: "Don't you know you'll get arthritis?" Now he sounds judgmental. He is telling my mother that I am a very good student, but he is worried about me: I should stop trying so hard and worrying about every point on a test. Perhaps it is his tone that communicates disapproval, but I feel shamed and put down; evidently I have failed to meet yet another set of cultural expectations.*

It was not until quite recently, when Frida encountered Richard Rodriguez's discussion of the "scholarship boy," that she came to understand some of the nuances of this communication. As discussed earlier, Rodriguez's drive to succeed came from his working-class background and its distance from the values of the classroom.[12] For Frida, the push "to kill herself studying," as she characterized her high school and college years to Linda and Beth, devolved from a perfectionism modeled after her mother, but also founded on the need to succeed as an immigrant. Frida's drive to position herself at the center of academic life and thereby gain status and belonging was indicative of her having acquired a new "identity kit" that could compensate for her status as an outsider.

Frida's high school experience was rich and complicated, positive and alienating. On the whole, despite some of the moments of cultural nonbelonging that she has narrated, those years afforded her a relatively safe transition into American culture. It was also a time when her identity as an intelligent, competent youth was firmly established through academic success, membership in multiple honorary societies, and the external affirmation of a generous college scholarship award in her senior year. On the home front, life was mainly calm and worry free. Both of Frida's parents worked very hard outside the home, so she had to contribute to the household, mostly through kitchen chores. At fourteen, she was cooking for the family. "I was not the only one to experience relief," she recalled,

> when a couple of years later my mother's parents moved to the States and took up residence with my aunt's family, just a few blocks away. From then on, Grandma Ella, a wonderful cook, walked over regularly to prepare meals for my family. From then on, I only had the less demanding tasks of table setting and dishwashing.

Frida was devoted principally to schoolwork during her high school years. Her parents did not require her to work for pay, "I suspect because they wanted to spare me the experience they had had as teenagers, when they had to quit school and get jobs to help support their families," Frida recounted. "I guess their ideal was to give their kids the time to devote themselves to their studies, and we were able to live up to that ideal." So Frida spent most summers attending summer school until right before her senior year, when she began working as an operator at the telephone company, a summer job she held for several summers.

By the end of high school, Frida had become successfully acculturated to American society; she no longer felt like a stranger and had acquired the language and cultural apparatus needed to function fairly effortlessly in her adopted country. A good deal of the credit belongs to her, for her hard work in her studies and her efforts at adaptation through extracurricular activities and social interactions. Her loving and supportive family should not be ignored, however, for this gave her the safety to venture out into new and risky places. Her parents—especially her mother—also provided her with a model of perseverance and a "can do" attitude in the face of difficulties (Sara had, as we have seen, managed to traverse cultures not just once, but twice over). Her parents' emphasis on education, undoubtedly influenced by their Jewish backgrounds, authenticated Frida's educational aspirations. Externally, she had adapted so well that one of her high school teachers disparagingly—and mistakenly—suggested that she was "plastic," presumably bending here and there as needed to fit in. In reality, things were more complex. Years later, after watching *American Graffiti*, Frida went into a depression. The movie featured high school life in 1950s small-town America; the time and locale were not her own, but nonetheless it tapped into Frida's repressed pain, reminding her of the layers of alienation she had felt in her adopted culture, at least in the early high school years.

It is essential to focus on the uniqueness of a single life in order to learn about the human condition. But this perspective is ultimately limited; focusing exclusively on a single life fails to account for the diversity of human experience and for the role that difference plays in shaping our lives and our responses to our environment. As we examined our lives, we saw both similarities and vast differences at play. This was especially so during our adolescent years. Linda and Beth, like Frida, had to contend with marginalizations that exacerbated the pain of maturing that adolescence entails. Despite the fact that Linda and Beth are both American born, they had less in common with each other during those years than did Linda and Frida, for whom success and the privilege of a supportive environment were central aspects of their high school experiences. By contrast, in those years, Beth knew little of either support or success.

Linda the Geek

Linda's conscious choice of a magnet business high school was pragmatic— she hoped that the large number of minority students would help her escape the racism of her earlier schooling. Her family's class marginalization had also been reduced by the time she began high school. Her father had died and her mother was receiving his Social Security; her older sisters had become the family breadwinners. The family no longer lived in aching poverty but had stable, if limited, sources of income. High school promised Linda the secretarial skills necessary to enter the work force after graduation, while also offering some college preparatory classes. During her sophomore year, Linda and her friend Sylvia, attempting to replace the external emblems of the lower class, decided to buy navy blue blazers and burgundy skirts, "so we could look like we went to one of the prep schools in Manhattan." They wanted to look like the rich kids on the long subway rides that took them from their homes in the Brooklyn projects to Central Commercial High School (CCHS) in Manhattan. Clearly, class marginalization and awareness of her distance from the mainstream continued to shape Linda's consciousness, even after she moved out of extreme poverty.

Linda poignantly captured her high school experience as a time "marked by the extremes of high achievement and quiet despair." In high school, she was an exemplary student, a leader, and a high achiever. She was articulate in speech and writing, often taking center stage in oratorical events and essay contests. At home, the family lived frugally and at times painfully. Material want and emotional illness constantly threatened their well being; one of Linda's sisters suffered from severe depression. The Baptist church, where Linda was a faithful member—with a significant place in the young adult choir—mediated between the two worlds. She always received loving praise and recognition in church, where she could allow "the poignant gospel harmonies to give expression to a profound shadow of sorrow that followed me at every turn."

By the time Linda reached high school, the emphasis on language she had acquired at her mother's knee was paying off. Her competence in the use of language had, ironically, set up a boundary between herself and her friends. This is how she puts it:

> *I knew, without question, that I could manipulate language to write and speak forcefully. This was a source of enormous power, but it was also the most significant point of distinction between me and most of my peers. Certainly, few of my friends in the projects, not far from Coney Island, shared or appreciated this distinction. Then, as is still often the case, I was accepted by my community friends, but regarded nonetheless as the oddball egghead, who marveled at Ravel and Tchaikovsky as often as Smokey Robinson and the Temptations. With the exception of Sylvia and Orease, who both encouraged me to value my achievements, most dismissed me as an amusing, gregarious geek. I could not be otherwise; I relished the writing assignments, and wrote adolescent poetry. All the while I was falling deeply in love with words. Writing was a sensuous experience. Approaching each writing assignment, I would begin to imagine the shape and direction of the piece and feel a low, visceral excitement. Titles took center focus, openings stumped me while I worked my way toward pithy closings. My sense of myself was safely balanced in words, and my high school identity was constructed primarily in the language arts classroom.*

Often to her own astonishment, Linda stood out in other areas, as well, winning the Miss CCHS title in her senior year, a distinction for business acumen and decorum: "We were judged by our appearance in business suits, complete with pill box hat and white gloves, as we answered the questions on office protocol from the corporation representatives assembled before us." In addition, she graduated with a number of awards, among them the medal for top student in biology. Yet she recalled that by the end of high school she had given up on her earlier fantasies of becoming a physician:

> After all, I was engaged to be married and everyone knew I would be an English teacher. It was 1965, and I was a poor Black girl from city housing who

was distinguished enough by her scholarship to go to college, never mind an am-
bition to go to medical school. Only very recently, when my old high school
friend reconnected with me, was I reminded that I dreamed of being a doctor.

We see here the confluence of gender and class issues in shaping the scope of
choices available to Linda. Given her class and racial backgrounds, the encouragement and support she received from her school to attend college was
mainly due to the extraordinary nature of her scholarly accomplishments.[13]

Linda remembered never hesitating to enter speech or essay contests
throughout high school. She had willing coaches who were generous with encouragement and praise. "My English teachers were my greatest allies, my
most patient of mentors, who looked over my shoulder, reading, marking, and
declaring me word-worthy, again and again. It was as if the teachers had se-
cretly conspired with my mother." She recalled her mother, even more than her
teachers, telling her to "say something else," to "put a little more in," after
reading her written work. It wasn't until she reached college, or even graduate
school, that Linda realized "how much this steadfast belief in me had buoyed
me forward. I was very fortunate to have gotten constant attention, coaching
and praise. I loved each of my English teachers. In them I saw modest elo-
quence and grace." Linda's senior year was a fitting culmination of her commitments to multiple clubs and college preparatory and honors courses.

In addition to this rigorous schedule of classes and extracurricular activities, Linda held a part-time job in Manhattan as a telephone information operator, working three or four hours a day after school. She also continued her
active involvement in church, where with the choir she traveled to other
churches, often at some distance from home. At her "sweet sixteen" she became engaged to her boyfriend of two years, whom she would marry just two
months after high school graduation, "even though by my senior year, he was
already showing signs of disaffection, and I, considerable doubts." Linda's
beloved older sister got married and left home before finishing high school,
only to return a year later in the midst of an emotional breakdown, joining the
sister who had earlier been diagnosed with clinical depression. By all ap-
pearances, and in certain respects, Linda lived a rich, ordinary life, but the at-
mosphere at home was often emotionally taut. Her mother worried about her
sisters' condition, for which there seemed to be no consistent help because
money and other resources were always short. In retrospect, Linda recalls that
her mother seemed understandably relieved that her youngest child was "doing well, engaged to an upstanding college boy and headed toward college
herself. Mother needn't worry about Linda. She was taking good care of herself, or so it seemed."

As high school graduation drew near, Linda was encouraged by her teachers to apply to college: "I thought, I don't know how I'm going to get to col-

lege, but I'm thinking about it, and the teachers think I should go, and I remember my mother saying I'd have to get scholarships." Indeed, upon her graduation Linda received a New York City Mayor's Committee on Scholastic Achievement Scholarship. But none of Linda's achievements were unalloyed; as she recalled, "When I went into the doors of Central Commercial High School, I was just such a perfect kid, but then I walked back into a world that was filled with all sorts of difficulty and stuff that I didn't understand." In the vortex of this paradox, she nonetheless followed through with the plans for college: "I was headed somewhere, but I scarcely knew the direction, the obstacles, or the rewards."

Beth the Dingbat

Beth's high school years held little joy or promise. "This was not an Ozzie and Harriet adolescence," she acerbically asserted, speaking of her problematic home life and the challenges of high school in a conservative small town. Her high school years were difficult. Her father had retired from the Air Force; his chronic unemployment and alcoholism were just two of many contributing factors to acute family dysfunction. Beth's immediate family lived with her grandmother, and the house was also shared with other extended family members. It seethed with tensions. The adults around her were preoccupied with their own problems or the addictions—to alcohol, cigarettes, and gambling— that were fueled by private demons. Privacy was unavailable; there literally was no place to hide. From the age of thirteen, Beth escaped into a series of after-school and weekend jobs in retail sales or office work that kept her out of the house. School always took second place.

While Beth did well in her classes and got good grades, she was neither challenged academically nor encouraged by most of her teachers. As very little was expected of her, she lacked dreams and expectations. Her parents expected her to get a full-time secretarial job after high school graduation. Beth saw little charm in this but, given the family's economic circumstances, she could not envision alternatives, and high school seemed a bleak and barren passage. A couple of "snapshots" capture some of the tensions in Beth's life during her adolescent years:

It is 1965. I am a sophomore at the public high school in the small, conservative South Jersey town where my parents have retired. My father's Air Force pension is small, not enough for the family to live on. He is permanently unemployed, a man in his late forties with a high school education and a tendency to overdo the vodka. My mother manages the florist's shop on Main Street. I endure an obligatory annual conference with my guidance counselor, a well-dressed, middle-aged woman who wears her hair in a matronly bun. She asks if

*I have thought about my future. I make up a plan on the spot, saying that I hope
to attend Mount Holyoke College and study French. One day I want to be an in-
terpreter at the United Nations. The guidance counselor seems surprised. She
coughs gently and then suggests that perhaps I am "aiming too high." "Girls
like me" should be thinking of getting married. Typing and shorthand would be
more "realistic" for me than college, "given where I come from." She does not
say "the wrong side of the tracks." She does not need to.*

Had Beth been middle class, the counselor likely would have encouraged
her, as intelligence is frequently associated with class status. Deb Busman
writes that she was almost forty years old "before I truly questioned the lies
that had been told about my intelligence—I was too 'slow,' I wasn't smart
enough to go on in school, I would never 'amount to anything,' higher education wasn't for 'people like me.'"[14]

When the exchange with her guidance counselor took place, Beth had completed nearly two years of the secretarial training track. Her parents encouraged her in this, since college was "not in the family vocabulary." "Just for
the hell of it," Beth took the SAT in her senior year. Her high verbal score
prompted the school counselors to suggest that she apply to college. By then,
it was too late: "There was no family support and things within the family
were not real good at that point in time; there was no money." Beth was bored
by the secretarial training curriculum and sought refuge in novels, poetry, and
her journal. When Frida and Linda marveled at Beth's remarkably capacious
memory for facts—what Beth calls her "unending supply of tedious trivia"—
she explained that she began reading voraciously very early in life. While
there were obvious gains, she also paid a price.

*It is 1966. My U.S. history teacher, who also coaches junior varsity football, of-
ten keeps me after class. He puts his arm around my shoulders, not sexually but
in an avuncular manner. He is fond of me, he says. He cautions me repeatedly
that it's not good for an attractive girl like me to be such a "brain." He warns
me that if I become too intellectual I will have trouble getting a boyfriend. He
tells me I have to "act more feminine." I take this advice to heart. I shut up in
class; I experiment with lipstick and mascara; I start reading* Seventeen *magazine the way born-again Christians read the Bible.*

Beth recounted her efforts to deal with this dilemma. The "class act" she
eventually perfected implicated gender, sexuality, and class in a complex set
of performances and representations.[15] In southern New Jersey, in the early
sixties, whiteness and heterosexuality were both normative and uninterro-
gated. As an adolescent, Beth took being both white and straight entirely for
granted. Yet, she remembers, "In my heart, I knew that I was *not* straight; the
dark secret of mortal sin had haunted me as a pre-pubescent and would sus-

tain a ghostly presence in my soul until I came out while in college in the early seventies. I was concerned (if not always consciously) with 'passing' for what I was not along multiple dimensions of identity." Beth worked very hard to look, walk, and talk like someone enrolled in a New England prep school. She won a coveted salesclerk position, working part time during school terms and full time during summer and holiday vacations at the high-end women's sportswear shop that sold the dyed-to-match Villager skirts, knee socks, and sweaters that were essential to her performance. Since a deep employee discount came with the job, she could afford the expensive preppy look that would otherwise have been beyond her means.

Beth remembered:

> I profoundly believed that if I could somehow present myself "properly," convincing people that I was precisely as I appeared—a normal preppie—I would belong. No matter how hard I worked at it, though, I was never fully a success. I fooled a lot of people a lot of the time—but I never really fooled myself.

It was only in the process of acknowledging and trying to come to terms with her ambivalence about "passing" in connection with lesbian sexuality that Beth began to see the dangers of passing in connection with class. Today, she sees both forms of passing as intricately connected, interwoven, and even more dangerous in combination than either might be if considered separately. As she put it,

> The forms of denial that I learned from my parents—mainly but not exclusively around class—were centered more on style than substance, on performance over content. Their denial sprang from the pain attendant on accepting the hard truths of life. My father drank to dull that pain; my mother sought simply to keep up appearances. My way out, away from truth and into my own "class act" of denial, was found in fantasies of white, middle-class, feminine "respectability," fed by magazines marketed to teenage girls.[16]

Linda and Beth shared the need to pass with regard to class. Frida did not, perhaps because, raised in a culture with no *Seventeen* magazine, she had no expectation that one "needed" to have multiple outfits or "look a certain way." She was shocked by the absence of uniforms in U.S. schools, aware even at age thirteen that the system of wearing street clothes to school exposed economic inequalities and encouraged unnecessary preoccupation with self-presentation. She took her mother as her model: have a few good things to wear, change your good clothes when you get home, wear an apron while you cook or eat (which she still routinely does; consequently some of her twenty-year-old clothes still look "like new"—surely a survival strategy for the financially strapped).

More was going on for Beth than her efforts to pass class-wise, or to adopt the looks of conventional femininity. She was located in a matrix of marginalized identities—as a working-class young lesbian not readily embraced by the norms of the American mainstream. Her emergent sexuality was implicated in her profound isolation. Early in her sophomore year, she was caught necking with a girlfriend at a school event. As punishment, she was banned from all extracurricular activities: "My graduating class was ninety-four students. This was not a secret. This was a very small town, and a very small fish bowl." More punitive sanctions have been and are still imposed on teenagers for being gay, lesbian, bisexual, or transgendered. On one hand, Beth was grateful not to have been expelled from school. But on the other, the opportunity to participate in debates, speech contests, and other activities had militated against both the boredom she was experiencing in the classroom and the dysfunction and denial that colored her family life. As a result, passing, often with a vengeance, for what she was not became even more of an imperative.

Recalling what it meant to inhabit an environment where she could not be truly and openly herself in various aspects of her life, Beth acknowledged that during her high school years—in fact, until she started college some five years after graduation—she "lost a sense of myself as an intelligent human being." She told Frida and Linda of how a girlfriend, and subsequently her parents and other family members, referred to Beth by the nickname "Edith," after the Edith Bunker character in *All in the Family*, "because I was such a dingbat."

"You're kidding!" Frida interrupted, incredulous.

"That's hard to believe." Linda, too, was shocked.

They were both astonished—even a brief acquaintance with Beth reveals her impressive and eloquent intelligence. "I *was* a dingbat," Beth asserted. "I felt that the only way that I could survive was by denial. It was a form of passing. I was passing for an anti-intellectual, often stupid person because that was the point of entry into cultural acceptance, because there was so much about me that I perceived was so wrong. . . . I *became* Edith." It wasn't until she enrolled in college, some years down the line, that Beth would finally enjoy a taste of the academic success and attention that Linda and Frida experienced repeatedly in their high school years.

We shared our stories of high school and college across several seasons in which Linda and Frida were often preoccupied by their adolescent daughters' transitions from high school to college. As we began our conversations, Linda's daughter had just graduated from a small, select private high school and was headed for an Ivy League university, while Frida's daughter was beginning to consider colleges to which she might apply. The contrast between the girls' experiences, as daughters securely located "within" highly educated, professionally oriented middle-class families, and our own, as "outsider" daughters of economically marginalized families, brought class issues into sharp focus. The two girls have grown into confident, articulate young women, aware that options and choices are open to them. They see the world as available, and welcoming, in ways it has never appeared to us. As Linda and Frida compared notes on the ritual progression of "college visits" they had made, describing in detail the many excursions to schools up and down the East Coast or across the Midwest, the extent to which our own options for higher education were constrained by class became acutely, even painfully, clear.[17]

OF CULTURAL AGORAPHOBIA: BETH'S STORY

Beth applied to college at age twenty-three "as an act of desperation," fed up with the dead-end secretarial positions in which she'd worked since high school. Her path to higher education was marked by more than one false start. Her parents had actively opposed the idea of college, believing that her high school secretarial training would be enough to fall back on should the need arise. Thus, a conditional acceptance from Douglass College, requiring that she make up more than a year of high school units, was easily declined. Acceptance into the honors Home Economics program at Drexel University seemed attractive, but turned out to be heavily laden with science and math courses. Beth, utterly unprepared for such study, was compelled to abandon the idea. In addition to the logistical problems that rendered Douglass and Drexel impossible, Beth battled deeply embedded doubts and insecurities that blocked her repeatedly. When she eventually enrolled at the newly established community college in Mays Landing, her anxieties blossomed. Tension was palpable as she told of being unable to leave her car and simply sitting in the parking lot, "scribbling dreadful, depressing poetry," for hours on end instead of going to class.

"What was going *on*?" Frida wondered.

"I was scared to death," Beth shrugged. "And I felt, I think, completely inadequate. I felt that by defying my parents and doing this, I was leaving the family."

In an essay entitled "Class and Education," bell hooks says more about this familiar fear, felt by parents as well as their young adult children, over the possible consequences when the children of the poor and working classes attain higher education. hooks recalls her parents' concerns over her leaving home to attend college at Stanford University: "Like many working-class folks, they feared what college education might do to their children's minds even as they unenthusiastically acknowledged its importance."[18] As difficult as it was for Beth to find the courage to step into the unknown, this probably filled her parents with dread over the possible loss of their daughter. Beth's recognition of their attendant sense of loss was further complicated by her own fears of disconnection:

> It's very hard for me now to look back on the person that I was at eighteen, or nineteen, or even twenty-three, and articulate much beyond a sense of being awash in terror and the knowledge that there was a whole lot wrong with me. I was the problem; if I could just behave, dress, look appropriately somehow, everything would be solved. By the time I was twenty-two, I knew that that was wrong. I knew that there had to be other and better ways of making a life for myself in the world. I didn't know what they were, though. My fear was taking myself away from my family, even though my family was no safe haven; it was no place of grace for me.

Eventually, Beth was able to bring herself to apply and follow through with her acceptance to a new state college in southern New Jersey, recognized particularly in its early days for its liberal climate and experimental programs. But this process, too, was fraught with false starts and ambivalence. Enrolling at Richard Stockton College (then Stockton State College) was nothing like the planned, conscious, and extended decision-making process that Linda and Frida were undertaking with their daughters. Motivated by the sense that she had to find a way to a different life, in the fall of 1972, Beth took time off from her office job and drove out to the Stockton campus. She did not make it past the parking lot of the Admissions Office: "I pulled into the parking lot and immediately had the mother of all anxiety attacks. I sat there for over an hour, shaking, unable to get out of the car, so eventually I just drove away."

In retrospect, Beth recognized that this paralytic moment reflected complex anxieties that coalesced around class-based fears. As ignorant as she was regarding higher education, she knew intuitively that enrolling at Stockton would pull her out of a world that, while debilitating, was nonetheless familiar. College represented a completely foreign world for her. Indeed, it has been noted that a common experience for working-class students in college is to feel like they are "immigrants," for they encounter "different notions about money, privacy, creativity, family, work, play, security." Valerie Miner has coined the term "cultural agoraphobia" to characterize that experience, for "the landscape seems dotted with land mines that might blow up in our faces at any time."[19] A month after her failure to approach the Admissions Office, it occurred to Beth that she could request a college application by phone. She was quickly accepted without conditions under the Open Admissions policies in place at the time.

However, there was another issue to address. Beth feared telling her parents about her plans, a well-warranted concern since her father reacted to her news by leaving the room. Her mother attempted to dissuade her, questioning Beth's motives. At twenty-two, Beth realized that college education would change her relations with her parents, and she feared further alienation. As she put it, "Dysfunctional as it was, my family remained my family. Angry as we sometimes were with each other, my parents were people I dearly loved. Although I hadn't lived with them for years, and despite their total inability to understand or support my choice, I did not want to sever that connection." Working-class writers have validated this intuition in accounts of their own lived experience, suggesting, as does Suzanne Sowinska, for example, that her parents offered her no support, moral or financial, because they "did not want to participate in my separation from them."[20] Without her parents' emotional or financial support, Beth managed to complete an illustrious college career, earning her BA in three years of study.

Beth quickly came to characterize her first terms at Stockton as "the world turned upside down," a time when she discovered that she had a mind and could be rewarded for using it. She walked around the campus, which was still under construction, with no hint of "ivy-covered halls," in a constant state of awe and excitement. She recalls how "my mind literally came to life. I soaked up knowledge like a thirsty sponge. For the first time I could remember, I felt fully and blissfully alive." While her transition to college was quite different from Frida's or Linda's in that both went on to college immediately after high school and had the moral (if not financial) support from their families that Beth lacked, the three of us shared an absence of parental advice or informed participation in our decision-making processes. In making the transition between high school and college—and beyond—each of us was very much on her own.

WANTING IT ALL: LINDA'S STORY

Linda described how, even as she was receiving awards at her high school graduation, she nonetheless returned to the community where she was engaged to marry her first steady boyfriend. Though her mother supported her ambitions and Linda was determined to go to college, her options were limited:

> I went to Long Island University. I had been accepted at Hunter College, which in those days was a far better school, but LIU was a private school and gave me a $1,750 per year scholarship. I still remember the exact amount. It would have been ungrateful for me not to take this money and say "thank you." There was

nobody to say, "go to Hunter instead of LIU." Going to college was almost
like—you go to whichever school you were pointed to, you know?

Linda acknowledged that she "always felt that certain kinds of choices
were unavailable to me because my first commitment was to my marriage."
Nonetheless, she felt that she had something to prove, given her marriage, to
those who questioned her ability to persist at LIU. She received a small scholarship from her church, and felt that "with that kind of public eye on me, I
couldn't be the one where they'd say, 'Oh, she got married and had a baby.'
I had to say, 'I'm going to do both, college and marriage.'"

CONSTRAINT, SERENDIPITY,
AND SOCIAL JUSTICE: FRIDA'S STORY

Frida was equally determined to succeed in college, despite also having little
guidance or support around making the choice of which school to attend. Her
success in high school, coupled with her parents' aspirations (even though
they held working-class jobs), left no doubt that she would continue to college, but her enrollment at the University of Southern California (USC) was,
at best, accidental:

> I had gotten a state scholarship. I thought at first that I'd go to UCLA, as my
> brother had. But it was a long commute, and my parents probably couldn't eas-
> ily afford room and board. I knew somebody in high school who was going to
> USC, which was much closer than UCLA. In a casual conversation with this kid,
> what came up was that maybe I could use the scholarship money at USC and
> have a shorter commute. So, I transferred the scholarship over, and that's how
> my college decision was made.

This serendipitous development allowed Frida to live at home and commute
to campus, an arrangement that saved her parents the cost of university housing, which would have been a burden. It also permitted her to stay within her
family's ambit, a choice that seemed appropriate at the time, since they were
only a few years removed from the traditional family-based Chilean culture.

Frida's parents were, to the best of their ability, a source of both financial
and emotional support:

> *My father lent me the money—$500, as I recall—to buy a used car. It was a red
> Corvair. At age seventeen, I joined the hoards of commuters clogging the con-
> gested freeways of Los Angeles. My parents rejoiced with me in having this op-
> portunity. From them, I inherited the view that it was possible "only in Amer-
> ica." Had my family remained in Latin America, it is unlikely that I would have*

become a university professor. My life would have been shaped by narrower vi-
sions and possibilities.

Reflecting on her years at USC, Frida grew pensive. "Did I get a good education? Would I go there again? No. I would go to a small, liberal arts college where I could get some attention, like Beth got at Stockton." This is ironic, for Frida remembered learning, as a college senior, that her scholarship could have been applied to Occidental College, "a small, liberal arts, very fine college" that was closer to her home than either USC or UCLA. She would have thrived in a place like that, but she didn't know Occidental existed—and there was no chance meeting with an Occidental student as there had been with the schoolmate on his way to USC.

Practical matters motivated our college choices; the locations were accessible, the institutional reputations were acceptable, if not exactly stellar, and the costs were within reach. Like so many other first-generation college students, we were motivated more by practicality than by measured selectivity. After all, our parents were unable to navigate for us, knowing neither the direction nor the landmarks. The most they could do was stand aside and watch us meander ahead, as they struggled with their own uncertainties.

As constrained as our choices were in applying to college, we nonetheless managed to grow and thrive while earning our degrees. Thanks to the times and our teachers, for each of us this was a period of significant personal and intellectual growth. The late 1960s and early 1970s was a time of enormous social and political ferment; our consciences were captured by movements we saw swirling around us—civil rights, women's liberation, anti-war, and the nascent lesbian and gay liberation struggles. Each of us recalled professors who inspired and encouraged us to make important connections between personal experience and a larger political agenda. "I had a very influential teacher," Frida said, "who was passionately committed to social transformation. I think it was through his influence that I majored in sociology because I wanted to change the world." She became active in social change movements, but it was through taking classes with this particular professor that she was able to make connections between her own life experiences and the wider world. For each of us, recognition by especially nurturing teachers helped ease our discomforts and contributed to our growing sense of stability in a new and often strange environment.

A TIME OF TRANSFORMATION: BETH'S STORY

At the turn of each college corridor, Beth discovered another aspect of the "possible person" she ached to be. In its early days, Stockton State was ablaze with the energy of students who were appreciated for their queries and their insights, however radical. Veterans fresh from Vietnam, along with older, "nontraditional" students excited that a four-year college had opened in the community, added a rich, diverse flavor to the student body. Stockton's faculty took student passions and dissidence seriously and supported students' efforts to have a significant voice in college governance.[21] There was a nascent women's union and a gay students' organization. Beth found herself in a veritable liminal space wherein she was no longer alone in her interrogations of middle-class and heterosexual assumptions. Anthropologist Victor Turner sees the liminal as a place of broad possibilities. He refers to it as a *subjunctive state* because it provides for the expression of "supposition, desire, hypothesis, possibility, etc."[22] For Beth at Stockton, traditional, conservative values were routinely interrogated, thereby legitimating previously silenced voices. This allowed Beth, for the first time in memory, to find a firm footing.

Beth explained to Frida and Linda,

> I don't remember ever having something firm to grab onto that gave me a sense of who I was or that it was OK to be who I was until I was twenty-three years old and finally enrolled at Stockton. Over the course of the first year or so, of the things about me that I had been taught to think of as wrong, or despised—all of a sudden it was the world turned upside down, because I was getting rewarded for them.

At Stockton, Beth found mentors, teachers from whom she not only received praise and recognition commensurate with her talents, but in whom she also recognized depths of concern, involvement, and commitment. This afforded her models of how professors may assist a student's enculturation into college discourse. Equally importantly, they may encourage the student's oppositional discourse in a safe space, facilitating the student's successful passage through the institution. Beth encountered professors who were willing, as Mikhail Bakhtin would suggest, to orchestrate the inherent *heteroglossia* of the institution. That is, they were sympathetic to the range of existing voices and they took the responsibility of creating an environment where students could voice divergent points of view very seriously.[23]

For Beth, Professor Bill Daly became just such a model. Recalling the end of her first term at Stockton, when she was preparing a final paper in his class in political science, Beth described a period of considerable struggle, marked by serious self doubt. The assignment represented both the first long paper she'd ever prepared and the preponderance of the grade she would receive. Daly offered his students at least as much as he asked of them, but it was still an arduous and challenging project. Twenty-five years later, Beth recalled verbatim her professor's summary comment on her paper: "Finally, Beth, you write extremely well. At times, I found myself abandoning the critical eye with which I usually approach student papers and simply savoring your style." As she shared his words, she realized that they retained a powerful element of validation, even after so many years. Daly's words marked the moment when she could begin to think of herself as "a possible person," someone worthy of a place at the academic table, even though she could hardly have imagined that she would complete her degree in three years, building an impressive academic record and becoming an effective student leader and activist along the way.[24]

There were others who would help Beth come to terms with college and serve as role models. In the mid-seventies, there were few women political scientists; Beth became acutely aware of the risks her choices would entail when she witnessed at close hand a brutal battle that resulted in the only female political science professor being denied tenure at Stockton. Over the long term, the incident afforded Beth profound insights into navigating the rough tides of academic politics. At the time, however, she was shocked and stunned by the misogyny of the overwhelmingly male faculty. "This woman had high standards. She was rigorous. I learned so much in her classes," Beth recounted. "I heard men in their late twenties describing a woman in her mid-forties as 'an irascible, demanding *woman.*' They spat out 'woman' with such venom; it was horrible." Beth shuddered as she spoke. "For me to hear this, at twenty-five, was frightening. I just thought, *this is what I'm going to face. I didn't think I had the strength.*" Beth eventually realized that some good did come out of this ordeal: "Of course, the professor left Stockton," she concluded, "but she had a distinguished career, and I was able to tell her how she'd inspired me, and say thanks, when I ran into her at a political science conference a few years ago."

Beth's college experiences were, on the whole, life affirming and transformative; she eventually found the courage to claim identities she had been taught to despise:

> Stockton literally gave me life, because for the first time in twenty-three, twenty-four years, it was OK to be who I was, it was OK to be a woman, it was OK to be smart, it was OK to have read stuff, it was OK to want to talk about what I had read, and it was OK ultimately to be able to come out as a lesbian, and not be punished and in fact be all the more respected.[25]

"I ALREADY HAVE THE MRS.": LINDA'S STORY

In contrast to Beth's transforming experience in college, her coming to know and to accept her peculiar insight, her voice and energy as a leader, Linda had

little to note regarding her undergraduate years as a time of particular significance in her coming to recognize herself as a thinker or writer with specific
talents. Nonetheless, those years for Linda were passed productively, with
noteworthy achievement and some measurable development as a nascent
writer. Yet, her early marriage overshadowed her college years and rendered
each semester and each course something to "get over with," in order to get
on with the business of marriage and earning an income. It was the first time
that her education moved from foreground to background, becoming merely
a means toward an end. Linda worked nearly full time, along with going to
school, and her resources were stretched to the limit. As she recalled:

*It was the mid-sixties, and in spite of the rise of the second wave of feminism,
many of us reached the end of our high school years with steady boyfriends and
even engagement rings to match. We took for granted the inevitability of marriage and the development of a significant aspect of our identity through our association with a man. I can remember my mother privately lamenting my early
marriage, but reassuring us both, "Marriage too is a career, you know." I held
firm to the decision to go on to college and regarded that as my private war
against the cultural mandate to subjugate my desires and goals to my husband's.
Yet I could not go so far as to foreclose on the marriage. Three years of "going
steady" and intimacy could only culminate respectably with marriage to this
young man, my first boyfriend. Moreover, he was a college boy from an upstanding family. He loved me and I loved him in return.*

*Few questioned my decision to go on to college. I felt I could not disappoint
the small community of my family, friends, and church members who anticipated
the professional I would become. From the start, however, I took my college life
as a pauper slips a second pair of shoes from the charity box. I was taking something I didn't need, was not entitled to. After all, I had expert secretarial skills
from the business high school I'd attended. I could type and take Pitman short-
hand as rapidly as the executive secretaries. I stayed on the periphery of college
life, attending classes regularly, but rejecting extracurricular activities. When I
saw young women and men emerge from the high-rise dormitory on campus, I
quickly diverted my attention, not even wanting to imagine what it would be like
to live away from home, but unmarried, within a community of students.*

*With nearly full-time employment and a husband who expected dinner on a
snack table in front of the TV after work, I saw regular study hours as a coveted
luxury for the first two years. By the second year, my thirst for something of the
ordinary undergraduate's life led me to the pledge line of the oldest African
American Sorority, Alpha Kappa Alpha. By this time, as well, considerable feedback from my English professors reinforced my decision to major in English, minor in secondary education, and fancy myself a writer. Prof. Joan Templeton, the
only female professor I studied with in the literature department, rewarded my
writing with one "A" after another. With her ironic, tongue-in-cheek humor and occasional profanity in front of the class, I saw a new kind of woman, a professor*

who smoked cigarettes during break and knew how to ignore rude, boorish com-
ments from late adolescent boys unused to female authority. She told me I could
write. In conjunction with the literature major, I took a minor in secondary ed-
ucation, and while most of the courses left me uninspired, my own readings in
psychology and the sociology of education started to provide a framework for
my passion for learning, my love of language, and my hopes of inspiring New
York, inner-city kids to read enthusiastically and well and to write with clarity.

Many young women of my college generation hoped to find a husband in col-
lege, or so I was told. Those of us who challenged this assumption went around
denying we were after the MRS., but rather looked forward to the BA or BS, just
as did our male counterparts. Therefore, when my education seminar professor
asked us all to articulate our reasons for going to college, I haughtily asserted,
"I'm here for my BA; I already have an MRS." Even then the irony did not es-
cape me: my husband was already more absent than present from his evening
seat in front of the television.

Shortly after her college graduation, Linda recalls coming to a new and different consciousness of the meaning of marginalization in her life and the
lives of those around her. Her first child, a son, was born in June, literally days
before her college graduation ceremony; that December, Linda began substi-
tute teaching in Ocean Hill-Brownsville, one of the most difficult sections of
Brooklyn. She reflected,

It wasn't until I went out to work as a teacher that I began to see what Paul Willis
calls "learning to labor" in particular ways, and that's when I became deeply disturbed by the ways in which inequalities get reproduced. I thought that it was
absolutely my job, my responsibility, to try to do something to rectify that. I began to recognize that something was going on, and it was larger than what was
happening just in my life.[26]

WANTING TO CHANGE THE WORLD: FRIDA'S STORY

Diverging from a common stereotype of idealistic and indulged middle-class
college students of our day, the three of us were well aware of the price of the
ticket. As college students, despite receiving scholarships and other financial
aid, each of us worked at part-time jobs, in offices or retail stores, to secure
her education. Frida spoke for all of us when she described her intense focus
on studying while being involved in extracurricular activities and working at
the telephone company during summer breaks. Scholarships paid her tuition,
but she needed books and clothes. Poignantly, she adds, "I don't know
whether my parents expected me to work. They were living on the margin as
immigrants, so I never asked. I simply knew that this was what I needed to
do. I never resented it; it was just the way it was."

USC was not a comfortable place for Frida. It was huge and not especially nurturing. Frida told of how she coped by devoting herself to her studies. With no one to guide her in the choice of a major, Frida changed majors several times before she settled on sociology, "because I thought I was going to change the world." Even though this was a "rather positivist department," she apparently found a few professors who seemed more concerned with social justice than many of their colleagues. She took several courses with these faculty, earning top grades and considerable praise and recognition for her accomplishments. This success, however, was faintly jaundiced when one professor who so admired Frida's talents, and who could have served as a very helpful mentor, perhaps even helping her to construct plans for further study after undergraduate school, eventually halted their frequent office-hour meetings. Frida remembered it vividly, recalling that, "He blew me away. I'd gone to talk to him about some academic question and as I was leaving, he said, 'You know, I don't think we should be seen together so often because people might talk.' And something about my being so attractive, so that was the end of that." In this moment, a potentially productive mentoring relationship abruptly ended.

In spite of Frida's eventual success, it behooves us to mark the incident and to approximate the loss. It was the late 1960s, as Frida reminded us, and she had "no analytical map" to help her find an appropriate way to respond to this incident beyond simply staying away from the professor. It would be many years before sexual harassment laws would be enacted and educational institutions mandated to put in place policies to help young women like Frida articulate grievances. In the absence of such institutional support or a more sophisticated personal compass, in addition to her social class and immigrant status, gender also constrained Frida's opportunities.

Each of us earned, along with the bachelor's degree, a deep commitment to making the world a different—and better—place. It's hard to tell if our shared idealism was an outgrowth of, or resistance to, our educational experiences during or just beyond college. What is clear is that it was out of a desire for social justice—expressed not just for ourselves, but on a far more encompassing scale—that each of us sought graduate education. As we began to enter this new and unfamiliar terrain, class issues would once again surface, in ways both similar to and different from what we had experienced while applying to, or forging successful careers at, our undergraduate schools.

PATHS TO GRADUATE SCHOOL

One consistent theme across college and graduate school, for all of us, was an overwhelming lack of choices, or even good advice, about what programs or universities we should seek out and attend. Once again, we had no models, no family support, and only ourselves to rely on. Linda Frost speaks for us all when she describes her own path to graduate education:

> I understand now how different [my] reasons were from those of many of my colleagues and friends who, either because of their backgrounds or because they were at a different stage in their indoctrination to the profession, made their graduate school choices and decisions based on very different things, things like finding someone with whom they wanted to work, link their name, and consequently position themselves professionally right from the start. Some of them knew to choose a school that had a strong department in the area of their "interest"—again, something I discovered much, much later. None of these things played a part in my final decisions.[27]

Frida echoed this in telling of her all but accidental route to the doctorate she completed at USC, saying, "I wanted to go to grad school, but where should I go? Not for a second did it occur to me to do a national search for someplace to go. Never. I couldn't. I didn't have any models; I had no one to advise me, so I was just fumbling around." When USC offered her a teaching assistantship, she decided to enroll in the social ethics program offered by the School of Religion. "If I couldn't study social justice in the Sociology Department," she recalled, "maybe religious studies was the place to do it. I think I went into social ethics because it just happened! It's crazy, like what Linda did!"

Indeed, Linda told a similar story of constrained choices and accidental affiliations. "I didn't attend a lot of schools," she said, "but I applied to a lot of schools and was accepted at different places before I actually went. I couldn't afford most of them. However, I did the master's in literature at New York University and continued there, working toward the Ph.D., until we left New York after the massive, city-wide budget cuts of 1976." She eventually applied for, and received, a Minority Advancement Program (MAP) Fellowship offered by the State of New Jersey to students who wished to pursue the Ph.D. and were willing to commit to teaching in New Jersey colleges or universities after completing their doctorates. However, at the time that she was accepted into the program, funding was restricted to those pursuing degrees in the natural and social sciences. In order to get MAP support, without which Ph.D. studies would have been impossible, she had to shift her focus from literature to linguistic anthropology. Perhaps this "just happened," as Frida put it earlier. However, neither Frida's nor Linda's choices were accidental; rather, class-based constraints limited their options. Certainly, the outcome for Linda was dictated by the arbitrary rules of the MAP.

Beth's story is similar. As college graduation drew near, she had a vague idea that she wanted to go to graduate school in political science and become a college professor. She only applied to one program, at the University of California, Berkeley. This wasn't arrogance. Berkeley had a very early deadline; Beth was so overwhelmed by putting that one application together that she couldn't bring herself to complete any others. Although Berkeley accepted her, she couldn't surmount the financial obstacles to attending as an out-of-state student. A year later, she entered the master's program at the Harvard Graduate School of Education (HGSE). Beth completed that degree and then spent several years doing grass-roots political work in Boston's lesbian and gay community before returning to South Jersey to help out when her father became ill. She returned to Stockton to teach developmental writing and critical thinking in the Basic Skills Program and, for a time, administer the Verbal Lab in the Skills Acquisition and Development Center. At this juncture, she realized she belonged in higher education and determined to pursue a doctorate.

Beth's route to doctoral study was nearly as fraught as her initial forays into college. She recalled:

> *Shortly after I learned that I'd been accepted at Harvard and Rutgers but rejected by Princeton, my father died. He left no insurance and my mother's Social Security was only a couple hundred dollars monthly; it looked for a bit as though she would be nearly destitute. I felt I would have to continue working full time. Then word came that my mother would receive a Veterans' Administration pension, which, while not munificent, would allow her some measure of independence. Harvard was still out of the question; I still couldn't leave her in South Jersey while I went off to Cambridge. Rutgers had also offered me a fellowship, however, and New Brunswick was only a hundred miles away. So I went there in search of a Ph.D., while my mother moved into a housing project, and somehow we managed.*[28]

By then, Beth was profoundly aware of how class had shaped her educational and life experiences. Yet it had only been a few years earlier, as a master's student at HGSE, that she began to perceive class in terms of what she would describe to Frida and Linda as "analytic consciousness." This occurred in the context of a course on the History of American Education in which the professor assigned students to write their families' educational histories. The day that the essays were due, students were asked to share highlights of their stories. Beth simply listened, stunned by the rich details that many others could relate. In several cases, family traditions of college attendance spanned two centuries. One student spoke proudly of his relationship to Marcus and Narcissa Whitman, Protestant missionaries who journeyed the Oregon Trail, claiming a Yankee heritage of Christian virtue. By contrast, Beth had only vague links to any generation prior to her grandparents'.

Beth's story did not end there, however:

That afternoon, as the seminar wore on, I understood why I'd been unable, for three months, to climb the marble stairs at the entrance to Widener Library. Day after day, I'd stood at the base of the steps, saying to myself, "Okay, today you're going in there," and then feeling paralyzed, unable to mount the steps. I remembered Ethel Curley's crossing the Atlantic in steerage to work as a chambermaid in Philadelphia at about the same time as the young scion of the Widener family had perished in the Titanic disaster.[29] My grandmother and young Widener may have been close in age, but they lived at opposite ends of the class spectrum. I could imagine her emptying the night soil of people with whom his family routinely socialized, sharing elegant dinner tables or boxes at the Academy of Music.

It slowly dawned on me that I belonged to the servants, the workers, on whose backs the libraries and monuments were built. I, too, had a place in a hierarchy of class oppression. The weight of unacknowledged history had intimidated me. I had felt I didn't deserve to enter Widener Library, which symbolized the University as a whole; indeed, I felt as though I were trespassing at Harvard. Class was no longer an abstraction; it had become my lived truth. That Ethel Curley had been invisible to history did not preclude my acknowledging her place in it, or claiming my own. The moment the seminar ended, I raced across Cambridge Common, into Harvard Yard, and up those intimidating marble stairs. I knew I belonged with the domestic servants, the workers, and that I belonged inside the doors of Widener, equally and irretrievably.

Joanna Kadi argues persuasively that "[u]niversities are designed to make working-class people feel like we don't belong." She suggests that the cumulative effects of such marginalization emerge "not because we invented them in a moment of deluded paranoia but because our daily living has taught us the truth." For Kadi, "to walk around a university campus saying 'I don't belong here' was true."[30] This certainly reflects the centrality of embodied knowledge, and its relationship to class marginalization, in the life narratives that Frida, Linda, and Beth have shared. But there is another side to marginalization; as Suzanne Sowinska suggests, it is also the "lived experience of class-based oppression" that "forces many working-class women academics from a cultural understanding of the operation of difference to a political recognition of the way in which social relations are ordered." Through learning "to create rearticulations of our experience," we may discover a new sense of identity; in "leaving behind what is familiar to us for unfamiliar intellectual and economic survival strategies," we can discover both "a catalyst for critique and a desire to understand new terms in the subject/subjugated argument, allowing for the possibility of agency and real movement."[31] Thus, what may begin as a survival strategy—finding ways to persist in a place where one is made to feel powerfully unwelcome—may end up, as Beth learned when she broached the steps of Widener Library, as a claiming of one's power over the world.

Empowerment never comes easily; Frida spoke for us all in describing her Ph.D. experience, saying, "This whole story was not an easy one." While her basic economic needs were met through fellowships and teaching assistant-ships, she felt marginalized as a Jew in her program in social ethics; her cur-riculum was grounded in exclusively Christian, and predominantly Protes-tant, religious traditions. She told of "reading Augustine and Aquinas and Luther, without being able to connect with who I was; the stuff I was cram-ming into my head had no personal resonance." Her initial graduate courses represented a long slog through what she characterized as "disembodied knowledge." Before taking comprehensive examinations, she took time off and worked for two years as director of family planning at the Los Angeles Free Clinic. While the work was challenging, she felt intellectually con-strained because "there was nobody to talk about a play with, or about a book that I was reading." As Frida put it, "The social activist part of me really liked what I was doing, but the intellectual part of me was dying." At some point after her first year on the job, she came to a decision: "I guess my heart was in academia, but I needed to find a way to make it work for me. So I did a lot of reading in that second year, focusing on Jewish topics." Before returning to USC to take her comprehensive exams, Frida sat in on courses at Hebrew Union College, immersing herself in Jewish literature and issues. "I needed it like water," she recalled, "being in that environment." She realized that she could only return to the Ph.D. program by planning a dissertation connected to Judaism. "I can't compromise that," she averred; "it's too much who I am."

Back at USC and facing the comprehensive exams, she began having a re-curring dream in which, while driving a vintage automobile down a darkened road, she encountered two people suddenly crossing the road at a sharp curve too late to avoid hitting—and killing—them. "They were my parents," she re-called. Her anxieties, focused in the dream, represented concerns common to working-class students at such points of major transition. Frida was moving to a new level of academic achievement, one closed to her parents. Death by auto, in the dream, reflected her fears of separation from them, heightened be-cause the new threshold of comprehensives was looming.

Thus, class issues, less salient as Frida searched for and reconciled her need to find a way to remain authentically Jewish in an overwhelmingly Christian academic environment of social ethics, nonetheless remained at the heart of her graduate school experience. While she did splendidly on the exams, and completed her dissertation in only two years, in the telling, she reiterated:

The whole thing was hard, for all kinds of reasons—a lot of them having to do with identity issues. I think one of the reasons my research is always around Jewish issues is that I need to stay grounded. For me, the groundedness comes from connecting my work with who I am. I had to learn enough about myself,

*and my determination not to alienate myself, in order to be able to be honest.
So, all the work I've done since, even my research methodology, is always kind
of on the margins. There are no models for the kind of work that I do, but I can't
abandon who I am in this process in order to do something just because others
expect me to.*

Would Frida have had the courage to seek out her own path, to seek and
construct knowledge that resonated on her terms, had she felt a greater sense
of belonging grounded in class privilege from childhood on? Donna Haraway,
speaking of what she terms "situated knowledge," argues that objectivity demands not the disappearance of the self into some abstract realm where value-
freedom prevails, but rather "particular and specific embodiment." She argues that it is the "split and contradictory self" who can best "interrogate
positionings and be accountable . . . who can construct and join rational conversations and fantastic imaginings that change history."[32] This question of
"embodied," or "situated," knowledge strikes significant chords for each of
us. As Beth put it at one point in our conversation,

What Frida said about disembodied knowledge gave me words—thirteen years
after the fact—for understanding why I felt so frustrated with the canon of political theory I studied at Rutgers. I walked around feeling like I was losing my
mind. That's emblematic of how lost we can feel when we don't have road
maps, we don't have models, we don't have good advice.

Persisting—and resisting—in graduate school entailed more than figuring
out how to cope with a lack of guidance or a surfeit of disembodied knowledge, however. At times, each of us was caught between the simple impera-
tives of survival and a need publicly to challenge the erasure or trivialization
of working-class experience in the classroom. Beth recalled enrolling in a
seminar on Enlightenment political thought at Rutgers, taught by a well-
known theorist who was, as it happened, writing a book about democracy.
Students flocked to this seminar, and the room was packed for the first session. The famous professor lectured at length, describing the *philosophes* and
their projects—Voltaire, Rousseau, Diderot, and the *Encyclopedie* on which
they collaborated. A student asked what the articles in the *Encyclopedie*
looked like. The professor's response was caustic: "Oh," he sighed, "they were
really trivial; think of the project as resembling a collection of state college
course syllabi." He chuckled.

Everyone in the room laughed—except for Beth, who recounted her very
ambivalent feelings as if she were back in the moment:

I sat silently, growing angrier by the moment. Of the twenty or so people
crowded around the seminar table, I was the only graduate of a state college. I

was the only one who'd grown up working class. To me, the joke was not funny; indeed, it was no joke. Yet I couldn't speak up. I didn't dare challenge the famous professor; I couldn't risk alienating my classmates.

Patricia Williams suggests that deploying a nonracist agenda entails finding the courage "to spoil a good party" by speaking against white supremacy and its taken-for-granted privilege, on which so many social norms are predicated.[33] While the incident in Beth's seminar clearly represents an example of how class privilege ought similarly to be challenged, spoiling the good party can demand enormous reserves of self-consciousness, courage, and will. It is never easy or pleasant to call the privilege of others into question. Sometimes—as for Beth—too much seems at stake. She couldn't afford to speak up; she didn't want to offend the professor because she depended on his favor for grades and recommendations. Despite the gulfs of age, gender, and sexuality between them, she was also reluctant to sacrifice the camaraderie of her graduate student peers.[34] Ruefully, she said,

> To this day, I regret sitting silently as they laughed. I regret not having the courage to say the joke was not funny. That I still remember every word of the famous professor's dismissal of working-class experience says something about the pain—and the power—of class privilege as it is commonly, indeed casually, enacted within the university. That Rutgers is a public institution adds a particularly ironic twist to the tale.

Especially for those whose lives are deeply rooted in poverty, and who retain poverty in memory long after they have obtained some measure of the financial security and comfort that was denied to their parents, it can be humiliating to tell these stories. Shame runs deep, and cuts to the bone. One afternoon Linda sighed, shaking her head and picking up the thread of her narrative. "Because I have family still living in impoverished situations," she began, "the message of the dissertation, deeply ingrained in my mind, was that I was abandoning the family by further solidifying my survival. Those were such horrible days, they really were. It was all the more painful because we weren't kids; we were adults." Linda and Beth began graduate study at Rutgers in the same year— 1983. Linda had just turned thirty-six; Beth was thirty-three. Linda was the primary wage earner for her family of four; her (now ex-) husband was chronically underemployed in those years. Frida and Beth could only listen in awe, as Linda recalled: "I was in foreclosure court three or four times in five years. It was hard. You can't tell anyone; the bottom line is, 'Where's your paper?' At times I had no telephone or the gas was turned off; it was the most humiliating time of my life. I can remember sitting in the car with Beth, crying and saying, 'I can't do this, I can't do this, I'm so tired, I can't balance it all.'"

Linda and Beth shared vivid memories of one awful night when Linda's car broke down. Her round-trip commute to New Brunswick was 150 miles, at least two, and often three, days a week. She had a series of utterly unreliable cars, with no money for repairs, let alone the purchase of a dependable vehicle. When Linda telephoned from the gas station near New Brunswick to which her now-useless vehicle had been towed, Beth offered to put Linda up for the night, but she was desperate to get home; there was a function at her daughter's school the next morning. So Beth offered to drive Linda home—a three-hour round trip—without thinking twice, knowing how humiliating it was to ask for help. Nevertheless, Linda argued, for the first twenty-five miles of the drive, that "this really wasn't necessary."

Today, the two laugh about that night. At the time, it took all they had not to dissolve into tears. As Linda pointed out, however, there is another side to the pain encapsulated in these stories: "We made wonderful jokes of it," she recalled. "As much as it's important to talk about it, and to acknowledge how utterly, utterly painful it was, there was something so precious about the way we encouraged each other. If we had fifty cents for coffee, we were doing good." Neither can imagine surviving Rutgers without the other. As Linda summed it up,

> Beth, I don't think I could have done it, if we weren't able to sit under those trees on the Douglass campus and talk about how hard it was, and for someone to look into my eyes and understand and care, and realize that it made an impact on what I did. Everything that I wrote about, that had to do with language, difference, hegemony, and borders was fraught with pain, because it was all too immediate—and yet, we knew how necessary it was to write it.

As important as it is to remember, and tell, these stories, it is also necessary to deploy our narratives in a project of constructing new knowledge, new meanings that serve a present purpose. The real question is of setting boundaries around the "rhetoric of hardship," and claiming ourselves as agents of social transformation. Linda speaks of her relationship with Carol, a former student who is now a teacher:

> *I know what it's like when Carol calls me up, and says, "OK, what do you want to know first? My father's just been diagnosed with AIDS, and I have to make sure that he keeps taking his medication because he's psychotic. My brother's just kicked down the door and thrown my sister against the wall. I just came home from the emergency room with my sister, and the police have a warrant for my brother. And I'm supposed to get ready to read my students' essays?" I tell her, "Carol, guess what? You're going to read those essays, because that's your only way out." I can remind her, "You have the choice."*

We still have the choice: we can be crazy, we can be impoverished, or we can escape and then we can help whoever is still salvageable. So I have to be there for Carol. I have to be there to tell that part of the story.[35]

Indeed, it is the being there, the solidarity, the looking into the other's eyes, the telling that part of the story where transformation begins. We move forward as we find the courage to spoil good parties and speak truth to power, as we carry our shared commitments to teaching that furthers empowerment and social justice into each of our classrooms and throughout our individual lives. As knowing selves who must continually straddle complex and conflicting positions, as dissidents who must cross borders every day, we are, however paradoxically, well positioned to teach and enact solidarity.

Dorothy Allison speaks of the "two or three things" that she knows "for sure."[36] One of the things we know with certainty is that just as our "survival stories" need to be told, so also do the ones that speak of solidarity, dissidence, and transformation. We have learned, over the course of many conversations, that an important point of entry into any such project is the conscious, strategic shattering of the silence surrounding class wherever and whenever this can be effected. Indeed, our own testimonies speak to the power of that silence. Linda, for whom the category of class was crosscut by race, has carried her consciousness of class since she was a small child. Beth was in her late twenties and a graduate student before she could articulate any conscious awareness of what class meant as a concrete measure of her life. When we began our work, Frida was unsure of where she stood in relation to the question of her own class consciousness. She was aware of having felt marginalized as an immigrant, a Jew, and the daughter of a family that was economically stressed in Chile and the United States. As discussed in chapter two, it was working on this book that sparked a new awareness of what she had known, but been unable to claim. As she put it toward the end of a conversation that had built over several years,

What has helped me a lot is being able to name my experience along the axis of class. I haven't had a clear sense of where I fit, coming from a different culture, but in conversation here it is so clear that the issues and the struggles we've had are very similar. You know, it's getting the language. It gives me a sort of fighting spirit to speak to myself. It's not just that I'm hung up about money. If people are operating out of a naturalized sense of privilege or entitlement, that's wrong; it allows no other options. The current great silence is class. I know that now, in a personal way.

For each of us, education has represented both a way out of and a path back toward working-class experience. Our consciousness of how class has operated in our own lives, not only as a constraint, but also as a source of values, connections, and strength, has given rise to a shared commitment to scholarship and teaching that honors lives and experiences excluded from the mainstream. Our conversations have demonstrated that identities are never unitary and reflect the partiality and uncertainty of all knowledge; just as we must constantly revise and "re-vision" in our scholarship and critical analyses, so too are we remaking our selves.[37] We have learned to claim ourselves as agents of change, as educators who carry common and distinct commitments to social justice into our classrooms, advising, and collegial relationships. Perhaps most importantly, however, as we have shared our stories, laughter, and sometimes tears, we have embodied solidarity. The narratives we tell here not only give the lie to the myth of classlessness, but also open the door to ways by which class consciousness and resistance may be utilized in the cause of social justice.

As survivors and highly proficient navigators of a system that remains, if not fully closed to "others," still unwelcoming, we have today reached measures of professional success and economic stability that would have been difficult to imagine as we entered higher education. Our houses of words stand strong but they are far from impregnable. This may be a good thing. Moments of silencing, of marginalization, of insecurity serve as reminders of where we have been, and too many people remain. It may be a small beginning, but we believe that the solidarity we embody today is a place from which we can encourage others to think, and work, against those silences. It is a place from which we can help our working-class and first-generation students build their own houses of words—words, we hope, that refuse to demean, belittle, classify, or stigmatize anyone on the basis of class or any other marker of marginalized identity. Having come to consciousness of class within the context of our own educations, we see the academy as a place where class privileges may be either replicated mindlessly or resisted conscientiously. Perhaps bell hooks puts this best:

> The academy is not paradise. But learning is a place where paradise can be created. The classroom, with all its limitations, remains a location of possibility. In that field of possibility we have the opportunity to labor for freedom, to demand of ourselves and our comrades an openness of mind and heart that allows us to face reality even as we collectively imagine ways to move beyond boundaries, to transgress. This is education as the practice of freedom.[38]

NOTES

1. Richard Rodriguez's account in *Hunger of Memory: The Education of Richard Rodriguez* (Boston: David R. Godine, 1981) is perhaps the most extreme. See also many of the autobiographical sketches in Jake Ryan and Charles Sackrey, eds.,

Strangers in Paradise: Academics from the Working Class (Lanham, MD: University Press of America, 1996); C. L. Barney Dews and Carolyn Leste Law, *This Fine Place so Far from Home: Voices of Academics from the Working Class* (Philadelphia: Temple University Press, 1995); and Tokarczyk and Fay, eds., *Working-Class Women in the Academy*.

2. bell hooks, "Keeping Close to Home: Class and Education," in Tokarczyk and Fay, eds., *Working-Class Women in the Academy*, 102. hooks describes how,

> even though I received an education designed to provide me with a bourgeois sensibility, passive acquiescence was not my only option. I knew that I could resist. I could rebel. I could shape the direction and focus of the various forms of knowledge available to me. Even though I sometimes envied and longed for greater material advantages. . . I did not share the sensibility and values of my peers. That was important—class was not just about money; it was about values that showed and determined behavior. While I often needed more money, I never needed a new set of beliefs and values. [hooks, "Keeping Close to Home," 102]

We concur.

3. Frost, "'Somewhere in Particular,'" 232.

4. In *Social Linguistics and Literacies*, 2nd ed. (London: Taylor and Francis, 1996), 139, James Gee argues that acquisition of a secondary discourse is not unlike the acquisition of a second language; that is, "Discourses are mastered through acquisition, not through learning. . . . Discourses are not mastered by overt instruction, but by enculturation (apprenticeship) into social practices through scaffolded and supported interaction with people who have already mastered the Discourse."

5. Gee, *Social Linguistics and Literacies*, 127.

6. See Rodriguez, *Hunger of Memory*, where he borrows the term "scholarship boy" from Richard Hoggart's *The Uses of Literacy* (London: Chatto and Windus, 1957), 47–73.

7. Rodriguez, *Hunger of Memory*, 65.

8. For Beth's account of how she learned to read and discovered that her grandmother was illiterate, see *Education, Democracy, & Public Knowledge*, 97–114.

9. Pierre Bourdieu, *Language and Symbolic Power*, Gino Raymond and Matthew Adamson, trans. (Cambridge, MA: Harvard University Press, 1991).

10. Kelly, *Education, Democracy, & Public Knowledge*, 2–3.

11. Patricia Hill Collins, *Fighting Words: Black Women and the Search for Justice* (Minneapolis: University of Minnesota Press, 1998), 5–6. See also Collins, "Learning from the Outsider Within: The Sociological Significance of Black Feminist Thought," *Social Problems* 33, no. 6 (1986); *Black Feminist Thought: Knowledge, Consciousness, and the Politics of Empowerment* (New York: Routledge, 1991), 11.

12. Rodriguez, *Hunger of Memory*, 33–39.

13. See Deb Busman, "Representations of Working-Class 'Intelligence': Fiction by Jack London, Agnes Smedley, and Valerie Miner, and New Scholarship by Carol Whitehill and Janet Zandy," *Women's Studies Quarterly* (*Working-Class Lives and Cultures: Critical and Pedagogical Essays, Memoirs, and Poetry*) 26, nos. 1 & 2 (Spring/Summer 1998).

14. Busman, "Representations," 76.

15. For extended discussion of Beth's "class act," see "You Could Throw Them Away without Breaking Your Heart: My Life in Magazines" in *Talking Back and Acting Out: Women Negotiating the Media across Culture*, Ann Russo and Sandra Jackson, eds. (New York: Peter Lang, 2002), 71-83. A recent exploration of the phenomenon of "passing" is found in Brooke Kroeger, *Passing: When People Can't Be Who They Are* (New York: Perseus Books, 2003).

16. Desire and denial are, of course, intimately related. For a slightly different, but illuminating, interpretation, see Rosemary Hennessy, "Desire as a Class Act: Lesbian in Late Capitalism" in Rosemary Hennessy, ed., *Profit and Pleasure: Sexual Identities in Late Capitalism* (New York: Routledge, 2000).

17. Somewhat closer to Linda's experience was that of her son, Sean, who at ten years older than his sister, Robin, did not have the same opportunities. He attended the local public high school and a nearby state college for his undergraduate degree. It wasn't until he pursued his master's degree that he was able to attend a selective university in Massachusetts.

18. See hooks, *Talking Back*, 74. This book is one of the author's early efforts to discuss the relationship between the prohibition against personal disclosures in academic writing and the gendered social hierarchy.

19. Cited in Pam Annas, "Pass the Cake: The Politics of Gender, Class and Text in the Academic Workplace," in Tokarczyk and Fay, eds., *Working-Class Women in the Academy*, 171.

20. Suzanne Sowinska, "Yer Own Motha Wouldna Reckanized Ya: Surviving an Apprenticeship in the 'Knowledge Factory,'" in Tokarczyk and Fay, eds., *Working-Class Women in the Academy*, 156. See also Rodriguez, *Hunger of Memory*, for a typically male working-class account of the tensions between higher education and familial ties. Valerie Miner writes, "In becoming a writer, the working-class person makes an irrevocable shift, moving beyond the family's imagination." Miner, "Writing and Teaching with Class," in Tokarczyk and Fay, eds., *Working-Class Women in the Academy*, 77.

21. For an extended discussion of the college's early years, see Gerald Grant and David Riesman, *The Perpetual Dream: Reform and Experiment in the American College* (Chicago: University of Chicago Press, 1978), 325–346.

22. For Turner, *liminality,* the middle rite of the rites of passage as initially described by Arnold Van Gennep, is inherently uncertain and therefore usefully described as "subjunctive." Turner explains, "People and public policies may be judged skeptically in relation to deep values; the vices, follies, stupidities, and abuses of contemporary holders of high political, economic or religious status may be satirized, ridiculed, or con[t]emned (*sic*) in terms of axiomatic values." See "Rukujo's Jealousy: Liminality and the Performative Genres," in Victor Turner, ed., *The Anthropology of Performance* (New York: PAJ Publications, 1988), 102.

23. Bakhtin, *The Dialogic Imagination*, 298.

24. During Beth's tenure at Stockton State, the college did not have a "letter-grade" system; students received grades of "Honors," "Satisfactory," or "Not Satisfactory" (H, S, or N). After graduation, her record of all-Honors was translated into a 4.0 grade point average when the college adopted letter grades.

25. Here we borrow from the title of Michelle Cliff's book, *Claiming an Identity They Taught Me to Despise* (Watertown, MA: Persephone Press, 1980). This imagistic, mixed genre project examines the experience of alienation, loss, and self-reclamation in the author's life, associated with her lesbian as well as her mixed racial identity.

26. Paul Willis, *Learning to Labor* (New York: Columbia University Press, 1981).

27. Frost, "Somewhere in Particular," 225.

28. Beth had applied to return to HGSE for an Ed.D. and to two Ph.D. programs in political theory—Princeton and Rutgers. She further commented: "I had no clue at the time that I made this decision that Rutgers was one of a handful of universities in the country where one can do a meaningful Ph.D. in political theory. I had applied to Princeton and Rutgers because they were close to where my parents lived. My hope, prior to my father's death, was that I'd somehow be able to return to HGSE."

29. The Harry Elkins Widener Memorial Library website notes that Harry Elkins Widener, son of a wealthy Philadelphia financier, graduated from Harvard College in 1907. A bibliophile, he had traveled to England with his parents in the spring of 1912 to purchase rare books. Widener and his father, as well as the father's valet, Edwin Keeping, died in the Titanic disaster; his mother and her maid, Emily Geiger, survived in Lifeboat #4. After her son's death, Mrs. Widener donated two million for construction of a library at Harvard memorializing Harry and housing his collection of rare books.

30. Joanna Kadi, "A Question of Belonging," in Tokarczyk and Fay, eds., *Working-Class Women in the Academy*, 92–93.

31. Sowinska, "Yer Own Motha Wouldna Reckanized Ya," 157–158.

32. Donna Haraway, *Simians, Cyborgs, and Women: The Reinvention of Nature* (New York: Routledge, 1991), 190, 193.

33. As Williams puts it:

> I think that the hard work of a nonracist sensibility is the boundary crossing, from safe circle into wilderness: the testing of boundary, the consecration of sacrilege. It is the willingness to spoil a good party and break an encompassing circle, to travel from the safe to the unsafe. The transgression is dizzyingly intense, a reminder of what it is to be alive. It is a sinful pleasure, this willing transgression of a line, which takes one into new awareness, a secret, lonely, and tabooed world—to survive the transgression is terrifying and addictive. To know that everything has changed, and yet that nothing has changed; and in leaping the chasm of this impossible division of self, a discovery of the self surviving, still well, still strong, and, as a curious consequence, renewed. [Patricia J. Williams, *The Alchemy of Race and Rights* (Cambridge, MA: Harvard University Press, 1991), 129–130]

34. In 1983, Beth was one of only two women in the entering cohort of Ph.D. students; she was between eight and twelve years older than all the other students and the same age as several of her professors; she was also the first, and for several years the only, public lesbian in the Political Science Department.

35. "Carol" is a pseudonym.

36. Dorothy Allison, *Two or Three Things I Know for Sure* (New York: Dutton, 1995).

37. The concept of "re-vision" is developed in Adrienne Rich's seminal essay, "When We Dead Awaken: Writing as Re-Vision," in Rich, ed., *On Lies, Secrets, and Silence: Selected Prose 1966–1978* (New York: W.W. Norton & Company, 1979), 33–49. Rich argues that

> Re-vision—the act of looking back, of seeing with fresh eyes, of entering an old text from a new critical direction—is for women more than a chapter in cultural history: it is an act of survival. Until we can understand the assumptions in which we are drenched we cannot know ourselves. And this drive to self-knowledge, for women, is more than a search for identity: it is part of our refusal of the self-destructiveness of male-dominated society. [p. 35]

38. bell hooks, "Ecstasy: Teaching and Learning without Limits," in Phyllis R. Freeman and Jan Zlotnick Schmidt, eds., *Wise Women: Reflections of Teachers at Midlife* (New York: Routledge, 2000), 177.

Chapter Four

For Every Border, a Bridge: Identity, Hybridity, and Moral Selves

Hay tantísimas fronteras There are so very many borders
que dividen a la gente, that divide people,
pero por cada frontera but for every border
existe también un puente.[1] there is also a bridge.[1]

Gina Valdés

"Necessity is the mother of invention," or so they say. Does that account for my father, a South American Jew speaking halting, heavily accented English, starting a business selling Catholic Bibles, crucifixes, and religious scenes painted on black velvet? Julio had nothing to sell but his selling skills when the family arrived in Los Angeles in early 1962. He worked for a couple of years as a door-to-door salesman for a small firm, selling religious articles to the area's Spanish-speaking population. But he longed to be on his own. Hence was born Catholic Circle Company, housed in a small building—a couple of rooms—mostly used for storage of merchandise. In my memory, my father's business is associated with his frequent and extended absences from home during his selling trips, first near the Los Angeles area where we lived, and later more adventuresome expeditions to places as far away as Idaho; and with the wonderful produce he often brought home, bartered with customers who could not make that month's installment. Melt-in-your-mouth potatoes from Idaho, giant white asparagus from Indio.

THE JEWISH "CATHOLIC CIRCLE" COMPANY

Frida told this story to Beth and Linda on a hot afternoon in Ocean City. "I feel uncomfortable talking about this to Jews," she confessed. "It feels weird because it is crossing a major boundary. But in some ways I'm sort of proud of it because it bespeaks a lack of prejudice on my father's part, an absence of bigotry: he could make his living working with people of a different tradition, one with a history not exactly friendly to Jews."

Beth was stunned: "This is just staggering to me, because, you know, one of the reasons why I have such an ambivalent relationship to being Catholic is the endemic anti-Semitism, and to me, this bespeaks such enormous generosity of spirit."

Frida felt unsettled by Beth's response. It wasn't quite on target.

My father was a complex man in some ways. But he was somebody who could talk to people of any social class, without judgment. He never finished high school, but he was more educated than many of his customers, some of whom were migrant farm workers. He felt very comfortable; he had rapport with his customers; they often invited him to dinner.

A week later, in the quiet of her own study, Frida reflected:

I don't think there was anything heroic about my father. But there was something special in his capacity to accommodate himself to any social circumstance, provided the language was Spanish, as he was never fully comfortable in English. My father was heir to a family history of displacement and cultural accommodation, several times over. He and my mother were cultural, not religious, Jews; hence his attachment to his Jewishness was not on the basis of a religious ideology that sees one tradition as having the single key to Truth. In a real sense, my father was a pluralist, given the multiple borders crossed by his parents before him, but also those he crossed himself. Selling religious artifacts to Catholic Latin Americans and Latinos in the U.S. was a pragmatic way to earn a living. Beyond that, this work probably represented for him less a betrayal of his Jewishness than an embrace of the linguistic and cultural affinity he shared with Spanish-speakers. In a curious way, my father and his Catholic Circle Company open up for me, viscerally, the pluriform nature of personal identity, and the enormous simplifications involved in claiming that the self is like a picture painted with a single stroke.

Frida's story about her father—both its content and its telling—introduces some of the central themes of this chapter: the complex nature of identity; experiences of multiple border crossings, sometimes creating hybrid identities; real or potential conflicts with our home communities because of our commitment to inclusiveness; and the development and purposeful cultivation of our moral selves. Furthermore, it highlights the complexity of our conversation itself— demonstrating how we often misunderstand one another, at least initially, and highlighting, as we saw in chapter two, the importance of reciprocity and mutuality to this project of co-constructing meaning through shared narratives.

CONTEMPORARY IDENTITY AND ITS COMPLEXITIES

Some thirty years ago, Robert Jay Lifton introduced the notion of the "protean" personality, suggesting that modernity and its concomitant choices and mobility had destabilized people's traditional and long-lasting identities. He argued that increasingly, since the last half of the twentieth century, individuals make and remake their identities throughout their life cycles.[2] In popular culture and in ordinary people's everyday experiences, there is a sense that we are confronting an "identity crisis." People are uncertain as to who they are, feeling that the anchors that in the past sustained a consistent sense of self have increasingly become detached from their moorings. Thus, in the United States most people can no longer expect a life-long attachment to the same religious institution, workplace, neighborhood, city, or even the state. This mobility necessarily disrupts family coherence and friendship circles, detaching individuals from traditional patterns of affiliation. Increasingly, individuals have become the shapers of their own identities, "shopping around" for religious affiliation, constructing extended families via fictive kin, and intensifying or decreasing their identification with ethnic or racial groups at different points throughout their life cycles.

This concern with changing identity issues—cultural and personal—is intense in the academy. It represents one response to major structural changes taking place across the globe that challenge people's sense of self and place: globalization and its accompanying cultural mixings and economic displacements.[3] These changes have contributed to labor-based migrations in various regions of the world as well as to technological developments that connect people around the globe in new and dramatic ways—ranging from inexpensive air travel to the Internet. There is also fallout from the breakup of the Soviet Union and the Eastern bloc, including shifting political, ethnic, and religious allegiances in that region and beyond.

Common contemporary designations for both complexity and fluidity in individual or collective cultural identities include such notions as "hybridity," "*mestizaje*," and "diaspora."[4] None of these terms is used consistently. Indeed, there is a great deal of slippage in their usage across authors and academic disciplines. Not surprisingly, there is also a good deal of scholarly debate as to the usefulness of some of these notions as theoretical categories.[5]

An additional source of interest in identity comes, in part, from the postmodern rejection of permanent selves, or of the notion of the self altogether; some of these perspectives view the self as a performance, not a material reality, and hence argue that identity is, in its entirety, situationally constructed and deployed.[6] From another angle, many contemporary feminists, cultural critics, and sociologists see culture constructed within the context of power disparities—configuring race, class, gender, sex, and sexuality, or some combination thereof. For example, Gloria Anzaldúa has provided us with the useful notion of "mestiza consciousness" to describe her life at the borders of many of these power inequalities.[7]

The concept of hybridity has been used extensively by scholars to capture the permeability between cultures and hence the impure nature of personal and group identity. As Jan Nederveen Pieterse explains, "Hybridity follows older themes of syncretism in anthropology and creolization in linguistics. In cultural studies, hybridity denotes a wide register of multiple identity, crossover, pick-'n'-mix, boundary-crossing experiences and styles, matching a world of growing migration and diaspora lives, intensive intercultural communication, everyday multiculturalism and erosion of boundaries."[8]

Committed to the reality of hybridity in cultural identities, Paul Gilroy argues for a conception of "a changing same," to recognize that ethnic cultures are characterized by both sameness and differentiation; they are neither static nor pure, but reflect ongoing processes of self-construction. Elsewhere, he puts it this way: "Identity is the compound result of many accretions. Its protean constitution does not defer to the scripts of ethnic, national, 'racial,' or cultural absolutism."[9]

Some fruitful revisionings of identity and culture are emerging, as well, in and across other academic disciplines. Interest in hybridity is current among religious studies scholars involved in interreligious dialogue as an effort to discover understanding and foment unity across differences and divisiveness.[10] From a different perspective, sociologist of religion Wade Clark Roof argues for moving beyond traditional interpretive categories to account for the nature of contemporary religion, which includes "adhesional faiths and spiritual improvisations" not easily absorbed into the old language of church, sect, and cult. Hybrid realities, he suggests, are present in religious life, as well as in the secular culture. He claims that "religions are anything but immaculately conceived." "Purity," he concludes, "is a fiction."[11]

Linda, Frida, and Beth were brought up in vastly different circumstances, at real or imagined continents' remove. Various things brought us together, but a central bond formed as we talked about our respective experiences of border crossings. As we have already seen, circumstances did not allow us the carefree experience of childhood enjoyed by those in more privileged or stable situations. Our social marginality, whether devolving from poverty or economically straitened circumstances, religion or nationality, race, ethnicity, or sexuality, made for early awareness of our difference vis-à-vis the dominant culture and for complicated negotiations with the mainstream for the sake of our surviving and thriving as we matured.

The reflective part of our work in this chapter involves description and analysis of features of our identities—personal and cultural. This is driven by the *telos* that currently informs all of our lives: a passion for social justice has shaped our chosen fields of study, much of our scholarly work, and the subject of many of our classes and our pedagogical orientations. We are committed to making a contribution, however small, to healing a divided society and righting its injustices.

Our conception of identity suggests an evolving set of constructions shaped by family legacies—of culture, religion, nationality, social class, and so on, introduced in earlier chapters. We are who we are because we have been shaped in certain ways and because we have made choices as self-conscious moral agents. We are engaged in a continual process of identity construction and character formation involving each of us alone and in relationship to others. In other words, identity "is a matter of 'becoming' as well as of 'being.'"[12] As Gloria Anzaldúa suggests, "*es difícil differentiating* between *lo heredado, lo adquirido, lo impuesto.*"[13]

HYBRID IDENTITIES

While her father was alive, Spanish was the language spoken in Frida's family of origin. Although today Frida's Spanish is not nearly on par with her English, she remains decidedly bilingual. So is Beth, but in her case the reference is not to linguistic fluency, but rather a metaphor for bicultural positioning involving two unequal cultures. "I really believe this," she averred. "Everyone who is queer is, culturally, at least bilingual. Part of the difficulty, part of the queer/straight split, is that if you're queer, you know all about being straight; if you are straight, you don't necessarily know anything about being queer, even if you're straight and sensitive to inclusivity." Thus, Linda, as an African American, would also be "bilingual." Though grounded in Black culture, she must know white culture in order to survive in American society. As a Jew, Frida must engage in cultural bilingualism as well, living as she does in a predominantly Christian country; her very survival is not at stake, however, as Jews, though still in a minority position and sometimes culturally marginalized, are no longer—as a whole—outside the power mainstream. Location at the margins of dominant cultures necessitates bilingualism.[14] The metaphor may also be extended to our shared capacities to traverse middle- and working-class cultures. This kind of positioning across cultures, or at the intersection of cultures, constructs hybrid identities, which are neither easy nor automatic, since they require frequent negotiations and often call for living with ambiguity.

Scholars typically agree that cultural identity is shaped in relation to difference (i.e., that a nation, religion, ethnic group, or racial group develops a sense of self in relationship to those it represents as different).[15] These representations of difference provide the borders or boundaries that define membership within the group, demarcating insiders by contrast to outsiders. Because of its provenance within a matrix of power relations, "difference" is not a socially or morally neutral concept. Himani Bannerji's critique of the appreciation of difference for difference's sake is well taken:

> The concept of "difference" . . . clearly needs to be problematized. Where does such "difference" reside? Who are we "different" from? Upon reflection it becomes clear that the "difference" which is politically significant is not a benign cultural form. The "difference" which is making us "different" is not something inherent or intrinsic to us but is constructed on the basis of our divergence from the norm.[16]

Personal identity today is shaped through people's membership in multiple groups and institutional affiliations—what Pierre Bourdieu calls "fields"—families, peer groups, religious bodies, educational and work settings, political groups, and so on. Any individual's identity at a given moment may well depend on a "subject-position," or the context in which the self is located.[17] Personal identity is also influenced by how others view us—by our ascribed identities. The complexity of an individual's identity, which may be comprised of multiple group memberships, is often ignored, while only one dimension of the person's identity is singled out for recognition. This is especially the case when the individual is perceived to be different from the norm, in which case people tend to rely on what James C. Scott calls "public transcripts," or representations of reality favored by dominant groups.[18] Given that tendency, George Lipsitz observes that "every representation leaves something out." He goes on to suggest that every struggle to tell a story "is also a struggle to displace a story."[19]

Take the representation of African Americans in the United States today. Then contrast Linda's stories pertaining to her identity as an African American, which demonstrate a powerful capacity to displace whatever public transcripts are produced and reproduced as stereotypes in the popular media. On a number of significant levels, her stories challenge any one dimensional, or homogeneous, representations of African American identity. As Linda told it:

> *I have often called my home culture hybridization, and now it still seems a fitting description for the most part. Yet, I believe I must be very careful with that characterization, for its potential to obviate both the shared culture among African Americans and our unique history of enslavement, creative adaptations*

*and survival. I'll have to return to that, but the varied cultural threads woven
into my family tapestry were undeniable. My father essentially spoke a nearly
pure Black Vernacular. When he read silently (and he read a great deal), he sub-
vocalized because of his fragile literacy. He once explained that he was only
able to complete the third grade. Ironically, on many occasions, he would sprin-
kle his speech with Yiddishisms, learned when, after leaving Mississippi as a
young man, he worked in the Catskill resort area, visited, we were told, by Jewish people from across the country, if not beyond. I can only imagine that young
man, lonely for the family he hastily left, forging bonds to a certain extent with
the people who employed him. Here he picked up new language inflections and
some of the cultural knowledge of his employers. He understood to some degree
the imperative of keeping kosher and the significance of the community's most
significant rite of passage, the* bar mitzvah. *We could expect him to occasionally
refer to us as* mamele, *or Papa's* shaynala, *and he taught us to count in Yiddish,
from one to twelve.*

*Nonetheless, I had a legitimate southern heritage, but it remained latent un-
til the day that my father died, taking it with him and beyond our reach forever, or so it would seem. The Mississippi family remains an abstraction, never
concretized by the hug, the handshake or a face-to-face greeting. Not even a
photograph existed to bridge the distance. In the place of actual contact with
our southern Black heritage, my father imparted to us many of the rich and
valued artifacts of the Mississippi of his youth and the Delta Blues of his years
of exile, when he rode the "blinds," stopping in railroad yards with other blues
men before coming north. It was out of this personal history of singular lone-
liness and wandering that he brought us his mellifluous harmonica with its
blues harp melodies and the acoustic guitar, playing backwater, homegrown
boogie-woogie.*

In contrast to her father, Linda's mother "spoke, in her own terms and by
anyone else's measure, the so-called Queen's English, with a Jamaican accent. She listened to WQXR, a classical music station in New York, while my
father sat to the side, playing guitar and talking about Robert Johnson and
Muddy Waters, stars in the constellation of blues men." All in all, Linda recounted, "With Mother listening to her favored classical music, reading the
Brontés and the British romantics, enunciating high back 'A's' of the
Caribbean, I was born into a cultural hybrid zone, where rural south moved
north and Europe pushed onto the shores of the Caribbean."

We learned in a previous chapter that Linda's mother passed the legacy of
public language to Linda by raising all her children to speak, write, and read
the language of power. For much of Linda's childhood and adolescence, her
family lived under the eye of the welfare department. However, as she put it:

I was aware of our literacy. We relished words and we spoke, as our mother
spoke, in something close to the language of the same relief investigators who

interrogated us, and in the words of our teachers at P.S. 58. We were Black people who spoke the language of the privileged, even though we lived in cramped rooms with strangers with whom we shared all the other emblems of economic and political marginality.

These accounts leave us with a compelling image of a complex hybridity. Linda's extended family further challenged monolithic descriptions of Blackness:

For as long as I can remember, my nuclear family and extended kin together brought forth a range of skin colors, hair textures, and even languages. We were, as my mother would say in the fifties, "Negro and proud of it." However, my Aunt Paula spoke Spanish and Aunt Cissy's Chinese heritage was apparent. The cousins from England were white, like my mother's father,[20] whom I never met. All of this presented us with a dizzying array of affiliations, some that we had to learn to shun as they rejected us; others we embraced, for the world outside our doors, made two major distinctions, particularly in the fifties and to a large extent, today—you were Black or you were white.

It was not until the 2000 U.S. census that respondents had the option even to indicate multiple self-identifications with regard to race.[21] Our culture, with its penchant for binary classifications, has yet fully to recognize and affirm people with multiple racial identities, let alone those characterized by more complicated combinations of identity markers. Moreover, among African Americans, there has been significant in-group pressure to avoid listing the other ethnic influences in one's identity. The history of segregation and a residual color hierarchy continues to alienate lighter- and darker-skinned Blacks from one another.[22] Often, one's insistence on naming his or her "mixes" is viewed as an attempt to be something other than Black, especially since the trans-Atlantic experience during enslavement and the subsequent decades of adaptation to a hostile environment inevitably resulted in the mixtures that most African Americans can readily identify.

Although for Linda the only appropriate racial marker is Black, or African American, problematic and often painful experiences have been reported by those who fall outside expected and accepted terms; for example, those of mixed race or ethnicity. Judy Scales-Trent, a culturally Black woman who looks white, writes: "I exist at the intersection of race and color, and because I understand, in a very profound way, that in order for me to exist I must transgress boundaries." She asks, "When do I tell someone that I am Black? And how? And how will they respond? And if I don't tell people (the apartment rental agent, the cab driver) aren't I 'passing'?" Elsewhere she describes the discomfort, and sometimes the incredulity and anger that her asserting her Black identity may ignite in others.[23]

A clear tension emerges between Scales-Trent's self-identity and her social identity—the way she is perceived by others. Katya Gibel Azoulay noted similar tensions among respondents in her study of individuals having Black-Jewish parentage. "Everywhere I go somebody says, 'What are you?'" reports an interviewee named Lindsey. "Everyday; happened yesterday. Happened the day before and I say, 'What do I look like?' . . . cause I think it's very clear. If you look at me it's clear as can be. I am Jewish and I'm Black. That's what it is. And then people first guess Puerto Rican or Spanish or Mexican."[24] Nonetheless, Linda is quick to remind us that she, unlike Scales-Trent, embodies the significant markers of Blackness—her skin color, hair texture, and features rendering her a fairly typical Black woman in the public eye. In addition, she freely codeswitches into Black Vernacular English. These attributes have often protected her from the attendant distrust and scrutiny that follow her lighter-skinned Black brothers and sisters.

Linda views her positioning within a hybridized family in a positive light. The very familiarity with difference that came, in her home, to be perceived as "natural" enables a new vision of human possibility drawn directly from the sort of racial, ethnic, and aesthetic mixing that describes her family. As she put it in the context of an early discussion:

> If there is any larger gain to be had from this dubious melding of cultures in one family, it is the development of our humanism. *That* comes with the experience of growing up in a family where, along the lines of extended kinship, there were others who looked different, who sounded different, yet whom you knew to be kin, family, even when they shunned you. Such an experience allowed us on some level to imagine our unavoidable human connectedness.

Scales-Trent provides an insightful approach to her own hybridity that is consonant with the broad vision of possibility that Linda identified. For many years, she experienced marginalization as a white Black woman in both Black and white communities because, as Scales-Trent puts it, "I accepted the definition of others." She then decided to "take control of the business of definition and valuation. . . . I think that if you turn the word 'marginal' over, you find the word 'bilingual'—and at the same time you emphasize inclusion and richness rather than exclusion and isolation." She concludes with the view that "it is valuable, and a great advantage, to be bilingual and bicultural. It is better to see and hear the world in stereophonic wide wrap-around sound, than in mono."[25]

Despite her fluency in Spanish, it has taken Frida decades to become bilingual in a cultural sense; that is, to feel comfortable as a Latin American as well as a Jew in the United States. By contrast, she more readily acquired cultural bilinguality as an American Jew. Marjorie Agosín, a scholar and writer now living in the United States, was raised in Chile a few years later than Frida. Agosín remarks that when she was growing up, "They always asked me, 'Are you Jewish or Chilean?' . . . [W]e were always viewed as Jews, not Chileans."[26] Although most Chileans are of mixed European and indigenous heritage, Jews were, historically, defined as falling outside of permissible categories for constructing "authentic" Chilean identity. In other words, there was no recognition that one could be both Chilean and Jewish, although this was the inner experience of many Chilean Jews, such as Frida and Agosín.[27] This hybrid subjectivity as a Chilean Jew began to unravel for Frida, however, in the wake of her sudden departure from Chile at an early age, with the concomitant trauma described in chapter one. At that juncture, her absorption into an English-speaking extended family in California, along with her need to learn a new language and otherwise adjust, and her experiences with anti-Semitism, both in Chile and in the United States, all necessitated new configurations of identity.

In the United States, Frida's Latin American identity was nurtured in a variety of ways: she spoke Spanish with her father; partook of her parents' friendships with a number of Latin Americans—Cubans, Puerto Ricans, Uruguayans; took a college course in Latin American history; held several jobs in her twenties that utilized her Spanish fluency; and after college made plans to spend a year in Chile, to visit her brother, who had moved back. (These plans were abandoned in the wake of the 1973 coup that toppled Salvador Allende.) At the same time, however, she forfeited opportunities to stay connected to her Chilean background, for example, by studying French instead of Spanish in high school and college, or by not reading in Spanish and hence not keeping up and developing her skills in that language. A lot of this is explained by her sudden exile from Chile at age twelve and the absence of any processes that might have facilitated her coping with the emotions of grief and loss this departure entailed. Unconsciously, she undoubtedly chose forms of avoidance of her earlier identity to deal with this emotional pain and the need to acculturate into her new environment.[28] Neither avoidance nor escape was absolute, however. As she recalled:

For many years, I listened to Chilean music, especially the folk tradition of protest that followed the coup in Chile. Several times, while living in Los Angeles, I went to see groups like Quilapallún and Intillimani. I remember periods when the sound of Latin American music, or even listening to the news in Spanish, would leave me weeping with a deep sense of nostalgia and unresolved loss. These musical and linguistic moments allowed me emotional entry into my childhood experience and cultural milieu, raising unanswerable yet urgent questions about who I would have been—or could have been—had my family stayed in Chile.

As the years went by, I started speaking less and less in my native language, not even with my family, a not unusual phenomenon among immigrant youth, challenged as they are by the demands of their new culture. I still feel OK speaking a very basic Spanish, but my sense of inadequacy as a fluent and adult speaker has made me shy away from open engagement in Latin American cultural events, even at the university. I feel I have no right to claim a Latin American identity, for my passion for Chile remains largely connected to that country as the site of my birth, childhood, and traumatic separation from all that was familiar to me, save members of my nuclear family.

As we saw in chapter one, the tensions surrounding Frida's Chilean identity began early in her life. Salman Rushdie captures Frida's diasporic experiences in writing about his own exilic past: "I am no longer what I was, and . . . by quitting Bombay never became what perhaps I was meant to be."[29] Such concerns are typical of immigrants who have left their homelands at a young age.[30] Several years ago, Frida's childhood friend Gaby sent a picture book of Chile as a gift to Frida's daughter in Chicago. For over three years, the book rested on the living room coffee table, its beautiful cover staring Frida in the face. However, she could not bring herself to even touch it. "Emotionally paralyzed" is how she described herself, saying, "I was unable to pick it up. Only when I decided to make my first return trip to Chile in the summer of 1999 was I able, gingerly, to pick it up, to look at it, and, with hands atremble, to actually enjoy it."[31]

Identity construction is a complicated and sometimes unpredictable process. A person's past clearly influences formative dimensions of self-identity, but ongoing life experiences call for responses and choices; some acts are conscious, others not. Frida's ongoing relationship with U.S. culture involves complex negotiations as to who she is to be at a given point in time. These involve emotional, linguistic, ethnocultural, and religious dimensions. In addition, while remembering and sharing stories of her early adolescence—the time when this process was put into motion—Frida extended the process of identity construction. As Agosín speculates, "Maybe memory and its arduous paths of retrieval are ways to invent ourselves."[32]

Frida's Jewishness emerges here as a central factor in her construction of self. Frida and her brother, as we saw in chapter three, were on occasion called "*judíos*"—Jews—by harassing neighborhood children while they were growing up in Valparaíso. "This is my first memory of anti-Semitism," Frida recounted. "*Judío* has a hard sound in mellifluous Spanish—much like the word 'Jew' has come to sound for many in the English-speaking world. We called ourselves *israelitas.*" *Recall that in her Chilean public school experience,* Frida's identity as a Jew was marked by her classmates' accusations of "Christ-killer" and her isolation on the playground during catechism classes.[33] These painful memories played a major role, later on in her life, in shaping Frida's adult identity. As her account here suggests:

> *There is a moment that is defining for me, when tentative efforts to connect to my Chilean identity were sabotaged and I made a choice, whether conscious or not I do not know. It was 1973. I was twenty-four. Salvador Allende had been toppled; he was said to have killed himself. The following year brought news of disappearances and concentration camps. My brother had been living in Chile and came to see that the better part of wisdom was to leave—too many of his friends had "disappeared." I was trying to find a way for him to gain entry into the U.S. My friend George, a university professor, had a Chilean graduate student, and George thought he might have some clues. The Chilean student—his name escapes me—graciously invited George and me and Roy, my boyfriend (who later became my husband), to dinner to talk things over. The student and his wife were models of Chilean hospitality—warm, gracious, charming. Another Chilean grad student and his American girlfriend completed the dinner party. Dinner was served: ham with all the trimmings.*
>
> *By this time I had stopped eating* treif, *foods disallowed by Jewish law; pork is one of them. So Roy and I unobtrusively reached for the trimmings and engaged in lively conversation. That is, until the American girlfriend insisted on knowing why we are not eating the ham: "Is it an allergy?" "No, it's for religious reasons," we said. She wanted a specific answer: "What do you mean?" "We are Jewish," we responded. After some moments of silence, the host piped in,* "Sé un chiste sobre un judío, pero no lo contaré. No lo contaré. No lo contaré *(I know a joke about a Jew, but I won't tell it. I won't tell it. I won't tell it).* Y lo contó *(and he told it)." I don't remember the joke. I do remember the awful silence that gripped Roy and me, and the embarrassment I could sense from George. I don't know what else transpired, except that we left soon thereafter. And then the epithets thrown our way by neighborhood kids and the inquisitorial moments on street corners merged in my consciousness with the "Jewish" joke and its telling. And it felt as if I had to make a choice between my Latin American and my Jewish identities:* "Chilena o judía." *I chose* judía.

Frida made this claim retrospectively. Identity construction is rarely so uncomplicated or so pristinely a matter of conscious choice. On reflection, she now recognizes that selecting her Jewish identity over her Chilean one was a process—probably unconscious in nature—that had taken years to unfold. That choice was, likely, not as dichotomous as it might appear at face value. Enduring the telling of the anti-Semitic "joke," Frida probably felt that she had to choose; in that instance, *judía* came first. This accent on her Jewishness stuck for more than two decades, until 1999, when Frida returned to Chile for her first visit since emigrating with her family in 1961. Her friend Gaby had been urging her for some years to go for a visit, but there were always excuses that got in the way: she was too busy, it was too expensive, she was traveling elsewhere, and so on. Frida is now certain that what facilitated her return, and hence the resolution of some of her Chilean-Jewish identity conflicts, was the series of conversations conducted through several years with Beth and Linda. This suggests to us that the process of "speaking across difference" can have a major influence in the ongoing process of identity construction. This realization, tested out empirically in Frida's life, supports the feminist notion that the self is relational and not strictly autonomous, as understood in the traditional Enlightenment conceptions of individuality.[34]

The self as relational suggests that individuals are socially constituted and interdependent with those in their relationship networks—family, friends, coworkers, etc. We have already seen that, in the course of discussions with Beth and Linda, Frida came to the realization that her family's background, in some significant ways, was working class. Peering into the worldviews and experiences of her colleagues destabilized her own sense of self as middle class; that label, she came to see, did not explain the occasional feelings of displacement and discomfort she experiences in the middle-class world she now inhabits. Our many conversations about class moved her to a more complete view of her own class identity. In short, she experienced a change in consciousness. Similarly, the conversations and ensuing reflection and writing about her childhood in Chile resulted in her making a decision—a return visit to Chile—that before had been too frightening and threatening to her sense of self. She needed to go beyond the years-long question of "who I would have been—or could have been—had my family stayed in Chile." She needed physically to go there and challenge her apprehensions.

"Return trips are always about recovering our abandoned childhoods," suggests anthropologist Ruth Behar, who was born in Cuba and whose family migrated to the United States when she was a child.[35] Frida returned to Chile in pursuit of her lost childhood but she also hoped to bridge her current identity and the Chilean one she left behind. That bridge proved to be her Jewishness, which she had not anticipated but nonetheless eased her longing for a less fragmented sense of self. During her visit, thanks to her friend Gaby, who made arrangements on her behalf, Frida spent time with many Jewish Chileans and made her way to synagogue services in two cities. For the first time ever, she heard sermons and prayers in Spanish[36] and, after thirty-eight years, heard others who, like herself, chanted liturgy and sang religious songs in Spanish-accented Hebrew. "I wept through much of the first service I attended," she said, her voice full of remembered emotion. "They were tears of loss but mostly of healing." Frida felt akin to Susan Rubin Suleiman, who described her return to her Hungarian birthplace for an extended visit: "[D]uring those months, I discovered Hungary as a place where there were people like what I am now, as opposed to people who only hearken back to my childhood or past."[37] For

Frida, returning to her homeland meant that "Chile became normalized, de-mystified. Like anywhere else, it is a regular place where ordinary people live their lives. It is no longer simply the sedimentation of my childhood memories and longings." Afterward, Chile would be transformed, becoming a place where she could feel safe and vibrant as a Jew. She could both practice her religious traditions and affirm her cultural heritage. In traversing national, linguistic, cultural, and religious borders, the trip to Chile allowed Frida to affirm the complexities of her hybrid identity in new and liberatory ways.

OUR BODIES, OUR SELVES? EMBODIED IDENTITY AND THE POLITICS OF DIFFERENCE

Because human beings are embodied, certain aspects of personal and cultural identity are readily defined by and revealed through the body. We must thus address some issues pertaining to our identities through our embodied experiences—our lives within and through our bodies. The issues here are complex, involving mutual and reciprocal interpretations of both "self" and "other." One of the central meanings of the body for human beings, according to the ethicist William F. May, is that it reveals the self to others. "We not only have bodies," May writes, "we are our bodies."[38] This contemporary view departs from a long tradition in the West, shaped by Christianity and philosophy, of locating the "real" self in the soul (or reason), while viewing the body as an inferior, though necessary, vessel. Over the last several decades, under the influence of both feminist and postmodern thought, the connection between the human body and identity has taken an additional turn, as the body has increasingly been understood as more than a physical entity that reveals a person's subjectivity. Indeed, the body has come to be seen as a site for the inscription of sociocultural meanings and social relations of power. Put simply, the body has become a "political signifier."[39] So, while made of flesh and blood, bones and sinews, brain and other organs, limbs and apertures—without which we could not be selves—our bodies are also conduits of cultural meanings and values. As such, human bodies are socially constructed, reflecting the sociostructural arrangements of society, or what Mechthild Hart felicitously designates the "topography of power."[40]

In many societies, the dominant culture uses binary modes of classification in its conceptual understanding of and its judgments about reality, including the reality of human bodies. In the United States, for example, bodies are placed in a hierarchical ordering, marking the first set of the following binary opposites as positive, the second as negative: white bodies vs. colored bodies, male bodies vs. female bodies, able bodies vs. disabled body, young bodies vs.

old bodies. Heterosexual bodies and homosexual bodies, though not necessarily visually evident, are not necessarily included in this dichotomy. Perhaps it would be more accurate to say that while the second set is negatively marked, the first set frequently remains unmarked and hence implicitly operative as the norm, against which all others are compared and evaluated.

THE STORIES OUR BODIES TELL: FRIDA *LA RUSIA*

On a wintry day in Chicago, we gathered at Frida's kitchen table, cups of steaming tea at hand. Frida opened the conversation: "I want to talk about issues of appearance, which for me have been interesting as boundary crossings. Because I never *looked the part*, if you will." Her words evoked a chorus of laughter. "It's kind of interesting," Frida continued, "about the cultural representation of certain kinds of groups, and what happens when you don't fit the role, when you don't fit the representation." Frida spoke of how, when she was a child in Chile, strangers often called her *rusia,* which at the time she interpreted as meaning "blonde." (Chile is largely mixed, ethnically and racially. There are also many people of unmixed European background; however, light blondes are rare.) "On the whole," Frida said, "I don't think the issue of appearance was a big deal for me; I mean, I was a child." She did, nonetheless, experience some disquiet about her appearance, about the label. "This probably sent a strange message to me: 'What does this mean, being called *rusia*?'"

Decades later, Frida began to make some sense of experiences from her Chilean childhood, when she read accounts of other Jews who grew up in Chile around the same time she did. Marjorie Agosín, for example, also a fair-skinned blonde, writes, "All foreigners were 'gringos' in Chile and all Jews were considered Arabs, Turks, or Russians. . . . We felt like outsiders. . . . There was no national debate about people like us, people who didn't fit."[41] In light of this insight, Frida now wondered whether being called *rusia* was a distortion of the Spanish for Russian, *rusa.* The intent was the same—to mark her difference from other Chileans; in that context, her body rendered her a foreigner, an outsider. In the United States, by contrast, non-Jews and Jews alike tell Frida that she does not look Jewish.[42] She explained: "When I was in grad school, I remember having a conversation with one of my professors about that. He insisted, 'You don't look Jewish at all, you look WASPish.' Whatever that means. And the way he was saying it—I may have been over interpreting—it seemed almost like a compliment. This was a compliment."

To this, Beth replied, sarcastically, "Well, to him you looked *normal.*"

Frida's account of the complexities devolving from her appearance—whether perceived as Jewish or not by others, and hence, depending on the context, as an insider or an outsider—takes her to the summer of 1980, when she and her husband spent two weeks in the former Soviet Union. They were ostensibly attending the Olympics, however, the real purpose of their trip was to visit and provide moral support and Jewish cultural materials to *refuseniks* (Jews who had applied for exit visas but whose application had been refused, rendering them *personae non grata* to the Soviets).[43] Whenever they managed to escape tour group activities, Frida and Roy went visiting. Frida's Slavic-looking features—high cheekbones and fair coloring—served her well, at first. She was able to navigate the huge and labyrinthine Soviet-style apartment complexes without suspicion, only encountering difficulty if someone on an elevator addressed her in Russian. On these occasions, passing for Russian was a strategic choice, made in hopes of avoiding detection and ensuring the anonymity and safety of the *refuseniks*, lest they be reported by neighbors for receiving foreign visitors.[44] Such situations readily reveal the performative nature of identity that allows for conscious self-construction in particular situations.

The very ease with which Frida blended into her Russian environment ("Russians didn't look at me twice") made for a more complex set of negotiations in contexts where her Jewish identity was involved. This came to the fore during a Sabbath service at the Choral Synagogue in Moscow, which was then routinely patrolled by KGB agents intent on intimidation because synagogues were places where Soviet Jews could meet with foreigners. As Frida recalled, the congregants' reception was initially less than hospitable.

> This was a traditional synagogue, in which women are separated from men. So I went upstairs to the women's gallery and I saw some old women sitting there. I thought, "I'll try to make contact with them." They were very suspicious; they wanted nothing to do with me. After my original shock at their coldness, it dawned on me that to them I looked Russian, *not* Jewish, and therefore they likely had seen me as a possible threat.

Frida was aware of the power dynamics implicit in how her body was interpreted by others but remained undeterred. She switched tactics, engaging in a different performance of identity:

> There was an old man sitting with the women (men are permitted to sit in the women's section), who was near me. In my rudimentary Yiddish, I managed to recall a phrase from my childhood and adapt it. "I'm a nice Jewish girl from California," I told him. He broke into a huge smile and told the women what I had said. They certainly warmed up in a hurry.

Another experience of not looking the part while in the Soviet Union occurred in Baku, Azerbaijan. Roy had been invited to teach a Hebrew class one evening at the home of a *refusenik*. Frida recalled that one guest, who was about to request an exit visa, "seemed terrified when he saw me." He immediately began physically backing away from her. "I had to give him a genealogy of my family, including the fact that my grandparents had been Jews born in the Ukraine, for him to be persuaded that in fact I was a bona fide Jew, and that he had nothing to worry about." Frida knew what the "topography of power" looked like in the Soviet Union. Nonetheless, from the perspective of her own subjectivity, "It felt terrible because there I was in a context where I was taking risks and endangering myself on behalf of others, and at the same time being suspected of not being one of them, of being marked as an outsider by my own people."

These identity-bending experiences—"being marked as insider or outsider, but on the wrong side," as she put it—are not without moral ambiguity for Frida. While the connections between her identity as a Jew and her appearance have caused her confusion and displacement at various points, she understands that her looks have, on the whole, been a safeguard for her in the U.S. context. She has been able, unwittingly, to "pass" in public in the everyday course of her life; that is, her European looks provide her with protection against being marked and thus potentially marginalized, or worse. As Victoria Brownworth suggests, "Society rewards passing. And passing is viable because it perpetuates social separation—among different classes, races, religions, sexual orientations."[45] We have discussed instances of passing—and their problematics—by Beth and Linda in earlier chapters. The moral danger here is that for Frida and others with white skin privilege and Euro American features, it is easier simply to assimilate to the American dominant culture—because they can—rather than to combat its exclusionary and oppressive practices. The moral opportunity is to engage in what María Lugones calls "'world' traveling." "The reason why we travel to others' worlds is as a way of identifying with them," Lugones writes, "because by traveling to their 'world' we can understand what it is to be them and what it is to be ourselves in their eyes. Only when we have traveled to each other's 'worlds' are we fully subjects to each other."[46] And only when we fully see the other can we enter into alliances with them to transform the world into a place that treats everyone with equality and justice.

WORLD TRAVELING

Lugones's "world traveling" is neither easy nor automatic, even when individuals have been engaged in multiple border crossings. As we have learned in previous chapters, all three of us have had to negotiate complicated identities as we moved into cultural spaces defined by middle-class values and expectations. Throughout many hours of talk, we listened eagerly and sympathetically to one another's narratives, opening up our hearts and minds and successfully engaging in a form of world traveling. Much of the time we could utilize our own experiences with border crossings to facilitate the passage to another's experience or understanding. We marked this via linguistic conventions, as discussed in chapter two. At times, we interjected stories of our own that signaled empathy or cross-identification. One such moment came about with regard to embodiment and identity after Frida shared her experiences in the Soviet Union. Beth revealed her identification with Frida's "world," turning to her and saying, "It would be funny if you could somehow go back and reconstruct the number of times people have commented on you as a non-Jew on the basis of your appearance, while I tallied up the number of times that people have assumed that I *was* Jewish."

Beth shared a story that illustrates an instance of multiple misunderstandings:

When we were grad students, my friend Michael Forman and I were going to the Film Forum, in Manhattan. He had to leave early to visit his grandmother in the Bronx. Of course, I didn't mind going along, so we drove all the way to the Bronx, and I met Grandma—a darling, spirited octogenarian who spoke of her visits to Israel and her friends who had died in the Triangle Shirtwaist fire in 1911.[47] The best, and worst, part was how excited Grandma was, thinking that Michael was finally bringing "a nice Jewish girl" home. We didn't dare disappoint her!

We shared a good laugh. Then Linda turned to Beth and confessed. "When I first met you—I don't know if I ever told you this—I thought you were Jewish." Beth's last name—Kelly—persuaded Linda that her assumptions were mistaken. Again, we laughed—but our hilarity inscribed a more complex set of associations. We recalled how Beth's Jewish grandfather and Irish grandmother had connected on the basis of their common claim to an "English" identity—a story told in detail in chapter one—and then turned to other elements of Beth's embodied identity. As the conversation unfolded, Linda again turned to Beth, asking, "Now, OK. How can you extrapolate from that, or generalize from that? What is this saying to you about physical identity, about body—the body you live in, how you are seen, that sort of thing?"

Beth thought for moment, then suggested, "Well, for me it's just one more piece of what I experience as a pattern of misreadings. Just now, as Frida was talking, I was thinking about the number of times that I've been told I don't look like a dyke—and not just by straight people! When I was politically active in Boston, gay men, especially, would frequently tell me that I didn't look like a dyke." Beth paused, shaking her head:

> I was confused by this, because I was making such a conscious effort to stop passing. When I challenged one person—this was after a *Gay Community News* collective meeting, and he was someone I knew fairly well—he said, "You don't look like a dyke; you look like a schoolmarm." It was just staggering, in 1979, to hear "schoolmarm" and "lesbian" as mutually exclusive categories.

Excited, Frida jumped in: "Do you know what just flashed into my mind? Beth's students' thinking she's a nun, with assumptions that these are mutually exclusive categories, too!"

Beth grinned:

> I think the nun confusion may have *something* to do with how students see "lesbian" and "nun" as irrevocably exclusive categories. But I also think students believe that people over forty have no sexuality—it would be less of an issue that I'm lesbian, because sex has already been erased. To DePaul students, it would matter a great deal if I were a nun, since there are so few. If were a nun I'd be more exotic.

Stories and exchanges like these demonstrate the treachery of classificatory schemes, grounded as they are in efforts to articulate a cultural identity in binary and exclusionary terms, and often hierarchically as well. The three of us have become highly capable of transcending such simplistic readings. Most of the time we are able to traverse our own boundaries, "visiting" the worlds others inhabit, as we have already discussed above. Our understanding broadened in another conversation, where Linda and Frida empathized with Beth's description of the difficulties she experienced, as a large woman, of "claiming the space in my life. That has engendered more silences and more erasures than anything, including the big erasure of class that you know about." Beth reminded Frida of an incident that had taken place a few years earlier:

> This was before you and I became close friends. We were teetering on the brink of that friendship, but it had yet to really bloom. The writing group was meeting in your living room, and I can't remember exactly the context, but you asked how my colleagues had responded to my being large.[48] I appreciated your marking that so much! It was one of those absolutely breathtaking moments where something that's erased by silence is put on the table. This almost never happens! A large woman is an embarrassed silence, to most people.

Frida did remember the context, because it was a discussion about issues pertaining to the body, related to her work on *Facing the Mirror: Older*

Women and Beauty Shop Culture. She also remembered that issues of size—she is small in stature—have at times also marginalized her. So she took a personal risk at the writing group meeting in hopes that her candor might open up silenced aspects of Beth's experience without alienating Beth. Frida's transgressive marking of Beth's size had an ethical intent as well, aimed at contesting cultural norms that valorize the slender female body as they derogate the heavy body, norms that in fact essentialize female beauty, consigning those who don't conform to the status of failed femininity.[49] These transgressions represent border crossings, moving the speaker from a position of safety to one of risk while simultaneously destabilizing the expectations of both listeners and speakers. As this instance demonstrates, such moments can be profoundly liberatory.

In Sea Isle, in the summer time, we often talked for hours on the sun porch or at the kitchen table, the stories spurring us on. When we needed a break, we took long walks on the promenade that ran along the shore, just a block down from our rented beach house. Linda often had occasion to mark her isolation as the only person of color on the beach or boardwalk. Back on the porch one steamy afternoon, Beth "traveled" to Linda's world, drawing links between seemingly discrete sets of experiences. We had been discussing how issues of appearance are often mediated by class. Beth was reminiscing about first grade in public school in rural Missouri, where her Buster Brown oxfords and hand-smocked pinafore dresses both reflected Maude's hunger for the "class act" of middle-class respectability and set her apart from her schoolmates. "I felt weird," she began. "I was a big, fat clunk of a kid, two or three heads taller than anybody else in first grade. Playgrounds were an agony because I didn't look like anybody—I didn't see *me* there. I was thinking about how that might give me some insight into what you might have felt, Linda, when we went to the concert at the Music Pier."

Linda signed on, shaking her head and saying "Oh, yeah!"

Beth recounted the moment she and Linda were remembering:

It was the Fourth of July. There's a big concert at the Music Pier, sort of Ocean City's version of the Boston Pops on the Esplanade—everyone goes; it's a tradition. Linda was visiting for the weekend, so we collected Maude and went to the Pier. Shortly after we got there, Linda and I both got the willies. Here was this sea of people, the Pier packed to the gills—

"Literally, every seat was taken," Linda interjected, picking up the story where Beth left off. "I was the only person of color, the only Black person in the whole place. It wasn't just that—I didn't even see anyone who looked academic—wearing sandals, or long earrings. Everyone seemed to be wearing those nylon sweat suits, with lots of gold trim."

In this exchange, Beth "traveled" to a moment of connection with Linda's experience. In the immediacy of its telling, their shared story resonated with new and powerful meanings. A couple of years later, back in Sea Isle, Frida circled back to this conversation about the concert, articulating her own account of traveling to a place she might have missed otherwise. We were at the kitchen table; Frida exclaimed, "Your story made an impression on me! I am aware of my own sense of being isolated at times, and you probably have the same sense, as a lesbian, right, Beth?" As Beth nodded, Frida addressed Linda: "I'm fairly sensitive about those issues, but today I was very cognizant of thinking, when you and I went walking two days ago, 'Linda is the only person of color here, and I wonder how she's feeling.' And, over there's a little Black boy, so she's not the only one now, but still, you know, it's only two spots." Here, Frida was echoing an earlier reference Linda had made to a common Black practice of using the term "spots" to signal the presence of people of color against a sea of whiteness.

Linda responded appreciatively, adding, "Your presence mitigates the isolation, even though you're not Black. Because you're not with me in a simplistic way, but in a much more complicated way, you know."

Beth offered a short-hand amplification: "Well, there's somebody watching your back." Alliance and solidarity across difference can thus begin by acknowledging the other's vulnerabilities and experience of isolation, by being present to, and with, the other.[50]

Here, as elsewhere in this book, we see how all of us have engaged in "'world' traveling," entering each other's lives or experiencing and expressing solidarity. At times understanding across difference was achieved only when one of us called attention to a misunderstanding or silencing—however inadvertent—of her experience. As discussed at length in chapter two, food preparation during times we spent together was one such issue. Linda felt that her spontaneous cooking style was being "silenced" by Beth's and Frida's careful meal planning, and it took some time to reach the point where this could be discussed. Ultimately, we all came to understand the process of constructing meanings and mutuality in a new light.

It is risky to express one's discomfort, even among friends, when boundaries of cultural experience or understanding must be crossed to reach comprehension. Beth often used the term "silencing an invisibility" to denote the experiences of marginalized people who are neither seen nor heard by those at the center. In another conversation, she recalled a tough exchange that took place between herself and Frida in the wake of Yitzhak Rabin's assassination in November 1995. Beth heard the news, noted its political import, and thought no further of it. Because she couldn't imagine it as having more tragic immediate connotations, she saw no need to express either condolence or support to Frida—who, it turned out, had experienced the Rabin assassination as a major tragedy. On learning of this, Beth felt guilty and ashamed. Not only had she—however unintentionally—hurt her friend, but she was also amazed by how far off her radar screen it had all been. After some difficult encounters with Frida, Beth could see both the assassination and her failure to respond through Frida's eyes and understand Frida's feelings of "erasure." "I had to learn a tough lesson," Beth said, turning to Frida, "and it bothers me that in the learning of a tough lesson a friend was overlooked. I mean, *I hurt you*. Why is that so hard to say?"

The matter did not end there; some time afterward, Beth realized she had gained insights that could help her comprehend her own experiences of invisibility and silencing. At a college faculty meeting devoted to discussing DePaul's Roman Catholic identity, Beth—who was at the time untenured—faced an audience of nearly two hundred colleagues and spoke of feeling accepted "as a working-class woman, a lesbian, and a feminist." Prior to that moment, she had neither hidden nor made her sexuality so publicly explicit. Many in the audience were not surprised by this "outing," but some were; many gave quick expressions of support at the subsequent reception. Beth recalled being particularly moved when a Religious Studies professor, himself a former priest, came over and shook her hand, saying, "I was proud of you and what you said." Her colleagues in the Political Science Department, however, responded with an overwhelming silence, which hurt Beth deeply. However, thanks to what had earlier transpired with Frida, she was able to acknowledge her need to be seen and heard, regardless of the risk.

Despite our many successes when risking communication across difference, there were times when we failed in our efforts at understanding. Perhaps because we could not fully move off of our own positions or fully appreciate another's complex experiences. These were painful moments, in which each of us might have felt misunderstood, frustrated, or vulnerable as we expressed disappointment in and sometimes anger at the other's limitations. One of our more difficult moments emerged, as described in chapter two, in the midst of a lively, candid, wide-ranging discussion about sexuality. A sharp disagreement emerged in the wake of Beth's contention that lesbian and gay sexuality has, historically, been sanctioned by state and federal law and thus cannot be seen as a terrain where privacy prevails. No closure was reached at this juncture; the conversation moved in new directions. Sometimes, it seems, remaining alert to responses of rightful anger and vulnerability around issues that have hurt us—and others—must suffice. Around some issues, and despite our best efforts, there may well be limits to our ability to become world travelers.

As theologians Rita Brock and Susan Thisthlethwaite soberly suggest, "It is possible to connect across considerable difference in sometimes unanticipated ways. We must also live with the knowledge that we can never completely bridge the difference and fully know the pain and the joys of another."[51] But that knowledge, we believe, should not keep us from trying, for the stakes are high, not only when it comes to relations among friends, but even more critically in reference to unknown others. As Patricia Williams cautions, "The hard work of listening across boundaries is not always perceived as necessary for those cushioned within the invisible privileges of racial and other hierarchies of power. But the failure to incorporate a sense of precarious connection as a part of our lives is a way of dehistoricizing, suppressing from view, and, if we are not careful, ultimately obliterating."[52] The challenge is to continue to engage in the hard work of listening, using our own complex identities as a resource. For we agree with Edwina Barvosa-Carter when she writes, "Contrary to the conventional wisdom that difference is inherently divisive . . . multiple identity— as difference within us—can play an integral role in coalition-building, which brings together different people to work toward social justice."[53]

IDENTITY AND MORAL CHARACTER

In this chapter, we have seen that contemporary reflections on identity forward a constructionist perspective, favoring fluidity over permanence and mutability over essentialism. We support this perspective, but we also want to recognize a dimension of identity often neglected in feminist and cultural studies, namely, the moral dimension of self that accrues through time, maintaining some continuity from past to present; we refer here to moral character. This position flows from our shared commitments to social justice and our sense that moral experience is central to personal identity.[54] Attention to moral character enhances the possibilities of volitionally developing one's moral agency and thus engaging in social transformation. The self-aware moral agent asks not only, "Who have I become as a moral person, given all my past choices and the influences on my self-formation?" but also, "Who should I become? What ends should I pursue?" As Joel Kupperman suggests, "For most people, self-definitions—what someone decides to be, or, at least, to see herself as being—play a major role in increasing or decreasing the frequency of various patterns of thought and action and, thus, in the formation of mature character."[55]

The work of the late philosopher Philip Hallie is helpful here, particularly his book, *Lest Innocent Blood Be Shed,* a study of Le Chambon, a mountain village in southern France that collectively saved some 4,000 Jews during World War Two.[56] Hallie focused on the experience and moral character of André Trocmé, the village pastor, grounding his analysis in narratives of

Trocmé's life, and, by extension, the life of his community. Hallie argues that it is through the concrete experience of living and the narratives by which experiences are organized, that we can locate living and breathing sources of moral character, moral predisposition, and moral action. Hallie's work challenges more traditional philosophical abstractions; he would likely have seconded bell hooks's commitment to the "passion of experience" and the "passion of remembrance," ways of knowing that are "often expressed through the body, what it knows, what has been deeply inscribed on it through experience."[57]

Hallie's emphasis on concrete experience influenced his approach to ethical analysis. "Don't just tell stories interpreted in the old words of ethical theories," he argued. "Show the intimate feelings of the storyteller." Rather than locating ethical obligations in abstract principles, as more traditional ethicists counsel, Hallie urged one to "find their force in the feelings, thoughts, and actions of particular human beings with their particular stories, or you find that force nowhere."[58] Hallie argued that narratives are revealing because "they show you something, something particular, and yet something of large significance."[59] As we see it, the point is not only to reveal people's lives, or aspects of those lives, as ends in themselves, but also as prisms that illuminate personal experiences within a social matrix of power relations and cultural meanings. Further, we agree with Russell B. Connors, Jr., and Patrick T. McCormick that, "In the stories we choose to attend to, believe in and repeat to others, we are expressing and shaping ourselves as persons and communities. Therefore, on the personal and communal levels our stories express and shape our moral character."[60] In what follows, we attempt to locate some of the sources of our moral character and our development of empathy and compassion, which have advanced our ethical visions and moral actions throughout our adult lives.

Empathy, from the Greek *empatheia,* "feeling into," has many possible sources. Some argue that it is genetically programmed and dependent for its development on parent-infant attunement[61]; others suggest that its sources are more exclusively social: important encounters with those who are different from oneself while growing up, modeling after mentors, or reading,[62] which inspires the imagination; family, religious, and/or communal culture—and their values—figure prominently here as well. An additional wellspring is one's personal experiences of pain, coupled with "sympathetic identification" with others.[63] As Linda told it, "Feeling one's own pain and the pain of one's experiences really allows me to recognize how people who are vastly differently situated are also deeply hurting." In some cases, this leads to compassion, the capacity to "suffer with" that moves one from feelings of empathy to action taken on behalf of others. Here, compassion carries with it a keen sense of responsibility to change the suffering of others by acting on their be-half.[64] In moving from empathy to compassionate action, we reach the heart of morality: ethical behavior. Certainly not all people who have endured pain turn into compassionate beings; there is some evidence that those who do so may experience their work on behalf of others as healing of their own pain.[65]

In our conversations, an expressed tendency to want to alleviate the pain of others was so consistent that we began to see a compassionate orientation as basic to our individual moral characters. "I take a philosophical position," Frida told Beth and Linda, "that you reach across differences in order to alle-viate suffering, no matter what. I probably fail at times to do that. I am sure I do. I believe that when I fail to do it, I've been irresponsible." Frida sees her own experiences of exclusion and pain as having contributed to a heightened sensitivity to the pain of others and an ethical mandate to respond to need wherever she sees it. She is convinced that the seeds of this ethic of care were planted in her own marginal locations: "I guess my sensitivity to the experi-ence of marginalized people is rooted in my own experience of being at the margins, so it's not a conceptual identification. I mean, it really is from the heart. Plus, being a Jew and knowing the history of persecution—for me it's a real bridge."

An example of this predisposition emerged one cold December afternoon as we sat in Frida's kitchen. The topic was money and conspicuous con-sumption, a theme that often emerged in conversation. Frida spoke of having experienced tensions when receiving an invitation to visit a friend's beautiful and well-appointed home. "I feel real ambivalence," she said. "On the one hand, it is gorgeous and aesthetic and magnificent, and I drool over the hard-wood floors and the high ceilings. And a piece of me wants that, but another piece of me feels repulsed. I know this is a crude type of Marxism, yet I can't help but think about the folks in Chicago who are starving." She continued, telling of how reluctant she is to wear her grandmother's diamond ring. Frida was (and remains) content with a relatively frugal life-style, far less than what her family's income might allow. Her sensitivity regarding other people's suf-fering reveals a view of social justice as equality. Linda ventured an interpre-tation: "You have a class consciousness that does not align neatly with where you are now, financially. And with that consciousness comes empathy."

Linda's early experiences of material deprivation have also shaped her re-sponses to others' needs. "One of the most difficult boundaries to cross and to negotiate has been the one that has symbolically taken me away from my family," she said. "It's not plausible for me to live with any degree of extreme comfort without sending something to the family in Brooklyn." Linda recog-nized her generosity in responding to others' needs—"not even family, I mean, extended family, fictive kin, people I've 'adopted'"—but adds that it's also informed by "a cultural value that is perpetuated from enslavement to the end of slavery that if you have resources, you share. Your resources are *not* just your own." She described how she often feels uncomfortable about extending this assumption into more mainstream settings, such as her workplace. "I will bring things in to share, like tissues. If I see someone else's tissues in the office, I'll use them, but then feel as though I have to replace them immediately. That's not the way that I operate at home, though. My friend will come over to the house and say, 'I need green peppers.' It doesn't cross my mind to think, 'Well, these are *my* green peppers.'" In this account, it is clear that both class marginalization and African American values are deep sources of Linda's moral character and behavior.

Religious traditions are important sources as well. For Linda, a Christian sensibility has informed her moral self from childhood on. She recalled her mother singing hymns to her children at bedtime, hymns Linda still sings in her head as she remembers her mother's voice:

> I don't use the Beatitudes, the New Testament, the life of Jesus necessarily to stop me at individual points in my daily life to say, "I've got to be careful of this decision" or "I've got to think in terms of what would be the model, the sort of New Testament model." *Not at all.* It's more a philosophical sense of a righteous—in the good sense of the word "righteous"—way of being in this world that is deeply satisfying. And, I do believe that in a general way, I hold the embodiment of Jesus as a role model. It's a background to my life, and it celebrates giving to others, alms, charity, generosity of spirit.

Crossing over to Frida's world, she asked, "Is the word *mitzvah*?" before continuing. "'I did something that's Christ-like' is an uncomfortable phrase for me to use publicly. But in my head it's not, you know."

"I can honestly say that I have never—even in my head—used the word 'Christ-like,'" added Beth, the most religiously skeptical among us. "I have always believed that the ethic of the Sermon on the Mount is one of the most powerful ethics of humanity; I wouldn't say that in Christian terms this consciously motivates me, but in a philosophical sense it's at the core of my being." After a momentary pause, she continued, "If you had a gun to my head and asked me to claim a philosophical standpoint, I'd go for Kant and the categorical imperative—to my mind, another way of saying the Sermon on the Mount."

Though Frida's upbringing was culturally and ethnically Jewish, it was not particularly religious. Since college, however, she has been deeply influenced by the Jewish prophetic tradition, coupled with the conviction that human beings are responsible for engaging in the work of *tikkun olam*, the repair or healing of the world.[66] In this regard, Frida's compassionate orientation is informed by a strong vision of social justice. A religious commitment to social justice "has been exceedingly powerful" for her. As she put it, "I did not get exposed to that until I was a young adult in the U.S. It may have been implicit in things that went on in my house—my mother was an educator, if only informally. She does have that gut level, knee-jerk reaction to injustices and cruelty."

Our conversations identified a number of other factors we believe have been significant in shaping our moral characters, and hence our predisposition toward compassion and openness to traversing difference. Given our cultural and socioeconomic locations, our formative years were spent outside the market economy's conspicuous consumption ethic in some important ways. For example, none of us grew up watching television and its invitations to consumption and upward mobility. We all came of age in the 1960s, an era that significantly influenced us, not the least in supporting our respective families' emphasis on group well-being versus the possessive individualism of the marketplace. We were all blessed with important role models—women and men who impressed on us the importance of intellectual and moral integrity and the centrality of a life devoted to important ends. And at different points in our lives, we all became involved with feminism and its commitments to diversity and the struggle against injustice. Undoubtedly, all these factors are significant in the formation of personal identity; we believe they were critical in our formation as moral agents as well.

Character is shaped not only in ways just noted, however, or even by the choices we make; it is also shaped by our responses to what has happened to us on our life's journey.[67] As Stanley Hauerwas puts it, "character . . . denotes a more basic determination of the self. . . . [Character] is thus the qualification of our self-agency, formed by our having certain intentions (and beliefs) rather than others."[68] We now turn to some of these.

COMMUNAL IDENTITIES: SAFETY AND INSULARITY

"I know any number of lesbians and gay men," Beth told Frida and Linda one evening, "who will say things like, 'I never want to talk to straight people,' or who criticize my involvement in this project: 'Why do you want to sit around talking to straight girls? How do you stand it?'" Linda reported that some of her friends, "professional women, black women, wouldn't ever have the experience of working on this project. I'm just wagering a guess that they'd never have sat around a table with white people in a purely social setting. All my adult life I've had Black friends who would come to my home and be surprised to find whites or Asians or Latinos." Frida described knowing Jews who will not cultivate friendships outside the Jewish community.

In contrast to the exclusionist positions just described, each of us has established a pattern of reaching across difference in our personal and professional lives. Yet our primary communities—lesbian, African American, and Jewish, respectively—remain central in our ongoing constitution of identity and subjectivity. Beth has a history of political activism; her interests, at home or at work, reveal longstanding engagement with lesbian and gay issues. Linda is deeply immersed in her African American heritage through her religious community, friendship circles, and academic work. Frida is a visible and committed Jew, active in religious as well as cultural aspects of her tradition; her writing frequently involves Jewish themes.

All of us locate ourselves in the tension between two positions. On the one hand, we engage in a "refusal of assimilation," that is, an unwillingness to give up our deep commitments to our communities for the sake of acceptance into the larger culture. On the other hand, we support a "refusal of insularity." We do not wish to be defined *exclusively* by our membership in, or commitments to, our primary communities. In advancing these dual refusals, we often engage in resistance that shapes our subjectivities and demands continual self-invention, as selves and moral agents.

"I refuse to fully assimilate," Beth announced rather defiantly, referring to the dominant culture: "It may look, superficially, as if I do: I'm white, highly educated, and articulate." She shrugged.

> I did graduate work at Harvard. A friend there told me I behaved as though I'd been born with a silver bookmark in my mouth. Yet there are many levels on which I'm not assimilated! I'm not very "feminine." I'm a large, uppity, and outspoken woman—add to that being a publicly professed lesbian—it strikes fear into a lot of people's hearts. Yet it's my consciously chosen refusal to assimilate with the American mainstream.

At the same time, Beth recognized that "there are often consciously chosen moments where I don't want to be the generic lesbian. Some of my best friends are straight people!" We all laughed at the obvious allusion to Linda and Frida. At another point, Beth proclaimed, "I don't choose my friends according to gay or straight, and I know that in the eyes of some dykes this makes me a bad dyke." Here Beth asserted her commitment to a kind of cosmopolitanism that transcends her group boundaries.

We all feel propelled to turn inward toward our communities in a quest for safety and belonging and to move away from them in pursuit of personal enrichment and social transformation. These movements to and fro are not always easy for us; they sometimes involve complex negotiations of our values and identities as we confront difference. Within our own communities, this at times creates tension. In part this is because we may perceive a community's necessarily limited scope as restricting our broader sociocultural interests and concerns, as in the example just related. We are not comfortable with exclusionist or nationalistic claims, and we chafe when we perceive resistance to open dialogue or self-criticism. Most of the time, however this may be differentially expressed on a day-to-day basis, each of us feels suspended between the comfort zone of identity and these sources of discontent.

Frida talked of finding important spiritual sustenance: "My Jewish spiritual community is the place where I find complete freedom to be me without having to look over my shoulder, to feel defensive as a Jew; it's a safe place." Her fellowship group provides an affirming context for religious practice and familial support. Nonetheless, she sometimes finds it too insular. While members are politically progressive, there is little public discussion during gatherings of issues that Frida feels passionate about, such as the entrenched inequalities of race, gender, and class in American society at large and the need to redress them. She sees her commitment to reaching across difference—to stepping outside her own Jewish community—as a Jewish mandate. Referring to her own community, she said:

> I don't want to live there *only*, OK. And in fact if I stay there too long, my sense of ethical responsibility begins to rear its head. I locate the grounding for this perspective in Judaism itself. I see it as a Jewish imperative: I have to help heal the world, OK, because it is seriously broken. That's where it starts; it's a theological vision, an imperative that forces me to not be comfortable in my own small world. In the work of crossing boundaries, when I'm thinking philosophically and self-consciously, I'm doing it as a Jew.

Linda responded with empathy to Frida's reflections, for in some ways they parallel her own self-understanding. Linda also feels driven by a moral imperative housed within her cultural tradition: "I think it is very important to say that I do what I do as a Black woman, not because it is our burden alone, but because it's part of the spiritual mission that I inherited as a part of my African American culture. And that's overwhelming to me. It's always present, as an undeniable, unavoidable cultural imperative." Referring to the comfort of her community, Linda spoke of her group of community friends. Some are Buddhists, but many are church women: "In this group before we walk, we all join hands and pray together. And it's such a wonderfully safe place." However, she continued,

> I have been acculturated into other communities that I thirst for if I spend too much time in this sanctuary. I always want to say, "Don't go anywhere, I'm coming back, but I've got to go out for a while." So that is a big, big part of my hunger for a solidified, identifiable community that is intellectual—more polit-

ically Left—and has a social conscience. You know, in many ways my African American community is very, very conservative.

"Spoiling the party," Beth broke in.

"Spoiling the party," Linda nodded.[69] "So, in some ways I belong to a number of groups that overlap, but I am not focal—I'm not at the center of any of them." While her various African American communal groups offer Linda the safety and support she needs in many ways, they can sometimes become too narrow to contain her multifaceted passions and commitments.

Beth spoke of her ambivalence about identity politics, which devolves from her perception that this "involves claiming an identity the heterosexual world has taught me to despise. To some, advocacy of lesbian separatism means coalescing in solidarity around that identity. So it's hard for me to be critical of people who ask, 'Why are you hanging around with those straight boys, why do you want to go to New Jersey and work on this book with these straight women?'" Beth acknowledged that the perspective of lesbian separatists may be informed by a commitment to "purity" in identity, which she rejects, but also by a concern for her safety in a world where lesbians and gays remain vulnerable.

We agree that, as Frida put it, "There are historical moments in which questions of safety are absolutely justifiable." Such moments may well lead to a temporary advocacy of essentialized identity by a group, a "political necessity," according to Smadar Lavie and Ted Swendenburg, "particularly when the group or culture is threatened with radical effacement."[70] Our concerns arise when worries about safety are no longer warranted, yet communities continue to advocate an exclusionist turn, looking inward and thereby precluding dialogue and alliances that might further social justice by working to bridge differences. We are not comfortable when communities establish standards of authenticity—litmus tests, if you will—to judge their members.

Beth explained to Linda and Frida that she has no answer when lesbian friends ask her why she works with straight women: "Those are questions to which I have no answer," she sighed, "because I don't understand where the question is coming from particularly."

Frida identified with Beth's bafflement. "That's where I get stung. This is where the definition of 'authentic' identity assumes rigid boundaries and assumes that groups with different identities can't learn from one another. This kind of insularity I don't get either. I just don't understand it."

Linda picked up the thread of conversation.

In the Black community, the counterpart of the "good Jew," or the "good dyke," or the "good lesbian" would be a "righteous brother" or a "righteous sister." And "righteous" is understood immediately. The term is infused with spirituality. But

it's also righteousness being responsive to your community and doing something in a public, activist way, and in somehow acknowledging your Blackness
in public, emblematic, iconic ways.

Sometimes this might mean a kind of nationalism that shuts itself off from the
possibilities of working with outsiders.

A challenge all three of us face is how, responsibly, to criticize those very
communities that nurture us, which we represent in some ways, and which
fail at times to reach their potential because of their limitations. Beth suggested that,

> Sustaining a critical and analytic perspective is very difficult; I think that's what
> so many people find threatening about feminism, which offers a fundamental
> critique of so many established orders that it's unsettling. Unless the contradic-
> tions of your life are such that you seek some resolution (and for many of us,
> feminism offers a guide to such resolution), you'll want to live comfortably—I
> don't think we can fault people for that.

"But there's a difference between comfort and complacency," Frida
pointed out.

"You took the words right out of my mouth," Beth replied. "You know, it's
not the comfort that's problematic; it's the complacency."

"Exactly," Frida said, "and that's what gets me. That's what gets me, in the
larger Jewish community, and in other communities everywhere."

"But," Beth continued, "it's also a shutting down of possibility. I think it's
boring to hang out all the time with people who look, talk, dress, and act just
like I do."

We who are critical of aspects of our communities worry that we might be
considered "traitors to our race," so to speak. We worry that we might be
evaluated as "not Black enough," "not queer enough," or "not Jewish enough"
when we speak out within our communities, but doubly so, when we write
publicly about them, as we are doing here. Frida summarized our positions regarding community insularity in this way: "All three of us feel a real call, an
urgency, not to stay exclusively within our communities of safety." She
shared her apprehensions about how she might be judged by her community
members, should they read this book.

Linda responded with an insightful reflection: "That's the risk I feel every
time I put the pen to the page, that somebody is going to feel betrayed. We
have to identify as intrinsic to this very project that we will always be suspect; the refusal of insularity goes with being in a position of being suspect."

Beth then offered a way for us to move beyond our personal concerns,
identifying a fundamental tension. "How," she asked, "do I maintain my own

ethical integrity without stepping on somebody else's toes?" She went on to reference the centrality of social class to our experiences:

> For me, there's a larger question at stake here. Who's betraying whom? Working-class folks, especially in academia, are often made to feel responsible for offending or holding those who are middle class and privileged to account. I think there are real elements of this at work, removing it from the merely personal—"I don't want to hurt anybody's feelings"—to a very political moment.

As Linda noted, when we speak out, we become "visible" in contrast to others in the group "who aren't asking these same questions, because they don't occur to them." Understanding that there are power dynamics involved in these processes allows us to proceed with the confidence that the work is important even if personally risky. There is a cost to living with integrity, after all, of enacting our deepest values in ways that both reveal and reshape our moral character. Bernice Johnson Reagon captures these sentiments when she speaks metaphorically about the difficulties of coalition work—work done across difference: "Coalition work is not work done in your home. Coalition work has to be done in the streets. And it is some of the most dangerous work that you do."[71]

Each of us has powerful commitments to our own communities—in central ways they define us and provide us a home. We do not see ourselves taking an either/or position, choosing between our communities and society at large. Rather, we see our position as both/and: we are grounded in the communities to which we belong; we are impelled to mark their limitations, when warranted; we will continue to traverse their boundaries as we connect with those who populate other worlds.[72]

As Lugones argues, "One can 'travel' between these 'worlds' and one can inhabit more than one of these 'worlds' at the very same time."[73] This view echoes Gloria Anzaldúa's notion of *mestiza* and our experience of our hybrid identities: "*La mestiza* constantly has to shift out of habitual formations . . . to divergent thinking . . . one that includes rather than excludes. . . . She learns to juggle cultures. She has a plural personality." Those who inhabit and often straddle more than one culture need to develop a "*mestiza* consciousness," according to Anzaldúa. "The work of *mestiza* consciousness is . . . to show in the flesh and through the images in her work how duality is transcended."[74]

NOTES

1. Gina Valdés, *Puentes y Fronteras: Coplas Chicanas* (Los Angeles: Castle Lithograph, 1982), 2. Unless otherwise indicated, in this chapter all translations from the Spanish are by Frida Kerner Furman.

2. The concept of the protean self was first introduced by Lifton in the essay "Self," in Robert Jay Lifton, ed., *Boundaries: Psychological Man in Revolution* (New York: Vintage, 1970); a more developed perspective is found in Lifton's more recent work, *The Protean Self: Human Resilience in an Age of Fragmentation* (New York: Basic Books, 1993).

3. In answer to the question, "What is globalization?" a Pakistani academic is quoted as recounting,

> An English Princess (Princess Diana) with an Egyptian boyfriend, uses a Norwegian mobile telephone, crashes in a French tunnel in a German car with a Dutch engine, driven by a Belgian driver, who was high on Scottish whiskey, followed closely by Italian Paparazzi, on Japanese motorcycles, treated by an American doctor, assisted by Filipino para-medical staff, using Brazilian medicines, dies! [Jan Nederveen Pieterse, "Hybridity, So What? The Anti-hybridity Backlash and the Riddles of Recognition," *Theory, Culture & Society* 18 (2–3), no.16 (2001), 240]

4. Lawrence Grossberg, "Identity and Cultural Studies: Is That All There Is?" in Stuart Hall and Paul du Gay, eds., *Questions of Cultural Identity* (London: Sage, 1996), 90–92.

5. See, for example, Pnina Werbner and Tariq Modood, eds., *Debating Cultural Hybridity: Multi-Cultural Identities and the Politics of Anti-Racism* (London: Zed Books, 1997); Floya Anthias, "New Hybridities, Old Concepts: The Limits of 'Culture,'" *Ethnic and Racial Studies* 24, no. 4 (July 2001); and Aijaz Ahmad, "The Politics of Literary Postcoloniality," *Race & Class* 36, no. 3 (1995).

6. Judith Butler's *Gender Trouble: Feminism and the Subversion of Identity* (New York: Routledge, 1990) is perhaps the best-known example.

7. Gloria Anzaldúa, *Borderlands/La Frontera: The New Mestiza* (San Francisco: Spinsters/Aunt Lute, 1987).

8. Pieterse, "Hybridity, So What?," 221.

9. Paul Gilroy, *The Black Atlantis: Modernity and Double Consciousness* (Cambridge, MA: Harvard University Press, 1993) and "Diaspora and the Detours of Identity," in Kathryn Woodward, ed., *Identity and Difference* (London: Sage Publications, in association with The Open University, 1997), 323.

10. Jerald D. Gort, "Liberative Ecumenism: Gateway to the Sharing of Religious Experience Today," in Jerald D. Gort et al., eds., *On Sharing Religious Experience: Possibilities of Interfaith Mutuality* (Grand Rapids, MI: Erdmans Publishing, 1992), 94.

11. Wade Clark Roof, "Religious Borderlands: Challenges for Future Study," *Journal for the Scientific Study of Religion* 37, no. 1 (1998), 5, 11.

12. Stuart Hall, "Cultural Identity and Diaspora," in Woodward, ed., *Identity and Difference*, 52.

13. Trans.: "It is difficult differentiating between what is inherited, acquired, imposed." Gloria Anzaldúa, "La conciencia de la mestiza: Toward a New Consciousness," in Gloria Anzaldúa, ed., *Making Face, Making Soul: Haciendo Caras* (San Francisco: Aunt Lute Books, 1990), 381.

14. Judy Scales-Trent, who considers herself a "white Black" woman, also uses the language of bilingualism to speak about biculturality. See her *Notes of a White Black Woman: Race, Color, Community* (University Park: Pennsylvania State Press, 1995), 9.

15. See, for example, the contributors to *Identity and Difference*, Kathryn Woodward, ed. See also Micaela Di Leonardo, *The Varieties of Ethnic Experience* (Ithaca, NY: Cornell University Press), 1984. Jack Douglas argued years ago that personal moral identity is also shaped in relationship to different others and that processes of evaluation of self versus others are at play in its construction. See Jack D. Douglas, "Deviance and Respectability: The Social Construction of Moral Meanings," in Jack D. Douglas, ed., *Deviance and Respectability: The Social Construction of Moral Meanings* (New York: Basic Books, 1970), 6.

16. Himani Bannerji, *Thinking Through: Essays on Feminism, Marxism, and Anti-Racism* (Toronto: Women's Press, 1995), 72.

17. Kathryn Woodward, "Concepts of Identity and Difference," in Woodward, ed., *Identity and Difference*, 21–22.

18. Scott's term is used by George Lipsitz, "Class Consciousness: Teaching about Social Class in Public Universities," in Amitava Kumar, ed., *Class Issues: Pedagogy, Cultural Studies, and the Public Sphere* (New York: New York University Press, 1997), 13.

19. Lipsitz, "Class Consciousness," 19.

20. Just after returning from a trip to Jamaica in August 2004, Linda learned that it is possible that her grandfather, who was described by her mother as a white man of English and Irish descent, might have had some African blood in him as well. In spite of this suggestion from relatives with whom she recently visited, Linda was also told that the white Godfreys were not always receptive to the "brown" ones, as they were called.

21. Pieterse, "Hybridity, So What?," 227.

22. *The Color Complex,* by Kathy Russell, Midge Wilson, and Ronald Hall (New York: Doubleday, 1993), offers a critical evaluation of the continuing problem of "colorism" among African Americans and the relationship between skin color and privilege within as well as outside the Black community. In her groundbreaking collection of essays and photographs depicting aspects of African American identity, *Picturing Us* (New York: The New Press, 1994), editor Deborah Willis includes three especially poignant accounts of family hierarchies and tensions resulting from sharp skin color distinctions. See "Gazing Colored: A Family Album," by Christian Walker, 65–70; "My Grandmother Died Last Night," by Lise Hamilton, 3–30; and "Finding a Space for Myself in My Film about Color Consciousness," by Kathe Sandler, 112.

23. Scales-Trent, *Notes of a White Black Woman*, 12, 28, 57–59.

24. Katya Gibel Azoulay, *Black, Jewish, and Interracial: It's Not the Color of Your Skin, but the Race of Your Kin, and Other Myths of Identity* (Durham, NC: Duke University Press, 1997), 152.

25. Scales-Trent, *Notes of a White Black Woman*, 114–115.

26. Marjorie Agosín, *Uncertain Travelers: Conversations with Jewish Women Immigrants to America* (Hanover, NH: University Press of New England, 1999), 136–137, 185.

27. See, for example, Agosín, *Uncertain Travelers*, 189. The notion that there are Latin American Jews is novel for many North Americans today, who express tremendous surprise if not incredulity when told of this hybrid identity.

28. Avoidance and denial are fairly common processes for coping with displacement in the experience of immigrant children. See, for example, contributors to *ReMembering*

Cuba: Legacy of a Diaspora, edited by Andrea O'Reilly Herrera (Austin: University of Texas Press, 2001).

29. Salman Rushdie, *Imaginary Homelands: Essays and Criticism 1981–1991* (London: Granta Books, 1991), 10. For an extended discussion of the experience of individuals who emigrated as children, see Furman, "The Long Road Home."

30. See, for example, Herrera, *ReMembering Cuba*; Agosín, *Uncertain Travelers*; Gustavo Perez Firmat, *Next Year in Cuba: A Cubano's Coming of Age in America* (New York: Anchor Books, 1995).

31. Anthropologist Ruth Behar reports that prior to her first return trip to Cuba she became agoraphobic for a period of time, a condition reflecting her anxiety over identity issues. See Behar, *The Vulnerable Observer: Anthropology that Breaks Your Heart* (Boston, Beacon Press, 1996), ch. 4.

32. Agosín, *Uncertain Travelers*, 156. In the same work, Agosín asks Susan Rubin Suleiman in an interview about the process of writing a book about her return to Hungary after many years of living in the United States: "Did you feel that you were preserving a memory of something gone forever?" Suleiman replies, "Actually, I think it was more like creating the memory than preserving it" (p. 145). Whether memories are recovered or created is open to debate. The point here is that identity construction involves a selective use of memory.

33. Renata Brailovsky and Silvia Zeldis Testa recall similar experiences during religion classes in Chilean public schools. Brailovsky reports that she was forced to attend these classes until her mother insisted that she be excused. In Agosín, *Uncertain Travelers*, 137, 187.

34. This notion has been particularly well developed in the literature on the ethics of care. See, for example, Carol Gilligan, *In a Different Voice: Psychological Theory and Women's Development* (Cambridge, MA: Harvard University Press, 1982); Mary Field Belenky et al., *Women's Ways of Knowing: The Development of Self, Voice, and Mind* (New York: Basic Books, 1986); Claudia Card., ed., *Feminist Ethics* (Lawrence: University of Kansas Press, 1991); and Nel Noddings, *Caring: A Feminine Approach to Ethics and Moral Education* (Berkeley: University of California Press, 1984).

35. Behar, *The Vulnerable Observer*, 141.

36. At the time that Frida lived in Chile, Orthodoxy was the only religious option in Judaism; its religious services were conducted exclusively in Hebrew.

37. Agosín, *Uncertain Travelers*, 153.

38. William F. May, "The Virtues and Vices of the Elderly," in Thomas R. Cole and Sally A. Gadow, eds., *What Does It Mean to Grow Old? Reflections from the Humanities* (Durham, NC: Duke University Press, 1986), 47.

39. Bannerji, *Thinking Through*, 61. There is a rapidly developing literature in this area. For insightful examples across different themes, see Susan Bordo, *Unbearable Weight: Feminism, Western Culture, and the Body* (Berkeley: University of California Press, 1993); Margaret R. Miles, *Carnal Knowing: Female Nakedness and Religious Meaning in the Christian West* (New York: Vintage Books, 1989); and Susan Wendell, *The Rejected Body: Feminist Philosophical Reflections on Disability* (New York: Routledge, 1996).

40. Mechthild Hart, "Transforming Boundaries of Power in the Classroom: Learning from *La Mestiza*," in Ronald M. Cervero, Arthur L. Wilson, and Associates, eds.,

Power in Practice: Adult Education and the Struggle for Knowledge and Power in Society (San Francisco: Jossey-Bass, 2001), 166.

41. Agosín, *Uncertain Travelers*, 2.

42. For a discussion about "Jewish looks," see Furman, *Facing the Mirror,* 75–85.

43. President Jimmy Carter had called on Americans to boycott the Moscow Olympics, in protest against the Soviet invasion of Afghanistan.

44. The irony of Frida being called *rusia* in Chile and passing as Russian in the former Soviet Union should not be missed. The former label, it should be remembered, was probably used as a catchall for Jews in Chile, if Agosín's assertion is accurate.

45. Victoria A. Brownworth, "Life in the Passing Lane: Exposing the Class Closet," in Raffo, ed., *Queerly Classed*, 77–78.

46. María Lugones, "Playfulness, 'World'-Travelling, and Loving Perception," in Gloria Anzaldúa, ed., *Making Face, Making Soul: Creative and Critical Perspectives by Feminists of Color* (San Francisco: Aunt Lute Books, 1990), 396, 401.

47. The fire at the Triangle Waist Company Factory on March 25, 1911, remained for ninety years the most deadly workplace disaster in New York City; 146 people, mostly young women, were killed. See David Von Drehle, *Triangle: The Fire that Changed America* (New York: Grove Press, 2003).

48. Frida was referring here to Beth's colleagues in the Political Science Department, with which she was then affiliated.

49. For cultural readings of women's body size and weight, see, for example, Furman, *Facing the Mirror*, 68–75; Bordo, *Unbearable Weight*; and Mary Louise Bringle, *The God of Thinness: Gluttony and Other Weighty Matters* (Nashville: Abingdon Press, 1992).

50. Poet Audre Lorde spoke eloquently on the heavily raced issue of "watching her back," or looking out for one's friend in case of possible trouble, in *Zami: A New Spelling of My Name* (New York: Persephone Press, 1982).

51. Rita Nakashima Brock and Susan Brooks Thistlethwaite, *Casting Stones: Prostitution and Liberation in Asia and the United States* (Minneapolis: Augsburg Fortress Press, 1996), 323.

52. Patricia J. Williams, *The Rooster's Egg: On the Persistence of Prejudice* (Cambridge: Harvard University Press, 1995), 200.

53. Edwina Barvosa-Carter, "Multiple Identity and Coalition Building: How Identity Differences within Us Enable Radical Alliances among Us," in Jill M. Bystydzienski and Steven P. Schacht, eds., *Forging Radical Alliances across Difference: Coalition Politics for the New Millennium* (Lanham, MD: Rowman & Littlefield, 2001), 32.

54. Many scholars in feminist and cultural studies have an ethical agenda of social transformation and social justice whose sources and commitments remain at an implicit level. Working from the perspective of virtue ethics, our intent here is to locate principal sources of moral character, with the assumption that moral commitments and moral actions flow from moral character.

55. Joel J. Kupperman, *Character* (New York: Oxford University Press, 1991), 50.

56. Philip P. Hallie, *Lest Innocent Blood Be Shed: The Story of the Village of Le Chambon and How Goodness Happened There* (New York: Harper & Row, 1979).

57. bell hooks, *Teaching to Transgress: Education as the Practice of Freedom* (New York: Routledge, 1994), 91. Hallie quotes from Montaigne's sixteenth-century essay "On the Art of Conversation": "We are always dealing with particular men, and it is a marvel how *fleshly* man is" (emphasis added). Philip P. Hallie, "Camus's Hug," *American Scholar* 64, no. 3 (Summer 1995), 432.

58. Philip P. Hallie, *Tales of Good and Evil, Help and Harm* (New York: Harper-Perennial, 1998), 85, 175.

59. Philip P. Hallie, "Scepticism, Narrative, and Holocaust Ethics," *The Philosophical Forum* 16, nos. 1–2 (Fall–Winter 1984–85), 45.

60. Russell B. Connors, Jr., and Patrick T. McCormick, *Character, Choices and Community: The Three Faces of Christian Ethics* (New York: Paulist Press, 1998), 75. This view is generally supported by narrative theology and, more recently, narrative ethics, which point to the significance of stories as both revealers and shapers of moral character.

61. Daniel Goleman, *Emotional Intelligence* (New York: Bantam Books, 1995), 102–104.

62. Daloz et al., *Common Fire*, 67–68.

63. The term is Mary Watkins's, cited in Daloz et al., *Common Fire*, 67.

64. Daloz et al., *Common Fire*, 69.

65. Daloz et al., *Common Fire*, 186–188.

66. The concept of *tikkun olam* is based on the thought of the sixteenth-century Jewish mystic, Isaac Luria. In his mythic conception of the creation, the world consisted of vessels containing divine light, which cracked open, scattering the light everywhere, along with the broken shards. *Tikkun olam*, the healing of the world, refers to the work that humans must do in perfecting a broken world (i.e., picking up the shards and bringing together God's light).

67. Connors and McCormick, *Character, Choices and Community*, 20.

68. Stanley Hauerwas, "Towards an Ethics of Character," in Ronald P. Hamel and Kenneth R. Himes, eds., *Introduction to Christian Ethics: A Reader* (New York: Paulist Press, 1989), 154–55.

69. The metaphor is from Williams, *Alchemy of Race and Rights*, 129–130.

70. Smadar Lavie and Ted Swedenburg, "Introduction: Displacement, Diaspora, and Geographies of Identity," in Smadar Lavie and Ted Swedenburg, eds., *Displacement, Diaspora, and Geographies of Identity* (Durham, NC: Duke University Press, 1996), 12.

71. Bernice Johnson Reagon, "Coalition Politics: Turning the Century," in Barbara Smith, ed., *Home Girls: A Black Feminist Anthology* (New York: Kitchen Table: Women of Color Press, 1983), 359.

72. Patricia Hill Collins, "Learning from the Outsider Within: The Sociological Significance of Black Feminist Thought," *Social* Problems 33 (1986): 514-32.

73. Lugones, "Playfulness," 396.

74. Anzaldúa, "La conciencia de la mestiza," 378–379. See also Gloria E. Anzaldúa and Analouise Keating, eds., *This Bridge We Call Home: Radical Visions for Transformation* (New York: Routledge, 2002).

Chapter Five

Work as Prayer: The Spiritual Dynamics of Professional Lives within and against the Academy

I am readying myself to write. No matter what the subject, each task rushes in on the waves of trepidation, and there is at least some of this in each starting moment in front of the page. Will my voice refuse me and remain silent, or worse, ring false or flat, ineffectual or commonplace? Somewhere along the route to the doctorate, on the suggestion of a friend known for the depth and complexity of her spiritual life, I began to touch the page, my written page, to sit still and imagine the ideas, the nuances, the purpose of the piece. At first I regarded this as a way to go within to listen to my thoughts. Then I enlarged the scope of my ritual. I would begin by first focusing on the revered cultural artifacts that surround my desk—my deceased father's guitar, more than sixty years old; the framed picture of Zora Neal Hurston, who dared to write about people thought unworthy of a scholar's attention. From the guitar, now long silent, I hear my father's blues and all his laments, his hopes and the sources of his fight to survive the most destructive forces of poverty and racism. From her photo, Hurston's brazen smile carries me to the rich, tonal nuances of the vernacular voice of her characters, re-created as few others could, then or since. I was seeking inspiration from the ancestors, the forebears. Listening to John Coltrane on sax or Miles Davis on trumpet, I would move into the sounds that originated—as I imagine—in a similar psychic and social space—and with the same urgency— as the words I would write about the lives of those who have been routinely ignored or held in low esteem.

However, somewhere along the way, my meditations took the shape of an actual prayer. With hands on the page from which I was working or even on the computer screen, I returned to the rituals and the words from many years gone by, and I asked a simple blessing on the work. Called to mind was the quiet chant we whispered in the Baptist church of my youth, a prelude to our recitation of the Lord's Prayer. "Let the words of my mouth and the meditations of my heart be acceptable in Thy sight, Oh Lord, my strength and my Redeemer." Many years before, I had renounced most formal religious practices, repelled by their inflexible dogma, their anti-intellectualism and spiritual elitism. Yet there I was now, reaching for a transcendent power, God, that is, to give me the necessary courage, clarity, and even inspiration to meet the challenge of my life's work.

LAYING HANDS ON THE WORK

We were sitting around the dining room table in Beth's steamy Ocean City rental apartment that first summer of our joint project when Linda told Frida and Beth about her practice of "laying hands on the work." She elaborated in this way:

As I regard the artifacts that are significant in my ritual, I realize that prayer in the context of my work is never an isolated or even a private act. The photo of scholars whose work inspires me or my father's actual guitar are symbolic of my cultural legacy of faith, which has managed to stay with me stubbornly even though I doubted its usefulness. As I touch the page and ask for guidance, I am returning to a source of courage and inspiration that has sustained generations before me.

In its simplest form, each prayer is a request that I, the writer, can find the fortitude to press forward. The need for courage derives, not only from the commonly understood writer's trepidation, the fear of moving forward, of hearing one's own voice from the page. The prayer is a weapon, as well, against the rising doubt that my written voice will resonate with truth and originality. I sense that without the courage buoyed on the prayer, I would sit defenseless against the relentless undermining of alternate cultural texts still prevalent in academic work, and I would contribute instead to their silence.

Another side of the prayer is a rendering, a gift that we seek to give to others. There is a hope that the prayer will help direct the shape of the work so that it might possess clarity and a subtlety that encourages personal and social transformation. In this way, the work represents a debt that we owe, a reconstitution of the gift of our foremothers and fathers. Through their lived experiences, secular and spiritual, they forged a survival route in response to various material and psychological threats. Our prayer, then, is central to the process of reconstituting a specific legacy of embodied knowledge, so that we might usefully build upon what we learned and further challenge easy, hegemonic conclusions about marginalized groups.

Linda's ruminations about prayer—its practice, its inspiration, and its purposes—introduce major themes for this chapter: the significance of our religious and cultural legacies in shaping us as human beings and as professionals; the nature of our spirituality and its role in our work as scholars and teachers; our experience in the academy; and our hopes, efforts, and commitments in our work lives.

CULTURAL LEGACIES OF FAITH

"I am very, very religious in terms of my belief in God and my practice of particular rituals," Linda exclaimed. "But I take the right to practice various sorts of things that are associated with more than one religion, and this makes dogmatic fundamentalists in either of the two religions that I practice very uncomfortable." Brought up in the Baptist church, Linda also practices aspects of Buddhism, including chanting and meditation. Frida was raised in a family of ethnically identified, secularized Jews. She began an exploration of religious Judaism in her college years and is currently a religiously committed Jew, active in a religious *havurah*—a small fellowship group of like-minded people—in this instance, unaffiliated with a synagogue. Beth remembers with fondness elements of her Catholic girlhood, but she has rejected that religion because, for her, "'Catholic' and 'lesbian' are oxymoronic. I reject the imperative that I should regret or atone for who I am."

From the inception of this project, the three of us have talked about religion, which has played a significant role in our development. None of us is *conventionally* religious, however. Linda navigates between two traditions and is dogmatic in neither. Frida has spent much of her adult life outside establishment religious institutions, preferring some of the more self-empowering, egalitarian, and spiritual group experiences influenced by the loosely organized, but broadly influential *Havurah* movement.[1] Beth envies the sense of belonging afforded Frida and Linda by their religious communities; she also longingly spies a kind of spiritual depth in the others' lives that she lacks. She does not feel a need to seek a religious affiliation at present. As a teenager, Linda was very active in her Baptist church, regularly attending services, singing in its choir. As she explained, "I was trying to find the best way to serve God. That was my adolescent quest." Linda's spiritual hunger is manifest in this restless pursuit, which has fueled her reluctance to remain within any preordained parameters: "I have a set of beliefs that doesn't fit neatly into any organized religion," she averred, "so I have chosen what is right for me. There is a God force that individuals can access through a variety of means. I happen to access that power through traditional prayer and through Buddhist chanting."

While her Buddhist practice is often a solitary one, Linda is regularly involved in her local Baptist church. She also participates in a neighborhood group of African American women who call themselves the "Women of Winslow." What began as a walking group evolved over a decade into a more formal organization aimed at nourishing both its members and the larger community in a number of ways.[2] Linda described the group's practice of joining hands and praying "before we walked, or before beginning any meeting." She spoke of how "the indigenous African American core of my spirituality" is thus "intricately tied to my [African American] community," adding, "It's a place where I can freely say, 'The Lord is in the blessin' business,' when the tax refund check comes at just the right time. And when somebody's acting crazy, I might say playfully, 'Girl, you just always keep me on my knees [in prayer].' Or when life's challenges seem about to overpower us—'You got to pray!'"

Linda continued, speaking of phone conversations with a "sister-friend" of nearly thirty years; Marilyn is a licensed Baptist minister and associate provost at a university in another state: "Marilyn and I have spent so many hours on the telephone just helping each other through all our challenges. After a while, she will say, 'Linda, can we have prayer?' We pray together over the phone, and whenever any one of us travels, we dare not do so without circling hands and praying with those whom we are leaving."

This reliance on one's spiritual community for sustenance is apparently shared by significant numbers of African American women. In an extensive study of Black women's self-perception, experiences of racism and sexism, and coping mechanisms, as well as other aspects of day-to-day life, Clarisse Jones and Kumea Shorter-Gooden report that 75 percent of the women surveyed identify "'faith,' 'prayer,' 'God,' 'my church,' or similar responses stressing the centrality of religion in their lives."[3] In a further effort to characterize her spirituality, Linda elaborated:

> *Before any momentous or transitional moments, there is prayer. When my children got their first cars, before you ride, we go and we sit in the car and we pray. We bless the journeys, the car, we ask for safety, we claim it. Above all, I don't pray prayers of begging and supplication. I pray prayers of claiming because fundamental to my belief—which is why I can move in different sorts of denominational directions—is that there is a good, a widespread ever-available good, what I call God's bounty, which we as human beings can claim to the extent that we can sustain faith. And, of course, there are all kinds of challenges to this, but I don't even entertain challenges to it, in any intellectual sense. I am thinking about the verse from Hebrews, about the "evidence of things unseen."[4]*

Enchanted with Linda's description, Frida eagerly asked her if she had ever written about this. When Linda replied in the negative, she urged her to do so, suggesting that womanists (African American feminists) are currently writing precisely about this kind of embodied spirituality.[5]

Linda's religiosity takes a very contemporary form, characterized by a postmodern perspective that is eclectic, designating the self as the seat of authority with regard to determining the beliefs and practices to which one subscribes. She thus joins the ranks of Americans who—as she puts it—"pick and choose" aspects of traditions that enrich and inform their own nascent religious sensibilities. However, for Linda, this is not a superficial religiosity. Much of her faith is grounded in the African American religious and cultural experience, as we have seen above and in previous chapters. As discussed in chapter four, it is an African American "spiritual mission" that impels her toward an "undeniable, unavoidable cultural imperative" to engage in social transformation, to connect her religious life to the well-being of others, within her community and beyond.

"I come from a family that is not 'religiously musical,'" Frida asserted, "but *I* am."[6] She explained that the great sociologist of religion, Max Weber, referred to himself as "religiously unmusical,"[7] adding, "I have appropriated Weber's resonant term *in reverse* to apply to myself. Beginning in my late teens, I began searching for a way to respond to my need for spiritual grounding. I don't mean a search for the traditional notion of a personal God. It's more of a conception of a force that makes for unity in the universe." Turning to Linda, who was nodding in response, Frida added, "Your kind of eclecticism doesn't surprise me at all. To some extent, I think I partake of that, not to the same degree you do, but I'm certainly sensitive to and appreciative of traditions that allow the spirit to be contacted. In my community, we want to pray Jewishly; we nonetheless experiment with certain forms that are not Jewish. So there are sounds and chants that we use, most of which are of Jewish provenance, some of which are not." Frida went on to describe a particular Hallelujah song that her religious group sings to a Native American melody. Explaining that prayer does not always work for her in establishing a connection to the sacred, Frida takes personal responsibility for that failure. Reflecting the theological perspective of Abraham Joshua Heschel,[8] she said,

> I take it, theologically, that there is this God—this force out there—it's always there. *We* are not always open to it. So it's my responsibility if I go into a prayer situation and *I* am unavailable, and nothing happens; I'm preoccupied, there's too much going on. What actually works for me best, always, is chanting. The Jewish tradition has a richness of music. And many folks, in recent years, have borrowed from the Hasidic musical tradition, especially in the use of certain melodies, *nigunim*—*nigun* in the singular—melodies that frequently have no words, or maybe one word, which is repeated almost like a mantra; and for those without words, we simply hum or sing, using "la la la's" and "yai di di dai's."

Linda interrupted, asking about the spelling of the word *nigun*. Frida spelled it out, differentiating between its Yiddish and Hebrew pronunciations before adding, "It's this chanted music, this chanted vocalization that reaches out as a spiritual-emotional connection to the sacred, and it's the medium that works most for me."

As a professor of religious studies, Frida teaches a variety of religions. She finds Buddhism particularly appealing from a psychological perspective. "I am not dogmatic in my professional or personal life," she explained, suggesting that she finds value in other traditions. "Buddhism is important to me at a personal level in terms of how I can better live my life—the kind of attitude I take toward my life or toward my condition at any one time; so, for example, I very much appreciate its emphasis on living in the moment." Yet Judaism remains at the core of her religious identity: "The myths that I live with, that I choose to assent to, the religious myths, they are Jewish." She amplified this:

> A lot of them are biblical. I haven't always experienced religious Judaism from within, but my calendar now follows the rhythms of the Jewish liturgical calendar. My inner world is often inhabited by biblical characters, so when I reflect on the tragedy of the Middle East—for example, the conflict between Israeli Jews and Palestinians—my imagination takes me to the struggles between Sara and Hagar, or Isaac and Ishmael. It's an interesting way of being in the world, that I choose to be part of a meta-narrative, if you will, which is my people's meta-narrative. I recognize that in all likelihood this is mythic and not literal, not historical, but it doesn't make any difference because I know that as a scholar, and as a practitioner, it's not literal truth that matters. It's the essential truth it provides me with.

While open to the wisdom of other religions, and involved in conversation and friendship across religions, Frida's religious, ethnic, and cultural home is, at heart, Jewish.

One August afternoon in Ocean City, Beth felt compelled to jump out of the conversation and play a recording of "By the Waters of Babylon," as performed by the folk group Sweet Honey in the Rock. She explained that the song's central question, of how to sing a holy song in a strange land, was particularly resonant to her.[9] Explaining how, as a lesbian, she feels alienated from Catholicism, Beth remembered hearing that song for the first time: "It gave voice to my question as someone who has *always* felt strange: How can I sing my holy song in this strange land where no one knows me, where no one wants me, or *what I do* is going to be abhorrent to many people, or *who I am* is going to be abhorrent? How can I then sing a holy song?"[10] This does not mean that Beth has rejected faith entirely, but, rather, that it finds expression through secular images, not the Western God-in-the-Sky. She finds holiness in poetry, for instance. "I think God might live in Adrienne Rich," she said, reciting from memory the words of her favorite poet: "never have we been closer to the truth/of the lies we were living, listen to me:/the faithfulness I can imagine would be a weed/flowering in tar, a blue energy piercing/the massed atoms of a bedrock disbelief."[11] Looking pensive, she softly added, "I want to be that weed, flowering in tar."

When we first began our conversation about religion and spirituality, Beth felt inept, conceding that she is a "devout coward about talking about such things, and I don't feel I have much to say." Frida acknowledged that these can be difficult topics to discuss. "I envy you your communities," Beth told Linda and Frida. "I hold out the hope that there will come a time when I will either find or create one that is more conscious than the unconscious spiritual community that I do have across friendships and relationships that have meaning to me."

Frida affirmed Beth's spirituality of interpersonal relations, citing Martin Buber's theology in *I and Thou*.[12] "For Buber," she explained, "God is present when the 'I' meets the 'Thou' fully, and I believe that. I think there are moments of tremendous spiritual richness — well, even the days that we have spent together — that are close to the spiritual. Now, that's different from ritualized practice, but no less valuable."

Beth was able to enter the conversation about faith through her connection to philosophers like Kant and Plato. Reflecting on her teaching of these philosophers in her political theory classes, she said, "We're acculturated to see a vast chasm between the political and the spiritual most of the time. I believe that politics and spirituality are often very connected, and the connection is ethical. That is what I try to live, that is what I try to teach my students."

Frida arrived at a similar conclusion, via a markedly different approach. She had been exploring the notion of "being divinely created and sustained" as very powerful for her. "That has a very strong dimension in Jewish liturgy — that the God who creates your being sustains your presence. When I'm in touch with that, I feel very centered." A bit further on, she suggested, "What I need in my spirituality that I don't find in normative synagogue life, but which I do find in my community, is the ecstatic. The ecstatic allows another dimension of life; I don't see it necessarily in opposition to reason. If I remember correctly, Paul Tillich talks about faith as being 'reason in ecstasy.'"[13]

"What a metaphor!" Beth exclaimed.

"When I'm feeling spiritually ecstatic — and that happens typically through music — and we go on and on singing, sometimes for a long time, and we can really get into it, like the Baptists and Pentecostals do, I haven't abandoned my reason," Frida continued. "I could stop at any minute. But it's an experience of being in touch with a dimension of existence that's simply not available through discursive thought. It's the experience of being connected with the entire universe, a sort of ecstatic spiritual moment."

"I love the way you put that," Linda interjected.

"It comes full circle to what you were talking about," Frida added, turning to Beth. "The spiritual is *not* opposed to the ethical because in the ecstatic moment, the experience of unity with all is grounded in the interconnection between myself and all—this is also very Jewish—and the deep responsibility that I have to all. So I don't think that they are necessarily polarized." After a pause, she continued, "Sometimes the political, often the political and the religious have been polarized—as has often been the case in fundamentalist Christianity—but in my experience, in my orientation, I see them as interconnected." Frida's allusion to the Jewishness of the connection of the ecstatic moment, its revelation of the unity of all there is, and the resulting move to social responsibility harkened back to her discussion of *tikkun olam* (see chapter four), which refers to the obligation to heal the broken world; unsurprisingly, that perspective emerges out of the Jewish mystical tradition. While Frida was describing her *personal* religious experience, she recognized that there is a dialectic relationship between that experience and the religious tradition within which it unfolds.

Reflecting her own background, Linda added that she has found reconciliation between reason and ecstasy in West African spiritual movements. "These domains or spheres of existence in the Western world view are traditionally opposed or bifurcated; on the other side of the world—and I think also certainly in the thinking and writing of many women—there is this reconciliation."

At times, as we have noted, our conversations took us to places we could not imagine, opening up previously unavailable dimensions of experience or imagination. Beth experienced an awakening to her possession of substantial spiritual resources in a manner that evoked Frida's discovery of social class as key to understanding her own experiences. At one point, Frida challenged Beth: "If I hear you correctly, you were saying that moral obligation for you is grounded in love. Now I want to know more what this love means to you." Initially, Beth felt reluctant to respond, suggesting that it was a question for people who were "more religiously sensitive or spiritually sensitive than I am." But she gave it a shot, nonetheless:

> I think that everything that exists is connected. I think that all animate things are connected by what I would call a life force, it might be energy, it might be spirit, it might be divinity, it might even be physics. In the rare, mystical moments when I am most myself, I know I am plugged into the planet. For me, love— whether it's in Hallmark Valentine's Day propaganda, Dorothy Day feeding street people in New York City, or Christians sheltering Jews in Hitler's Europe—exists because we want to recognize ourselves in the other. What we see of ourselves in the other is not a reflection in a golden eye or through a glass darkly or a silvery mirror.[14] When we see ourselves in the other, we are seeing that connection, that absolutely fundamental connection "to the Know that I exist! of all existing things."[15]

Beth went on to describe her vision of what this definition of love might mean, moving, as is usual for her, from the personal to the political:

> I would love to live in a world where civility was founded on mutual inter-action, respect for others in their persons, just as in the sense of Jefferson's sentence in the Declaration of Independence, "We hold these truths to be self-evident, that all humans are created equal, and they are endowed by their Creator with certain inalienable rights, that among these are life, liberty, and the pursuit of happiness"—take away the generic masculine—that, to me, is love. Not, however, in its political practice, where those principles have been per-verted by a culture that does not see people as human but, rather, as com-modities and consumers in the market economy. The world I imagine is an extended speculation, a jazz riff, if you will, on the possibilities of loving other people just as much as you love yourself.

After Beth exhausted herself in this discursive effort, she referred to Rich's poem about blue energy, concluding, "I can't separate social justice from love, from care, or vice versa." Finally, she acknowledged that perhaps she was not, after all, so spiritually deficient, concluding a bit ruefully, "I guess all this just absolutely undercuts my perception of myself as a spiritual nonentity."

We discovered that, for all three of us, our deepest spiritual experience, our most personal religious moments are linked to a mandate to move from the inside to the outside, from the quiet of our thinking or meditation, from the ecstasy of our worship or chanting to the messiness and disruptions of a bro-ken world, and to an effort to make a difference.[16] These times are moments of healing and inspiration when we experience wholeness and unity that con-nect us and our destiny to everyone else's. They prepare us to "fight the good fight," to work for social justice in our teaching and in our writing. For, as Steven Glazer suggests, "Viewing the world as whole, one begins to feel *a part* of something rather than *apart* from something. Feeling a part of the world creates a sense of place and relationship. Feeling in place and relation-ship begins to nurture the spirit. Nurtured spirit, then, begins to grow, and grow outward."[17] This observation is supported by Elizabeth Tisdell in her study of adult educators; she writes, "their spirituality is what gives many people further inspiration to stand up against injustice."[18]

It was dusk by the time we finished the conversation described earlier in this chapter. We had turned the tape recorder off; we felt spent, exhausted by the breadth and depth of our talk. For a few moments we simply sat at the table, too tired to move. Then Frida shyly offered to teach Beth and Linda a *nigun*, as a way of sanctifying the moment, marking a time of deep sharing and mu-tual understanding. Making up in soulfulness what she lacks in voice, she pro-ceeded, gently and quietly, to lead her colleagues in a wordless Hasidic chant.

MAKING ROOM FOR THE SPIRIT IN EDUCATION

In contrast to the population at large, talk of spirituality—particularly one's own—is rare among academics today. The most impersonal discussions around the topic are often met with dismissal, disdain, and even titters of embarrassment. Such responses are undoubtedly shaped by associations with "flaky" New Age explorations of the spirit; after all, we live in a culture that is still committed (at least in its educational system) to the modern dedication to abstract rationality, scientific method, and—ultimately—to positivist objectivism as the most legitimate approaches to the pursuit of knowledge and truth. In fairness, there is something to be said about the messiness of "spirituality" as a concept: it is frequently vague because we lack consensus about its meaning and usage. Yet the term is used widely in American society today. Only gradually have scholars in various fields begun to address the nature and significance of spirituality.[19] Each of us first entered our conversations on spirituality through an examination of our respective religious traditions and practices. Despite our distinctive differences, we ultimately experience spirituality as that which unites us to the rest of humanity and "all there is." Our talk of spirituality then grew to encompass dimensions of wholeness and connectedness in our work lives.

On a warm seashore evening, we spoke of the academic conferences that we regularly attend. Frida opened up, sharing the story of how this book was inspired at a professional meeting, by a deeply moving conversation she engaged in with two female colleagues. She explained, "The women's conferences that I have attended—and I'm including here not only academic conferences but a number of women's spirituality conferences as well—have a quality of affirmation that have been absent for me in academic conferences that I attend, which I do not find especially affirming of deep parts of myself."

Linda concurred. Referring to mealtimes at conferences she typically attends, she said, "You are sitting at a table with four people, and it always sounds to me as if everybody is trying to be smarter than the other person. That clicks into my insecurities: 'OK, I made it through this panel, but now at this table I'm really going to discover that I don't belong.'" She explained how badly she feels about such moments, where "you're pushing the IQ display," or you are measured by "how voraciously have you read?"

"Or who you know," Frida broke in. Implicit in their exchange was a negative judgment about the lack of authenticity nurtured in such settings.

"I need my academic work to be rich," Linda added. "I need it to be rich in that I need to feel overwhelmed, emotionally. I need to feel passion, or else why am I spending so much time, so much of my life doing this? The intellectual thing in and of itself is absolutely worthwhile to me, and valuable, and legitimate. But I can't be otherwise disconnected."

Frida agreed completely, arguing that what nourishes her is, not the academic game playing described by Linda, but "being willing to have contact with other human beings at a profound, real level, and having the courage to risk."

Linda immediately brought to mind her experience at the Black Women in the Academy Conference that we first discussed in chapter two. As she recollected it, she became visibly energized, enthusiastically emoting, moving her hands to and fro. She described the "many emblems that validated who I am: the fact that there were two thousand women in attendance, that nearly two-thirds of the women I saw had their hair in either braids or dreads, that these women came from Harvard and Yale and all of the big muckety-muck institutions." It was "the look of things but also the sound of things" that provided Linda with the kind of "cultural affirmation that I need." As opposed to her feelings of discomfort in more mainstream academic conferences, "what came to me in this setting was that in every room that I walked into I felt 'churched,'" which means that the emotionality and the commitment were fueled by spiritual energy; in this secular space, the sacred influence prevailed. Indeed, the Black cultural marker was very significant, but so was the female marker, "the acceptance of feeling, which was just so profound and nurturing. The women were standing up and just crying and talking about the ways in which they identified with the material of the formal presentations, which were anything but disembodied, so much so that it pulled out of the audience this highly emotive response that was not silenced."

"My women's conference experience is very different," said Beth, "and yet at the same time, it plugs into the questions of solidarity and difference that we are struggling with." She then told of attending the Berkshire Women's History Conference held at Radcliffe is the early 1970s, when she was an undergraduate at Stockton State College. As she put it, this was a time when "we were full of women's studies and that heady, fermenting, yeasty excitement of those days. But there was a very, very small handful of feminist faculty and students, and three of us students took off for the conference," where simply seeing "hundreds of women all in one place was in itself amazing." In terms of identity and solidarity, "the profound, moving moment" came for Beth during a slide presentation on images of women in American films. Somewhere during the talk, the speaker "got to a point—and I remember the sentence to this day—where she said, 'In the thirties, for the first time, healthy, asexual relationships between women began to be portrayed on film.' Now, if I'd heard that in any other setting, I would have thought, 'Yeah, that doesn't make me feel real good, but it's probably true.'" Beth became animated, expressively turning her hands to punctuate her narrative.

Sitting in the dark of the Harvard Science Center, the moment the audience heard "healthy, asexual relationships," the hissing began. It's traditional to hiss, it's a big Harvard tradition, to show displeasure. So there I was, sitting by myself in a dark auditorium, and the sibilant "hssss" was growing. All I could think was, "Holy Mother of God! I'm not the only one!" From that moment, I can date a wholeness that I had never before experienced.

On the drive back to New Jersey, Beth came out to the two students who had accompanied her to Radcliffe: "That was the first time that I ever positively articulated my lesbian self to another woman who was not my lover."

What Linda and Beth captured in these evocative remembrances is the sense of wholeness and connectedness otherwise absent from much academic or scholarly experience. This, indeed, is how spirituality is now widely understood; for example, sociologist of religion Robert Wuthnow suggests that, "The term 'spirituality' refers to an aspect of life that is concerned with transcendence, wholeness, or ultimacy."[20] Likewise, education writer Parker Palmer defines the "spiritual" as "the ancient and abiding human quest for connectedness with something larger and more trustworthy than our own egos."[21] Tisdell, an expert in adult education, expands on this definition when she suggests that, "The drive to spirituality is the drive to wholeness, to holiness, to health, and to making meaning of that wholeness."[22]

Recent intellectual developments are consonant with elements of the popular interest in spirituality. For example, feminist scholarship has for some time challenged the Western intellectual tradition's multiple dualisms—soul vs. body, intellect vs. emotions, theory vs. practice—on the grounds that they reveal a misguided and outdated understanding of the self, fracture knowledge, and perpetuate patterns of hierarchy and domination. Again and again, this literature reveals a commitment to holistic knowledge and to an understanding of the healthy self as integrated rather than fragmented. Recognizing that fragmentation is not a given, but frequently the result of particular forms of human cognition and action, prescriptions are often advanced for the healing of disparate parts of the individual, among and between people around the world, and of the earth itself.[23]

One dimension of this approach is the related interest in connectedness and interdependence that has surfaced in a variety of academic venues, including, for example, feminist scholarship, religious studies, and ecology. Feminist ethicists, for instance, descriptively and normatively identify interdependence as the appropriate relationship between individuals, in contrast to the assumption of independence and autonomy as the moral ideals of traditional ethics.[24] Some ecologists borrow from indigenous world views in their advocacy of metaphors of interconnectedness in the natural as well as the human realms.[25] Some discourse about globalization uses similar imagery to characterize connections across national borders.[26] In a study of activists with deep and sustained commitments to the common good, the authors conclude, "For them, the radical interdependence of all life is not just the way it could be, but the way things really are."[27]

Most appropriately for our purposes, recent publications by educators imply connections between spirituality and education that devolve from notions of integration and connectedness. An early entry was the vibrant discussion generated by the 1986 publication of *Women's Ways of Knowing: The Development of Self, Voice, and Mind.*[28] Based on extensive interviews with a cross-section of American women—college students and graduates—Mary Belenky and her colleagues concluded that a significant number of respondents felt alienated from the American educational system's emphasis on procedural knowledge, which is "oriented away from the self—the knower—and toward the object the knower seeks to analyze or understand." These women "felt as though they were answering other people's questions, and they could not make themselves care about the answers."[29] More successful were the women who engaged in what the authors call "constructed knowledge," an attempt "to *integrate* knowledge that they felt intuitively was personally important with the knowledge they learned from others. They told of weaving together the strands of rational and emotive thought and of integrating objective and subjective knowing."[30] While this work has been subjected to various criticisms,[31] it has also pointed to the important roles that experience and emotion play, alongside abstract rationality, in the learning processes of many people.[32] We refer to this kind of learning as "embodied" knowledge, that is, knowledge that seeks to integrate such traditional Western binaries as mind/emotion, abstract/concrete, or subjective/objective.

A case in point is Frida's experience in graduate school, described in chapter three, where she felt a disconnection between her Jewish self and the discourse about Christian theology and Christian ethics that permeated her program. While she found this literature interesting at an intellectual level, spiritually she felt disconnected. Only after taking a leave could she complete her degree by focusing on Jewish issues in her dissertation. This allowed her to integrate the Christian emphasis of social ethics with her Jewish identity. While segmenting aspects of the self from learning might work for some, many others cannot sustain such fragmentation with integrity. This awareness, which we all share, has important pedagogical implications. We believe Tisdell is correct to suggest that, "Attending to spirituality in higher and adult education, particularly as it relates to emancipatory and transformative approaches to education, is about the engagement of passion, which involves the knowledge construction processes of the whole person. The engagement of people's passion is generally not only about critical reflection or 'rational discourse,' it is also about engaging people's hearts and souls, as well as their minds."[33]

The question of connecting learning and the self brought unsuccessful teaching moments to Frida's mind when we spoke about what happens in our classrooms. "My worst teaching," she noted, "occurs when I am not optimally prepared. By that I mean when—because of the press of other work—I am unable to sufficiently integrate the assigned material for myself. Sometimes this happens when I have read the assigned reading for the first time in preparation for a specific class session. I have had little time to reflect on it, to make it my own." She paused briefly before continuing:

> I am virtually always enthusiastic in class and communicate an interest in both students and subject matter. But at these times my knowledge is *disembodied*, floating around but failing to find an anchor, a grounding in myself. As a result, I feel somewhat tentative in what I say and how I say it. What's missing at those times is the kind of passion that I think is necessary for good teaching. And I'm sure, at these times, students notice the difference.[34]

For Frida, the ideal teaching moment occurs, not only when *she* is holistically engaged in learning, but when her students are as well. As Parker Palmer argues, "Good teachers possess a capacity for connectedness. They are able to weave a complex web of connections among themselves, their subjects, and their students so that students can learn to weave a world for themselves."[35]

When Linda began to speak about her own experiences of difficulty in the classroom, she realized that they have often occurred in settings where she was one of three or four Black people in the room, especially when the subject matter focused on aspects of class or racial inequality. In such settings, students' willingness to challenge their initial assumptions and trust their professor's authority becomes crucial. However, such trust can rarely be taken for granted. Linda finds herself in a paradoxical situation; first, she must create a comfort zone in the classroom, where students are willing to speak honestly even when they express views contrary to hers. At the same time, she needs to challenge the students to examine their assumptions more critically and perhaps reassess their positions. Capturing the words that will encourage dialogue while maintaining a genuinely positive affect can be difficult; Linda feels that she sometimes falls short of this delicate balance. At such moments, she acknowledged, "I've failed to maintain a teacherly posture." Doing so would help her keep the discussion open, manage a mix of voices, and facilitate critical inquiry. It would also encourage students to accept her authority.

Linda is passionate and engaging in the classroom; she almost always manages to stay "teacherly," even when confronted with blatant, if naive, racist attitudes. Once in a while, however, a student's disdain for her authority or blatant indifference to questions of social justice evokes too much of her own lived experience. At such moments, frustration, evident in her tone of voice or body language, becomes apparent. That frustration has the power to foreclose on the students' opportunity to reason, encouraging their silence and rendering the classroom a difficult place to be.

"THERE IS MORE TO LIFE THAN STUFF AND SELF": TEACHING SOLIDARITY AND SOCIAL JUSTICE

In one of our last recorded conversations, we spoke once more about teaching—perhaps our favorite topic. We were supposed to be brainstorming an outline for this chapter, but, as usual, we associated freely. Harking back to a conversation in the early stages of our work together, Frida tried to extrapolate from her connection of ecstasy and ethics to the educational process. "The mystical is the vision of unity, the experience of unity of all. That connects then to the ethical, to my obligation to reach across to those who are suffering, because we're all one. That, then, is what connects me to my work. I want to see this world healed, and I feel an obligation; my students need to do some of the work, too. That's what drives me to do it. I can't do it alone. You can't do it alone. It's my mission to 'convert' others to this view."

Linda eagerly agreed with Frida, breaking in to say, "It is. It is. It is. It is," adding, "And we do come off strong, because we're not neutral. And it's more than not neutral!" We are often reminded, in this exchange as elsewhere, of Paulo Freire's contention that "There is no neutral education. All education is directive. . . . The role of an educator who is pedagogically and critically radical is to avoid being indifferent, a characteristic of the facilitator who promotes a laissez-faire education. The radical educator has to be an active presence in educational practice."[36]

Our aim as educators is to awaken students to a new awareness of social reality, empowering them to challenge conventional wisdom. When that works, Beth said, "You can see light bulbs going on. I like to think of it as throwing a switch. The current didn't flow through this channel before, but now it does." She indicated concerns about the "language of conversion" used by Frida, given her negative association with "aspects of conversion that are odious to me." But, in the end, we agreed that, although relying on different metaphors, we had conceptually arrived "on the same page." Encouraged by Frida and Linda, Beth spelled out her pedagogical aspirations:

> What I try to do in the classroom is bring out the decency that I want to assume
> is already there in most of us, and give students a picture of how to be decent—
> what to do with it. We are often an indecent culture; we're so individualistic, and

the messages that students receive have to do with getting stuff, or winning against others. They think that's what makes a good life—owning a BMW, for instance. This doesn't have anything to do with forging solidarity, or thinking critically about injustices. To do that, you have to think in new ways. Well, what I want my students to do is step outside of the box, go beyond the individual self.

Speaking for all of us, Beth added,

We see what we do as a vocation. It is a mission. I see the kind of teaching that we do—and many of our colleagues do; we're not unique—as flipping those switches, as challenging our students to see that it isn't about stuff, and it's not even always about self. There's more to life than stuff and self. And maybe part of that "more" is the solidarity that we talk about and try to engage, and try to enact, and try to inspire others to enact.

As teachers, we aim to politicize our students, to empower them to become social actors, individuals who will take an active role in transforming society in the direction of greater social justice. For that to become a reality, however, we must heighten our students' awareness of those who inhabit worlds outside their "radar screens," those they consider "other." We must help them develop empathy and compassion for those unlike themselves. We must encourage their engagement in solidarity with those who are unjustly marginalized or disenfranchised. This is how we understand transformative education.[37]

Beverly Tatum makes a connection between spirituality and some of our aims when she writes, "If we understand spirituality as the 'human quest for connectedness,' the challenge is to help our students see themselves connected to not only those like them but those different from them."[38] For Frida, this means an ongoing effort in the classroom as she attempts to awaken a transformation in privileged students that moves them from a sense of entitlement to social engagement. She explained, "I confess that I feel agitated by those who take their privilege for granted. I detest complacency and smugness everywhere. They bespeak of the unreflected life. My job as a teacher is to contest these, to challenge students to step outside their 'comfort zones' and hold up a mirror to their lives. And that often involves 'teaching what you are not.'"[39] We all struggle with the critical question raised by bell hooks: "What are we doing as educators to . . . bring a spirit of compassion, of interbeing, into our classrooms and administrations?"[40] Experiences of "interbeing"—a term that, according to Thich Nhat Hanh, "is not in the dictionary yet"[41]—"enable us to know we are connected in trustworthy ways and have some confidence that we can make a difference."[42]

Frida's reflections on her approach to teaching might be seen as a beginning response to hooks's question:

I pay attention to how I teach so that learning will be a living, dynamic process for students, not a dead, inert thing. I spend a lot of time thinking about how to link what students know and care about and what I want to teach them. This is not to say that all subject matter must connect directly to students' own lives. But I believe holistic learning happens when students' being is engaged in a way that matters to them. The engagement can be at any level—intellectual, emotional, spiritual. But an engagement is necessary so that students don't feel that disembodied sense of material having no resonance with their world whatsoever.

This orientation is consistent with hooks's treatment of "engaged pedagogy," developed in a different context, where she writes that students want "knowledge that is meaningful. They rightfully expect that my colleagues and I will not offer them information without addressing the connection between what they are learning and their overall life experiences."[43]

Continuing to reflect, Frida added that, "Teaching about difference, for example, can work much better if students can find points of commonality between their experiences and that of other people and perceive the humanity of those they consider 'other.' Only in this way can they tap into empathy." James Keen, co-author of *Common Fire*,[44] a study of activists committed to social transformation, reports,

Our most salient finding was the importance of enlarging encounters across the thresholds of difference, so that someone or some group that had previously been part of "they" became part of a wider, reconstructed sense of "we." From our research we are convinced that promoting encounters to help people learn to sustain relationships which reach across boundaries of irreducible difference should be among the most important aims of contemporary higher education.[45]

Like other faculty committed to transformative education, Frida, Beth, and Linda teach courses that address difference across a variety of social locations, including gender, social class, race, ethnicity, religion, sexuality, and age. In an effort to combat the various "isms" that oppress or marginalize people, we dedicate a good deal of effort to selecting appropriate reading materials for our classes and thinking about effective teaching methods to convey them. We find great satisfaction when our students "get it," or, to use Beth's metaphor, when the "switches are flipped." Some of our most successful teaching moments have been when an effective bridge has been created in the classroom that allows our students to enter the experience of others, or when they are awakened to realities from which they have been sheltered.

Frida recalled with satisfaction a group of white lesbian students in a "Values and Gender" class who expressed surprise and appreciation after learning about the experiences of African American gay men. More recently, she received the following comment in an unsolicited e-mail from a white, female, middle-class student who had just completed her "Women and Religion" class, which references the unit on womanist theology[46] that they had covered: "I just wanted to say that I really enjoyed your class and really have a new understanding for [*sic*] religion. Not being religious by any means, it really helped to open my eyes to all things. I didn't know that Black women suffered and had many dualisms to overcome."

Linda suggested that, "Some of my best teaching moments can be the ones that start out with the most tension and uncertainty." Usually the question at hand has to do with race. She described her "Language and Power" class, in which students were assigned *The Real Ebonics Debate*.[47] Several days had been devoted to a discussion of dialect. Linda set the scene: "I identified Black Vernacular English (BVE, or Ebonics) as a systematic way of speaking, with a grammar, such is found in any language system. Its devaluation, I explained, is associated with political issues, related to political and economic power, to race, to prestige, to authorized public language forms, and the like." Some students asked challenging, yet relevant questions, but others simply looked at Linda with obvious disbelief and disrespect or looked away, their disinterest and impatience manifest. The moment was painful, but, as Linda continued, "I seized upon two heuristics: First, in order to help them to recognize that BVE speakers were not simply dumb or lazy, as some believed, I put two constructions on the blackboard and asked if they believed that one or the other was easier for a young child to learn to say clearly." The first was, "He's always bothering me!" (in Standard English); the second, "He always be botherin me!" (in non-Standard BVE). After a bit of silence the students agreed that both sentences were probably of equal difficulty. "But Ebonics still sounds terrible," someone said. Linda remained receptive to all ideas, becoming demonstrably enthusiastic. Next, she simulated, as best she could, the pronunciation of an English phrase by someone whose first language was French. When she asked the students if they would call this speaker "dumb" for her inability to sound like an educated American, they said "Of course not."

At this point, Linda could hardly contain herself. Political and linguistic insight lay just around the bend. She began to speak in BVE, embellishing the content and describing herself as a young Black woman whose self-presentation was typical of the hip-hop styles then fashionable in urban centers. The students were riveted. Finally, one white youth literally jumped out of his seat. Amid an obvious epiphany, he shouted, "They don't look like us!" Linda responded, her arms outstretched, with a resounding, "Thank you. Thank you!" All issues of race and power were not resolved in that moment, but as Linda put it, "We had overcome significant obstacles, not the least of which was the recognition that our responses to language forms different from our own have much to do with our overall response to the people who speak those language forms."

While we enjoy these kinds of successes, teaching about differences is also frequently difficult and challenging for us. In our conversations we talked about how we repeatedly place ourselves at risk in the classroom because of our commitments to multiculturalism and inclusion: We all teach about women to men and about the poor to the comfortable; Beth teaches about gays and lesbians to straight students, Frida about Jews to Christians, and, as we have seen, Linda teaches about African Americans to largely white classes. We talked about how vulnerable we feel when students assume we are engaged in special pleading, when in fact we are concerned about justice. And, of course, we risk offending members of any of these groups when we, as outsiders, teach them about themselves. But we try to remember that, as Palmer puts it, "teaching is a daily exercise in vulnerability" because "a good teacher must stand where personal and public meet. . . . As we try to connect ourselves and our subjects with our students, we make ourselves, as well as our subjects, vulnerable to indifference, judgment, ridicule."[48]

According to Beth, "constructing new ways of communicating" with students "also entails constructing new ways of presenting ourselves as educators." When teaching courses in political science, for example, she might be the first female teacher some students encounter, and some of them might have to deal with their discomfort with a woman being in a position of authority. Beth continued:

> Being a woman is the least of it most of the time. My pedagogical question is: How much do I push the various envelopes? Where and when do I test the boundaries of expectations for professors by clarifying that I am a working-class woman? Where and how, if ever, do I push those boundaries further by either indirectly or directly coming out as a lesbian? Where and how do I push those boundaries by making it explicit that I am on the Left politically? Do I talk about Marx as one who is an "objective" student of Marxist philosophy or do I talk about Marx as a partisan of a social order where justice prevailed in ways that they cannot even imagine? So the package that I personally bring to the classroom is very complex. For me, pedagogical questions of presentation of self are a constant source of concern. It's always a very complex set of negotiations that even on good days I do not think I have really mastered.

Elizabeth Tisdell is cognizant of such issues of self-presentation in the classroom when she writes,

> Clearly the positionality of the instructor always affects what goes on in classes; however, the conditions under which instructors will *directly* discuss it in the class might vary. If I am an African-American woman, in what circumstances should I discuss my "Blackness" or my femaleness and what it has to do with

class? Or if I am a gay white man, under what conditions in the learning environment do I problemetize my whiteness, my maleness, my gayness?[49]

Linda responded sympathetically to Beth's concerns, saying, "I'm listening to you and I understand exactly what you're saying. I feel that I've had an experience similar to that. I feel, though, that I can't hide—not to say that you hide—but that *you* can sort of foreground or background aspects of your identity."

Beth readily agreed: "Yeah, you can't," fully recognizing, of course, that Linda cannot conceal her racial identity and hence has absolutely no control over how students' attitudes toward her race shape their receptivity to her teaching. Linda continued:

> I realize how much that becomes the challenge when I'm trying to ask students to consider a point of view that's oppositional to their own. I always feel as if I want somebody else in there. I always feel as if I cannot communicate, I cannot help them understand oppression, structures of oppression, voicelessness, power, privilege, the dynamics of privilege. I can't help them to understand this and to question it, up there by myself. I need a partner who is not Black. And it makes me angry that I even think that. But I know that some students have a really, really hard time legitimating what I am saying to the extent that it opposes their frame of reference; and it's because of who I am.

Linda does not simply give up in her efforts to open up students' awareness. She sometimes is helped by other students—Black students, generally—who provide support for her interpretations, but this strategy does not always work with some of the skeptical working- or middle-class white students in the mix. Linda attributes their skepticism to "a failure of imagination" on the part of those sheltered from close relationships "with people in groups other than their own." "What I do at that point," she explained, "is what I call the meta-discourse: 'OK, let's talk about what's going on here, let's talk about our own talk.'" Using her skills as a linguist, Linda works with students to deconstruct both the speech used in the classroom and the assumptions informing it. Sighing deeply, she admitted, "That's when all this stuff gets unearthed in ways that are very uncomfortable."

"On issues about self-presentation, the challenges for me are both parallel and different from what you two have said," Frida stated, as she shared her experience with her colleagues. "It's very easy for me to pass as a non-Jew, so I could pretend, or not offer that—but I can't do that. I'm committed to authenticity. There are few enough Jewish students on campus and they need models. They need some affirmation, especially in religious studies courses." DePaul is, of course, a Catholic university. According to Frida, in this predominantly Christian context, "It's never a comfortable solution to let my students know I'm a Jew." She does so—particularly in comparative religion courses—because, as she put it, "I teach inductively, and I like students to offer their religious experience and their knowledge as a source for people understanding one another, and I see myself as another player."

"That's right," Linda broke in.

"But I realize," Frida continued, "that part of my agenda is to offer an embodied expression of what a Jew is." Frida was thinking about modeling for both Jews and non-Jews in the classroom. "It needs to be done in a subtle sort of way, and my problem is—and this is where I can identify with what you're saying—I always feel that there's a danger of my students interpreting, whenever I teach about Judaism or Jewish issues or anti-Semitism, that I'm engaged in a self-serving enterprise, that the only reason why I do this is because I'm a Jew.[50] And, in fact, my fears have at times been validated." She reported about evaluations for her "Women and Religion" course some years ago when some students complained that the course title should be changed to "*Jewish* Women and Religion," despite the fact that less that one-fourth of the course was dedicated to the study of women in Judaism. At times like that, Frida added:

> I feel a tension between "should I continue to teach about Judaism, which then generates all of these feelings and tensions for me, or should I just take the easy path and not do it?" I told you about my commitment in all of my classes: I feel one has to fight injustice, one has to contest the taken-for-granted truths; there's a lot of anti-Semitism out there, and a lot of the time it comes out of ignorance, out of a lack of exposure. And I feel it's my responsibility. . . . I think if I were not Jewish I would feel the same way, just as in actuality I feel it's my responsibility to deal with racism in all my classes.

As is her wont, Linda readily offered empathy as well as an interpretation of why students seemingly misread our efforts to include work about and by nondominant groups in our classes: "It seems to be perhaps a function of our cognitive systems or something, some way in which we perceive reality and fit things into categories that, when we see something as *marked*, the marked as opposed to the unmarked looms much, much larger than it actually is." In Frida's experience, noted above, the Jewish material in her class was perceived by some students as disproportionately represented, whereas the culturally dominant—and hence, unmarked—Christian material that constituted the bulk of the course material was not seen as problematic (i.e., it was taken for granted).

The same process obtains for Beth when male students in political science classes grumble that the class should be offered in women's studies, instead, because a few women theorists are assigned on the course syllabus. More recently, as she has moved to integrate issues central to lesbian, gay, bisexual, or transgendered (LGBT) experiences into her political science and liberal

studies courses, she has encountered similar resistance from students unable
to move beyond their heterosexual privilege. As she described it:

> Most DePaul students are very open to, and very interested in, questions of
> LGBT history and politics, and those classes can be very exciting, but there are
> always a few who express anger at having, as one student put it on an evalua-
> tion, "to study this shit." A few, who haven't figured out my orientation, have
> asked why LGBT politics are on the syllabus—they assume I'm straight, so why
> should I want to engage them on these issues?

Beth laughed, but there was a hint of bitterness behind her humor.

Linda reported a painful case of a young white student who publicly ac-
cused Linda of being racist. "I asked for evidence. I said, 'Please help me to
understand where your accusation comes from.' He couldn't conjure up anything except for the material that I used, which was perhaps one-third by people of color. But the very fact that I have used material by people of color
means that I'm racist."

Despite such moment of despair, we forged on. As Linda wearily observed,
"It's a chore to do social justice work, it's a chore to do any sort of class consciousness work, all of which I do in all of my classes, regardless of what I'm
teaching. I'm in some way going against the grain and challenging hegemony.
It's just who I am in front of the classroom." She paused a moment, adding,
"It's been my challenge as a professional, as an educator, to find a way to let
these young people express their anger, to let their anger bounce off me without my silencing it, finding a way for them to facilitate their hearing the silences in some meaningful, pedagogical heuristic that keeps them there and
enlarges their thinking, rather than see them run and drop the class."

When we discussed these vulnerabilities and frustrations with one another,
"letting our hair down" about these and other difficult moments in our classrooms, we always felt somewhat discouraged. In one gloomy moment, Beth
sought inspiration in Gertrude Stein's aphorism, "Considering how dangerous
everything is, nothing is really very frightening."[51] She interpreted the quote
this way, "If you take teaching seriously, you're always going to be at risk, so
you might as well take your risks with ethical integrity. You might as well, because otherwise, how do you look in the mirror at the end of the day?"

Despite the tensions we live with and the vulnerabilities we experience, all
of us continue our investment in transformative pedagogy. In earlier chapters,
we have shown that we have long been infused by a common commitment to
social justice, informed by our own experiences of marginalization, religious
attitudes demanding justice, or role models who inspired work on behalf of
social transformation. In this chapter, we have examined how our various religious and spiritual groundings have contributed to this commitment. Our

ideals of social justice are not abstract or ideological; they are grounded in the embodied, formative experiences of our lives, and in the religious or philosophical wellsprings that feed our souls.

Each of us has been involved in social activism over the course of our lives. In the early years of Linda's career, she taught kids in group homes and adolescent addicts in a New York recovery program, so-called problem kids. This was an environment where she could serve, as she put it, the "excluded, the under-represented, the unspoken for." For a number of years, Beth worked tirelessly with a number of grassroots lesbian and gay organizations, primarily in Boston. She was a member of the *Gay Community News* collective, which was a memorable, "pre-AIDS experience of lesbians and gay men attempting to make common cause around feminist and socialist principles while putting out a weekly newspaper." Frida dedicated some years to women's reproductive health issues. The demands of academic life and other obligations, however, are such that we currently engage our passion for justice in the work of the classroom and research, not in the streets. At times, we have all felt some measure of guilt about these choices. But, as Frida told her colleagues: "I've come around to recognize that it is in the university that I make a difference; it is in the teaching, in the texts that I select, it's how I teach, it's the mission I have, it's the value-laden education. I have come to recognize that this is a form of activism, that we in fact are social change agents."

Linda agreed. She discussed some of the texts she assigns her students, hoping to engage them in empathetic learning, and then turned to a key pedagogical concern: "It is because I've come from particularly fragile places, vis-à-vis the academy, that there is absolutely no way for me to ever do what I do without passion, because this would be to deny my whole experience of reality and my construction of reality."

The experience of remembered pain has motivated much of Beth's teaching as well. For many years, she has had "a sense of social justice that was tuned to run on overdrive." When she probed deeper into why she does what she does, and how she defines her professional self, she concluded, "I see my work as an educator as *praxis*, because I don't want any young person to have to live the way I have lived."

In chapter four, we noted that one's own experience of pain may be a significant ingredient in the development of compassion; Beth and Linda may well have been alluding to this connection as it applies to their pedagogical commitments. We were all moved by bell hooks's elucidation of this dynamic within the context of U.S. culture: "One of the things that a culture of domination does to all of us—irrespective of our class, race or gender—is make us ashamed of our pain. In claiming our pain as a space where we can work alchemically, we begin to move against the forces of domination. We move against the forces of fear and shame. In fact, *we discover that it is precisely our pain that intimately connects us with others*."[52] Rachel Remen's view of compassion further extends our understanding: "True compassion requires us to attend to our own humanity, to come to a deep acceptance of our own life as it is. It requires us to come into right relationship with that which is most human in ourselves, that which is most capable of suffering."[53] As educators, we recognize that if the pain we have experienced has mobilized us for the work of transformative education, students accessing their own pain may open their eyes to other people's suffering. This view parallels Ronald A. Kuipers's aspiration, expressed in a recent article on ethical debates about homosexuality: "I only hope to encourage those at the centre to show solidarity with those who, in my opinion, suffer unnecessarily at the margins of our society." Paraphrasing philosopher Richard Rorty, Kuipers argues that "the difference between the heterosexual majority and the homosexual minority is unimportant when compared with the similarity both groups have with respect to their ability to suffer pain and humiliation. In the suffering of the homosexual minority, both groups may begin to recognize a shared humanity, one that transcends the difference of sexual orientation."[54]

Our discussion of pain and suffering brings us full circle to where we began this chapter—religion and spirituality—and their connection with ethics. Throughout our exploration of these topics, we have referenced pain that is socially and culturally constructed, and therefore *not* inevitable (e.g., social marginalization, material deprivation, discrimination). Yet the *experience* of human suffering often feels the same, whether it stems from social or existential sources. We thus enter the realm of the spirit, and religion, for in the end we are speaking about the human condition. All people, no matter which culture, religion, gender, ethnicity, race, or any other social indicator, are subject to and witnesses (if not perpetrators) of human suffering. Such suffering must be understood as a common denominator of our humanity, for this unfortunate element in human experience has the potential of binding the "we" and "they," the "familiar" and "other." The irony is that suffering, the scourge of human life, God's punishment for human disobedience in the biblical myth, may in the end be a major agent of human redemption, as we learn to extend our hearts and hands—indeed, our voices—in solidarity across the multitudinous differences that keep us apart.

SPIRITUAL WHOLENESS AND UNEASE IN THE ACADEMY

At the end of the academic year, Beth and Frida often carpool to DePaul's commencement ceremony, held in a cavernous arena some distance from the university. On a recent return trip, discussing the highlights of the event and joyous encounters with new graduates at the reception, they bemoaned the absence of many colleagues. Frida noted with relief that her department, Religious Studies, had been well represented, but this could not be said about most of the other departments and programs. Sometime later, when we were all together, Beth and Frida raised the issue with Linda, who readily agreed that it is a faculty member's moral obligation to be present at such events, for the sake of students and their families. We remarked on how many of our students, at DePaul or Stockton, are working-class or first-generation students, and on the need to recognize, as Beth put it, "the real sacrifices that have been made by their parents."

Warming up to her subject, Beth added, her voice rising with emotion,

> This is the one time when DePaul gets to put on a show that demonstrates symbolically to the families what this has been about. It's a closure, and a promise—an acknowledgment of achievement to date, a hope for achievement to come. To be so cavalier about the meaning of this for our students and their families as to not show up! I cannot find the language that is strong enough to express how reprehensible I think it is, how angry it makes me.

Beth's frustration about this revealed the deep-seated solidarity she believes faculty should develop with students. She interpreted the failure to attend graduation as a betrayal of that solidarity, as a breach of the connection faculty should dedicate their working lives to establish with students.

Linda expressed a similar view, refracted through her racial-ethnic pride and her ability to model high academic achievement for Black graduates and their families:

> For me, this is so much an act of community, when at Stockton the faculty processes in and we walk past all the parents. We're out on the lawn, provided the weather is good, and all the parents are in the bleachers. Most times, I feel as if I don't have the choice to say, "I don't feel like going in the procession this year." The students are out there with their parents, their uncles and aunts, their grandparents; and students who have graduated are back there. The Black faculty often—not always—breaks the line of vision, marches together, some of us with kente cloth stoles over our gowns, and the students and their parents are so responsive. I look in the eyes of the Black parents, many of whom I've never seen before in my life, and they just look at me expressing such pride, and it is a feeling that I cannot describe.

On a rather different level, the experience of donning our own academic regalia for the faculty procession fills us with a kind of joy and wholeness difficult to articulate. As Frida put it:

> I really enjoy the whole pomp and circumstance of parading back and forth. I love it. I love being seen by students. It's one moment in which you can visually communicate a kind of hierarchy that we have earned in a sense. We have earned it; it's symbolic. Even though I don't *believe* in the hierarchical marking, I do enjoy it. I have to admit that. And it probably has to do with the fact that I'm the only person in my family who has gotten this kind of education.

Identifying with Frida's sentiments, Linda enthusiastically broke in, "Of course! That *has* to have something to do with it."

Frida continued, "It's got to be part of it. There's a kind of joy in, 'Aren't I lucky that I was able to do this?' And I made it!"

"Oh, of course. That's just so right to me," Linda shot back.

Beth added an apt literary association, fully resonant for Frida and Linda. "The procession aspect of it also represents tangible evidence of what Virginia Woolf criticizes in *Three Guineas* as 'the long processions of the sons of educated men.'[55] And here we are, and here we are. And *I* am in the procession as an educated woman."

Our participation in such academic events involves experiences of spiritual wholeness for us, in that it affirms deep and essential elements of our being, providing opportunities for healing alienated dimensions of ourselves—dimensions pertaining to gender, social class, educational achievement, and, for Linda, race-ethnicity. At these moments we feel at home in academia. There are other such moments, of course. In a previous chapter, for example, we discussed the appreciation Beth experienced when her lesbian identity was acknowledged and affirmed by a faculty member from Religious Studies. We also have seen how some of the feminist conferences we have attended have encouraged us to celebrate important components of identity—such as our race, ethnicity, or sexuality—typically swept to the margins of mainstream academic gatherings.

At the same time, each of us continues to experience moments of discomfort or unease that sometimes lead us to question our own authority. In such instances, we often feel spiritually defeated or erased. This was the case for Beth, as we have seen, when her Political Science colleagues ignored her public coming out at the college faculty meeting.

Erasure was mirrored for Linda when, at a small, informal faculty gathering, discussion centered on a negative review of a scholarly publication. Reading closely, Linda responded to the negativity with a spontaneous, unself-conscious articulation commonly heard in African American discourse, particularly from women. All those present could hear the rise and fall of her tone contours, issuing a powerful, emotive response to the words on the page. As her head moved from side to side, a motion indicating concern, Linda uttered, "Um, um uh, uh, um!" On the heels of this, a white colleague burst forth with a mock religious testimony, "Hallelujah, Hallelujah!," clearly meant to mimic Linda's Black cultural expressiveness. Linda was left with feelings of ridicule and self-consciousness. She had done nothing more than exclaim in a manner that is taken for granted, and therefore would hardly have been noticed within the Black community, where there is no sharp divide marking the sacred from the secular domains of action and thought. Certainly, it would not have been mocked or trivialized. While Linda does not expect non-Blacks to hear this in the same way she does, she does believe that with greater sensitivity to cultural differences, the colleague who interjected the "Hallelujahs" would have recognized them as an insult.

Frida experiences such erasures most notably around her Jewishness. For example, she feels invisible when DePaul begins fall classes on the first or second day of Rosh Hashanah, which she observes. A few years ago, her department chair scheduled a departmental meeting on Yom Kippur, arguing that it would be more convenient for a majority of the rest of the faculty—another erasure, for no one would consider meeting on Good Friday, for instance, at a Catholic university. Most recently, the three of us were invited to present a panel on this book at a national conference on "Race, Gender and Class" aimed, among other things, at exploring ways in which persons and groups are marginalized by virtue of their social location. The conference, however, fell on Yom Kippur—an irony that the planning committee failed to note. When Beth pointed this out to the person who had invited them to present, she was told that no adjustment could be made because plans were well underway. We are sure that, had such a conference been inadvertently scheduled to coincide with a significant Christian holy day, things would have been otherwise. Linda and Beth chose to attend the conference in protest, planning to illuminate Frida's absence by designating an empty chair and starting their presentation by discussing issues of exclusion and erasure.

The theologian Ada María Isasi-Díaz writes about the "invisible invisibility" that Hispanic women and others outside the dominant culture often experience in the United States: "Invisible invisibility has to do with people not even knowing that they do not know you."[56] That's the kind of erasure we feel when central dimensions of our identity are entirely ignored. For us these reflections ultimately pertain to this chapter's topic—spirituality and education—and, hence, they lead us to ask about our responsibility to our students and to attend to the ways that they might experience invisibility and erasure. In probing our own experiences of unease, we hope to become sensitized to the many ways in which we ourselves may contribute to similar feelings in our students. Collaboration on this project has raised our awareness. It has encouraged us to work harder at listening to colleagues and students who come from worlds unfamiliar to our own, yet who long for understanding and, short of that, acceptance of their uniqueness and difference, so they, too, can feel spiritually whole. Beth's reflection on her own work—perhaps ironically, since she is the least "religiously musical" among us—seems to sum it all up: "I have always been moved by the saying *Laborare et orare*. Work is prayer. I believe it, and try to live it, whether I am knitting or teaching or trying to get just one more section of one more chapter of the book written." Work is prayer. However variously we believe in, or express, our different forms—or lack—of religious faith, it is at this juncture that our professional and spiritual lives all intersect.

NOTES

1. The *Havurah* movement arose in the late 1960s with calls for the spiritual renewal of Judaism, understood to include the empowerment of worshipers through liturgical skill development and experimentation. The movement is typically manifested by fellowship groups (*havurot*) that are small, nonhierarchical, and gender inclusive.

2. As the Women of Winslow grew, Linda explained, "Our outreach diversified: We have donated small recognition scholarships to local high school graduates; we have collected money for charities; on one occasion, we organized the community's Martin Luther King Prayer Breakfast; and, if any one of us became ill, we would provide a meal, chauffeur children to and from appointments, and, as member Judy Shell says, 'We have tried to be a blessing to each other.'"

3. Charisse Jones and Kumea Shorter-Gooden, *Shifting: The Double Lives of Black Women in America* (New York: Harper Collins, 2004), 261. For a detailed discussion of the genesis and the objectives of this study, see page 4.

4. The reference is to Hebrews 11:1, "Now faith is the assurance of things hoped for, the conviction of things not seen."

5. See, for example, Gloria Jean Wade-Gayles, ed., *My Soul Is a Witness: African-American Women's Spirituality* (Boston: Beacon Press, 1995).

6. Frida's sister shares this orientation.

7. Cited in H. H. Gerth and C. Wright Mills, eds. and trans., *From Max Weber: Essays in Sociology* (New York: Oxford University Press, 1958), 25.

8. See, especially, Heschel's *Man Is Not Alone* (Reprint, New York: Noonday Press, 1976) and *God in Search of Man* (Reprint, New York: Noonday Press, 1976).

9. The song has been recorded many times by a variety of artists. Beth's favorite is found on Sweet Honey in the Rock's 1992 CD, *Feel Something Drawing Me On*, Flying Fish Records.

10. For Beth, the Catholic Church is "this strange land."

11. Rich, "When We Dead Awaken" in *Poems: Selected and New*, 187–188.

12. Martin Buber, *I and Thou*, Ronald Gregor Smith, trans. (New York: Scribner, 2000).

13. Paul Tillich, *Dynamics of Faith* (New York: Harper & Row, 1957), 77.

14. Beth alluded here to the language of 1 Corinthians 13:12.

15. Rich, "Leaflets," in *Poems: Selected and New*, 118.

16. Educators interviewed by Elizabeth J. Tisdell "talked about the fact that the spiritual was found in creating a balance between inner reflection and outer action." See Tisdell, *Exploring Spirituality and Culture in Adult and Higher Education* (San Francisco: Jossey-Bass, 2003), 246.

17. Steven Glazer, ed., *The Heart of Learning: Spirituality in Education* (New York: Jeremy P. Tarcher/Putnam, 1999), 82.

18. Tisdell, *Exploring Spirituality*, 60.

19. In religious studies and sociology, for example, see Robert Wuthnow, *After Heaven: Spirituality in America since the 1950s* (Berkeley: University of California Press, 1998) and Clark Wade Roof, *Spiritual Marketplace: Baby Boomers and the Re-*

making of American Religion (Princeton, NJ: Princeton University Press, 1999). In adult education, see Parker J. Palmer, *The Courage to Teach: Exploring the Inner Landscape of a Teacher's Life* (San Francisco: Jossey-Bass Publishers, 1998); Glazer, *The Heart of Learning*; and Tisdell, *Exploring Spirituality*.

20. Robert Wuthnow, *Creative Spirituality: The Way of the Artist* (Berkeley: University of California Press, 2001), 23.

21. Parker Palmer, "Evoking the Spirit of Public Education," *Educational Leadership* 56, no. 4 (December 1998/January 1999): 6.

22. Tisdell, *Exploring Spirituality*, 48.

23. See, for example, Rosemary Radford Ruether's *Gaia and God: An Ecofeminist Theology of Earth Healing* (New York: HarperCollins, 1992) and her edited collection, *Women Healing Earth* (Maryknoll, NY: Orbis Books, 1996).

24. See, for example, Paula M. Cooey, Sharon A. Farmer, and Mary Ellen Ross, eds., *Embodied Love: Sensuality and Relationship as Feminist Values* (New York: Harper & Row, 1987); Linda Holler, *Erotic Morality: The Role of Touch in Moral Agency* (New Brunswick, NJ: Rutgers University Press, 2002); and Diana Tietjens Meyers, ed., *Feminists Rethink the Self* (Boulder, CO: Westview Press, 1997).

25. See, for example, contributors to Ruether, *Women Healing Earth*.

26. See Manfred B. Steger, *Globalism: The New Market Ideology* (New York: Rowman & Littlefield, 2002).

27. Daloz et al., *Common Fire*, 201.

28. Belenky, Mary Field, et al., *Women's Ways of Knowing*: The Development of Self, Voice, and Mind (New York: Basic Books, 1986).

29. Belenky et al., *Women's Ways of Knowing*, 124.

30. Belenky et al., *Women's Ways of Knowing*, 134.

31. See, for example, Nancy Rule Goldberger et al., *Knowledge, Difference, and Power: Essays Inspired by* Women's Ways of Knowing (New York: Basic Books, 1996).

32. For a recent discussion of some of these issues, see Martha C. Nussbaum, *Upheavals of Thought: The Intelligence of Emotions* (New York: Cambridge University Press, 2001).

33. Tisdell, *Exploring Spirituality*, 187–188.

34. Similarly, Parker Palmer reports one student's assessment of bad teaching as times when teachers' "words float somewhere in front of their faces like the balloon speeches in cartoons." See Palmer, "The Grace of Great Things: Reclaiming the Sacred in Knowing, Teaching, and Learning," in Glazer, *The Heart of Learning*, 27.

35. Palmer, *The Courage to Teach*, 11.

36. Paulo Freire and Donaldo P. Macedo, "A Dialogue: Culture, Language, and Race," *Harvard Education Review* 65, no. 3 (Fall 1995), 394, 379.

37. Paulo Freire captures our sentiments exactly when he says, "One of our challenges as educators is to discover what historically is possible in the sense of contributing toward the transformation of the world, giving rise to a world that is rounder, less angular, more humane, and in which one prepares the materialization of the great Utopia: Unity in Diversity" (Freire and Macedo, "A Dialogue," 397).

38. Beverly Daniel Tatum, "Changing Lives: Building a Capacity for Connection in a Pluralistic Context," in Victor H. Kazanjian, Jr., and Peter L. Laurence, eds., *Education*

as Transformation: Religious Pluralism, Spirituality, and a New Vision for Higher Education in America (New York: Peter Lang, 2000), 83.

39. The expression is borrowed from the book title of *Teaching What You're Not: Identity Politics in Higher Education*, Katherine J. Mayberry, ed. (New York: New York University Press, 1996).

40. bell hooks, "Embracing Freedom: Spirituality and Liberation," in Glazer, ed., *The Heart of Learning*, 121.

41. Thich Nhat Hanh, *Peace Is Every Step: The Path of Mindfulness in Everyday Life* (New York: Bantam, 1991), 95–96.

42. Daloz et al., *Common Fire*, 26.

43. hooks, *Teaching to Transgress*, 19.

44. Daloz et al., *Common Fire*.

45. James P. Keen, "Appreciative Engagement of Diversity: E Pluribus Unum and the EDUCATION as Transformation Project," in Kazanjian and Laurence, eds., *Education as Transformation*, 207.

46. Womanist theology addresses the theological and sociocultural concerns of African American feminists.

47. Theresa Perry and Lisa Delpit, eds., *The Real Ebonics Debate* (Boston: Beacon Press), 1998.

48. Palmer, *The Courage to Teach*, 17.

49. Elizabeth J. Tisdell, "Poststructural Feminist Pedagogies: The Possibilities and Limitations of Feminist Emancipatory Adult Learning Theory and Practice," *Adult Education Quarterly* 48, No. 3 (Spring 1998), 147–148.

50. In a parallel manner, Tisdell argues that, "If an African-American woman brings up her own identity or champions women's rights or race rights, she may be seen as 'pushing her own agenda'" (Tisdell, "Poststructural Feminist Pedagogies," 148).

51. Gertrude Stein, *Everybody's Autobiography* (London: Virago Press, 1985), 48.

52. hooks, "Embracing Freedom," 126, emphasis added.

53. Rachel Naomi Remen, "Educating for Mission, Meaning, and Compassion," in Glazer and Smith, eds., *The Heart of Learning*, 34.

54. Ronald A. Kuipers, "Violent Asymmetry: The Shape of Power in the Current Debate over the Morality of Homosexuality," in James H. Olthuis, ed., *Towards an Ethics of Community: Negotiations of Difference in a Pluralist Society* (Waterloo, Ontario, Canada: Wilfrid Laurier University Press, 2000), 171. Richard Rorty's work is referenced as *Contingency, Irony, and Solidarity* (Cambridge: Cambridge University Press, 1989), 192.

55. Virginia Woolf, *Three Guineas* (San Diego, CA: Harcourt Trade Publishers, 1963).

56. Ada María Isasi-Díaz, "Toward an Understanding of *Feminismo Hispano* in the U.S.A.," in Barbara Hilkert Andolsen, Christine E. Gudorf, and Mary D. Pellauer, eds., *Women's Consciousness, Women's Conscience* (Minneapolis: Winston Press, 1985), 51.

Chapter Six

Interwoven Lives, Cosmopolitan Visions

One August afternoon, as our work on this book drew to a close, Beth and Frida lingered in Beth's office at DePaul after a conference call with Linda in New Jersey. Late summer sunshine streamed in through the windows of the former St. Vincent DePaul Church Rectory. Both the church next door and Beth's office building are landmarks in Chicago's Lincoln Park neighborhood, a few blocks west of the Lake Michigan shoreline. As the two talked over the manuscript, their conversation was frequently broken by the ear-splitting roar of low-flying jet planes. Frida frowned in annoyance after a string of noisy interruptions. "What is going *on?*" she asked, her tone tight and face tense. "I can't even hear myself think!"

Beth replied, "They're fighter planes, rehearsing for the Air and Water Show on the beach this weekend. This will be going on all day today and tomorrow. It's driving me crazy; these are the kind of jets I grew up with. This noise takes me back to a place I do *not* want to go!"

Frida's response was quick and compassionate: "It must really resonate with the experiences you had in childhood."

Beth nodded. "I don't think it would bother me so much," she added pensively, "if I hadn't just been rereading that bit of our text in the first chapter. It brings it all back—I'm just realizing how deeply this affects me and how much this book shows how our past and present lives are interwoven."

"Yes!" Frida acknowledged. "We're not conscious of that most of the time. What's been distinctive about this project is that it's brought those connections to consciousness in ways that they are usually not available. For the past seven years, our pasts have been very much a part of our present. That's made the work rich, but it's been hard."

As we have noted along the way, putting this book together was a challenging, at times daunting, enterprise. Telling our stories, analyzing our experiences, and writing about them frequently demanded a great deal of emotional energy. However, immersing ourselves in the data was also pleasurable and delightful, especially in those moments where we grew to know ourselves and each other in new and deeper ways. To a remarkable extent, we came to inhabit one another's autobiographies, to the point where today, in conversation, we frequently draw on our shared experiences in a kind of shorthand that only the three of us understand. For example, "Snow Globes!" (from a narrative Frida shared in chapter three) has come to stand for any form of unexpressed, and thereby unsatisfied, yearning. The deathless phrase, "It's a two hot dog day," which evokes a highly charged moment Beth and Linda shared long ago as colleagues at Stockton, invariably serves to indicate stress that the speaker hopes to deflect, in part, with humor. From Patricia Williams, all three of us have borrowed the term "spoiling a good party," whose context and usage have been explained in several chapters of this book. We take this as evidence of how we have come to respect one another for our values, lived experiences, and thoughtful reflections.

While often rewarding, our collaboration was not without its difficulties. Three very different personalities, obligations, schedules, and work styles did not always mesh felicitously. Nor did our conversations always go smoothly or supportively, especially when we were tired or otherwise stressed; exhaustion sometimes got the better of us. Despite all the hard work and the occasional rough going, all three of us today feel profoundly transformed. How often, we wonder, does scholarship result in such feelings? We all enriched and informed one another; we have become friends of each other's minds in ways that we could never have imagined when we embarked upon this journey. A full accounting of our individual and mutual transformations is beyond the scope of this chapter, but some brief reflections seem in order at this juncture.

Frida began this assessment with appreciation for the process at the heart of the project:

> *In the harried pace of academic life, it is rare to find the time and energy to engage in long, deep, leisurely conversations—sometimes spanning days. Rarer still is finding such a high level of openness, trust, and solidarity in the context of a threesome—it was so moving and so powerful to be allowed into Beth and Linda's very minds and souls. I treasure the memory of those days and look forward to continuing my engagement in their lives and work.*

As to the transformative impact the project has had for her life, Frida is convinced that, without question, our triadic exchanges have been a source of two significant changes. The first pertains to her intellectual, ethical, and emotional relationship to social class. This is how she put it:

As I have said before, your solid grounding in social class analysis has been extremely helpful for me; it has provided me with a far more refined interpretive frame to understand my life, my responses, and the experiences of other people. Beforehand, I felt a strong ethical commitment to the eradication of poverty and a good deal of visceral indignation at the huge gap separating rich and poor, in the United States and elsewhere. I've taught about all this for years in my social ethics courses. What's different now is that I have grown so sensitized to class dynamics that I am able to "read" them in everyday life quite regularly. It's as though I have grown antenna that pick up social class signals. Of course this has been helped by all the reading and writing I have done regarding class issues in the last few years. As a result, I think my intellectual awareness is now linked to being more fully present to the experiences of those who suffer because of class disparities; I now experience greater identification with them, in part because I have come to see more forcefully that my family and I shared in those experiences. I have become a better analyst, but perhaps more importantly, a more compassionate person.

Frida's departure from Chile was the foundational trauma of her life; its pain, as we have seen, remained repressed or otherwise unresolved for decades. In her judgment, it was the process of narrativization—in conversations with Beth and Linda, followed by writing the stories of her childhood experience and so-called exile—and her colleagues' encouragement that finally freed her to make the return trip to her birthplace in 1999. Gabriella Ibieta, a Cuban-born academic, migrated to the United States with her family when she was a child. She notes that returning "does not bring closure to the conflicts of identity, but it does heal the pain of fragmentation."[1] "That's a fitting description for me as well," Frida observed. "My visit to Chile did heal a lot of that pain. It also released me to explore my Latin American identity, gingerly, in small steps, for I still struggle with questions of authenticity about my right to claim it."

As she continued:

Now I more comfortably attend Latin American events at DePaul. I have become close friends with a Puerto Rican colleague, with whom I speak exclusively in Spanish. I recently led a student group for a semester abroad program in Madrid, in part, so I could immerse myself in a Spanish-speaking environment. And I have inscribed my recovering identity as a Latin American on the walls of my university office: Chilean posters and copper plates, Mexican and Ecuadorian textiles, and a brilliantly blue-and-red pictorial rendition of Pablo Neruda's "Oda a la Sandía" ("Ode to the Watermelon"). These visual images are my latest narratives of self-construction, at this point still exploratory gestures, tentative efforts on my part to shape the evolving nature of my identity. Occasionally, I still feel self-conscious as I enter my office, but I hope that in time the inner and the outer pieces of myself, the "there" (Chile) and the "here" (the

U.S.) will become more integrally reconciled. Arriving at this place has been, for me, the gift of this book project.

Linda's reflections took a slightly different tack. She began with the challenge the three of us faced as we refused to be daunted by the predictable struggles of three personalities committed to continuous compromise. Linda then moved from the group experience to her own personal realization that the memory of past pain associated with poverty has deeply informed her abiding community commitments:

More than once I doubted that I could get through the project; the challenges were, as one can imagine, interpersonal as well as singularly private. In our meetings over the years, after long hours of face-to-face work, after saying goodnight, I went to my room in our rented home in Sea Isle, usually exhausted, but often invigorated and amazed at the magnitude of what we had undertaken. However, there were days when I was so weary from the effort, the perceived lack of understanding and our personal differences, that I was ready to quit. I'm thankful that I didn't. My inner struggle with the material of my life story was at least as daunting, but our steadfast commitment to the project's completion repaid my efforts double-fold.

Because this project insisted I revisit the past, I have developed keener vision; I have been better able to recognize the way that my early poverty has nourished—no, necessitated—my compassion. Because of this book, I not only mouth the words about poverty being violence against the human spirit, but also accept my own history without the shame that seems to shadow the poor. I had made these connections in my own life before we began our work, but there is something profoundly transformative when we stumble upon an insight, as in those processural moments of narrative co-construction that we identify in chapter two.

Even as I am better able to integrate the pain of my early years into the frame of who I am now, I believe I more fully accept the folly of privileging one kind of pain over another. The enslavement of my forebears is still present each morning as I assess the world all over again. However, this is no less true for a great many other groups of people. From long conversations with Frida and Beth, I know that they, too, meet the world with identities, visible or not, that leave them vulnerable, that are marked by considerable pain. While I can't know their experiences in the depths of my own life, I do hear with my eyes as well as my ears. Having arrived at this project so equipped, I am more convinced than ever that I cannot participate in a hierarchical arrangement of suffering. To do so would diminish me as a human being and in an odd way deflect from the vast distance African Americans have traveled over the last two centuries.

Moreover, the more I learn of my own family history, joyously revitalized on my recent trip to Jamaica, the more I am convinced that revisiting our legacies is essential in order to mend the fragmentation of dislocations. I don't know if I would have followed through with my new project, associated with Jamaica, had I not participated in this enterprise.

My dear friend and colleague, Pam Cross, jokingly tells me that I have the capacity, although I deny it, "to see the Christ in everyone." If, as I believe, the historical Jesus embodied forgiveness and generosity, then I will continue to follow that role model (though I fall short far more often than Pam acknowledges). Nonetheless, this project has confirmed that I am not foolhardy, that my ideals are not naive or vain. Even as my socioeconomic status has elevated remarkably since the days of my youth—I have crossed over at least two strata—I refuse to abandon the economic pattern of reciprocity and sharing. Indeed, the extra green pepper, or chicken, or bread will be available to others as long as I am able to provide. It is so easy to relinquish subsistence patterns born in dire need when those needs are no longer yours, even if others you know still require help.

In addition, this project helped me to see that teaching can be part of the available goods we share with those in need. In conjunction with my recent work on this book, I consulted one of the Women of Winslow to verify my description of our purposes. She freely offered, seemingly unrelated to our conversation, that I had "been a blessing to this community," referring to my assistance to young students working their way toward college. Her unsolicited feedback reminded me of the importance of this commitment, which I am not sure that I could have sustained, were it not for how, in this work, we have repeatedly shared and analyzed, as Frida has put it, "a personal ethics of care."

Beth's experiences of growth and change while engaged with this project played out rather differently from Frida's or Linda's. She cannot report significant transformations of her sense of self, class consciousness, hybridity, or bodily presentation. Her hair, it is true, today shows more "salt" than "pepper" than it did in 1997, but it is still cut short in the same "fifth grade in Catholic school 'do'" she has worn for decades.[2] Overall, Beth's personal and professional transformations have been subtle. "My mother has always believed that your life changes every seven years," she began. "Your body changes; your personality shifts; everything about you is different, even new." Beth shrugged, making a skeptical face. "I never bought that. But, still, seven years is how long we've been at this." She continued:

When we began working together, I had just gotten tenure and been appointed Director of the Women's Studies Program; I felt professionally secure for the first time. Those changes more or less coincided with our beginning work on this book. In a sense, they represented a significant border crossing, because I was so used to feeling like a supplicant in grad school or pre-tenure, and before that, demeaned as an office worker, that I couldn't have imagined what a difference security would make or how much my outlook would change. It took a while for the realization to sink in. It was really a "Look, Ma, no hands!" moment—liberatory, just like learning to balance on the bicycle without holding on.

Becoming professionally secure intersected with this book in a couple of ways. First, and most importantly, the actual process of co-constructing our narratives gave me a new voice. Sharing stories with Linda and Frida was empowering; we told one another things we'd never shared with anyone else, and we mutually validated each other. Claiming my values and aspirations in conversation with them—knowing that they heard me, in deep and meaningful ways—gave me the strength to claim what was most important to me, publicly and professionally. I had never felt comfortable in the Political Science Department, where misogyny and homophobia seemed always to run just below the surface of collegial relationships, occasionally bursting forth in ugly interactions with colleagues that left me feeling vulnerable, alienated, and alone. When I became Director of Women's Studies—which at the time had only one full-time faculty appointment, although today we have eight full-time professors—it seemed, for the first three years, as though I were doing two full-time jobs. I was working hard to be a productive member of the Political Science Department at the same time that I was working overtime to build and strengthen Women's Studies, to which I was deeply committed. I was afraid I would burn out from all the stress.

For the first time in my life I was able to see that I had choices and the power to change things. I recalled a conversation with Linda and Frida in which I had whined about never having had such choices, offering a litany of examples; they had challenged me to rethink my interpretations and suggested that perhaps I had not been so entirely powerless as I'd thought. Although at the time I argued against their interpretation, I now saw the truth in it. I realized that although I did not want to leave DePaul, remaining in Political Science would be debilitating. Once I was clear about that, I formulated a plan. I sought the support of Women's Studies colleagues in requesting that my appointment be transferred over to the Program. Since both Political Science and Women's Studies had reviewed and supported my tenure, the Dean could readily make this shift. I've been full time in what is now the Women's and Gender Studies Program for four years; had it not been for our work on this book, I would never have found the courage to imagine, let alone bring about, such a change.

At several points throughout this book, Beth spoke of her having made frequent moves—both with her family as a "service brat" and subsequently, as an independent adult. Our conversations were replete with her sense that as much as she longed for a home of her own, she would never be in a financial position to afford one. When we began this project, "being able to do laundry in her nightgown" was a cherished, yet seemingly impossible, dream. However, things are different today. As Beth put it:

A miracle happened. It didn't come directly out of this project, but it has powerful connections to the work, nonetheless. Two years after we began work on this book, my living situation became untenable. I was renting an apartment in a fifty-year-old complex in a suburb that was an hour's commute from DePaul.

The buildings were originally built to house returning veterans from Korea and World War Two, and while they had been fairly well maintained, heat was faulty, plumbing dicey, and maintenance sketchy at best. Even worse, homophobic skinheads had moved in downstairs; our common entryway was often "decorated" with homophobic and sexist graffiti. If I asked the management to clean up the graffiti, it reappeared immediately, but more virulently. I was afraid in my home. Finally, with a new shopping center going up across the street, the flat became infested with field mice, and that was the last straw.

I was a wreck; I felt utterly incapable of dealing with the situation. I wanted to move back to Chicago because commuting was awful, but apartment rentals in safe neighborhoods were more than I could afford. Things appeared hopeless until a very good and generous friend intervened. Seeing my distress, he offered to lend me money for a down payment on a condo, help with house hunting, and cosign a mortgage loan if necessary. He had the means to do this; he argued that it was foolish for me to pay rent when, for the same monthly outlay, I could own. As grateful as I was for this offer, my initial inclination was to turn it down. I did not want to accept what felt like charity.

Upon reflection, however, I saw that my friend's offer was precisely in line with what Frida, Linda, and I had been talking about. As a man of independent means, he felt obligated to share them; he had recognized my need and believed he could do something to help—out of his own sense of social justice. His generosity flowed from a moral sensibility akin to Linda's belief that the green peppers in her fridge should be freely shared with a neighbor in need. That was a "Eureka!" moment for me. Until then my class consciousness had been acute, but overly intellectual; I realized that declining this offer would leave me a victim, not of class, but foolish pride. I had been offered a gift that bridged a deep class chasm. Abrogating it would be a denial of the solidarity that I was enacting with Linda and Frida, through our work on this book. If I couldn't be responsible to myself, I nonetheless had to be responsible to them!

Only in retrospect do I understand the power of this. I gratefully accepted the loan; my friend helped me find a flat; this Thanksgiving, I will have owned my home—a modest condo in Chicago's most ethnically diverse neighborhood—for five years, and lived under this roof longer than any other in my life. A while back, I was able to refinance the mortgage and repay the initial loan; today, I enjoy more stability than I could ever have imagined. Best of all—I can do laundry in the buff if I so choose. While one friend provided the means to make this happen, Linda and Frida offered equally important gifts through our work on this book—thus, I was able to turn a rhetoric of solidarity into action, crossing a new kind of bridge.

As profoundly as each of us, individually, has been affected by our experiences working together over the past seven years, we have also learned important lessons about collaboration and dealing with differences that have much broader applicability. It has become fashionable, in the academy and beyond, to emphasize the importance of transnationalism in the world today. The September 11th attacks on the United States highlighted both the ignorance of many Americans about social, cultural, and political worlds beyond their borders and provoked, among many thinking individuals, a sense of urgency about becoming better educated and engaging with an interdependent global society in new and constructive ways. We affirm these concerns. At the same time, we believe that a commitment to transnationalism may well need to begin at home.

Without discounting the importance of a global vision and the imperative of combating U.S. xenophobia, we are often made uncomfortable by the tendency of some who have latched on to concepts of transnationalism to focus on "exotic others" living elsewhere in the world while ignoring equally important issues of difference found closer to hand. It can be relatively easy to read about patterns of discrimination and dehumanization affecting women on the other side of the world; it may be much harder to engage in boundary crossings with the person who sits across the kitchen table. As agents of change, we realize that the challenges of social justice entail not merely confronting particular issues and questions publicly; they also entail the choices we make as actors engaged in the process of such confrontation. We mean here, not just a *rhetorical* commitment to engagement, but a practical, political, ethical commitment that is demonstrated in the *doing*. Thus, the journey matters as much as the arrival—and at times, it may be even more important.

"Two's company; three's a crowd" is a well-worn cliché that we have all understood since high school, at least. After working on this book, however, we have come to understand that in some instances it is productive to draw on another, equally familiar cliché: "The third *person* is the charm!" One of the most significant lessons we learned about communicating across difference, in the end, was that there are limits to dyads—in our case, two individuals, but this might equally well refer to two groups of people who share the same cultural givens or philosophical positions. The most difficult moments in our work were our failures to communicate. In chapter two, we saw how Frida was, ultimately, able to break down an impasse between Beth and Linda in which Linda was speaking psychologically about the need for sexual privacy, while Beth was mounting political arguments against state intervention. Neither could hear what the other was saying, and both were deeply dug into their own positions. Frida, however, was able to recognize and define the problem; her insights pushed the other two to move past the limits of dyadic understanding; while there was no immediate resolution of our differences, all three of us came to view what had been a tense and difficult moment in a new light. This may be the most significant example of the importance of moving beyond dyads or binaries, but it is far from the only such instance, and we take this as evidence—if any more were really needed—of the need to think beyond the narrow logics of the "either/or." Had only two position-alities remained present in that difficult conversation—Linda's and Beth's— we doubt that we would ever have been able to move beyond a tense situa-tion or the personal vulnerabilities and potential emotional damage such failures to communicate may entail. Here we were reminded of Beth's sug-gestion that we go with a "third model" in the early stages of putting this proj-ect together. Whether prescience on Beth's part or happy coincidence, in the end, we agreed that we made the right choice, and for better reasons than we could ever have anticipated.

We are convinced that good will *alone* is insufficient for the hard work of building bridges of understanding across difference. Even with the best of in-tentions, such achievements will not come "naturally"; indeed, it is danger-ous to expect such outcomes. Rather, the work of understanding is a lived and learned experience—involving hard work, patience, and dedication. In the in-stance just cited, the key to moving our conversation forward was Frida's willingness to take on the tasks of meta-discursive analysis. She had to step outside her own involvement in a tense, uncomfortable exchange, analyze what it meant, and articulate her new understanding of the incident in ways that Beth and Linda could both hear and utilize to reach their own fresh un-derstandings of what had transpired. This was no quick and easy solution. "If we are to reach meaningful solidarity," Beth insisted, speaking for all us,

> we have to move beyond slogans, rhetoric, and even "good intentions." We must be willing to engage in the hard work of empathetic listening that is at one and the same time critical and self-critical. We need to find ways of moving beyond the comfort zones, be they individually or collectively framed. There are no safe houses here.

As Linda suggests in her reflection earlier on in this chapter, we each brought deep, sometimes painful family legacies to our work of border crossing— legacies that we all agree we would deny today to our peril. As daughters of di-aspora, however variously expressed, we quickly recognized that we shared an inheritance of what we termed "unconscious cosmopolitanism" embedded within our family histories. We respect all of the rich—and often fascinating— differences in those histories, described in detail in chapter one. However, at the same time, we find several common themes emerging from them: fluid identi-ties, boundary transgressions, and hybridities. These have all served to militate against the full assimilation of individuals within the mainstream, while allow-ing them to incorporate and adapt to the new or different in creative ways. Re-call, for example, the repeated physical displacements, across generations, of Frida's Jewish family and the creative adaptation her father made to the demands of earning a living by selling crucifixes to migrant workers in California. Think of the fascinating and rich mixes of race, ethnicity, and language that shaped Linda's Jamaican family, where "picnee Ivy's dawta" can claim Spanish, Chinese, African, British, and Caribbean inheritances—and then add that to her father's unique blending of Mississippi Delta Blues and Borscht Belt Yiddishisms. Then conjure up the moment when Beth's Russian Jewish grandfather and illiterate Irish grandmother, both passing as "nice English youth," meet on the lawn at Willow Grove Park while John Phillips Sousa's band played on. How could we not embrace and further the moves across borders begun by our progenitors? How could we forget that, for them, such moves were often involuntary, not willed and chosen, as many of our border crossings have been—and will be? Out of their worlds of pain, we have been provided a strong foundation that we consciously affirm and forward: a commitment toward an open, cosmopolitan and humanist approach to dealing with others—as individuals or groups.

Edward Said argues that those who have been exiled from their home country are characterized by a "plurality of vision": "Most people are principally aware of one culture, one setting, one home; exiles are aware of at least two, and this plurality of vision gives rise to an awareness of simultaneous dimensions, an awareness that—to borrow a phrase from music—is contrapuntal."[3] We believe that such a contrapuntal sensibility can also be developed among those who have not traversed national borders. As we have seen, the border crossings we have engaged in and discussed in this book include gender, race, ethnicity, social class, and sexuality, in addition to nationality. As self-conscious and self-critical social actors and moral agents, we have been deeply affected by our backgrounds, but we also rely on our religious, spiritual, ethical, and political commitments to direct our decision making. It is critical to recognize that our engagement in "world traveling" is, finally, volitional. Frida captured some of this complexity when she stated:

I have been committed to moving across difference since my college years. I attribute such orientation to a variety of factors: my transnational migrancy; other border crossings, such as social class and ethnicity; and my commitments to feminism and to the Jewish prophetic tradition, which calls for tikkun olam, *the fixing of, or transforming, the world. My politics are often informed by an urgency to recognize the humanity and, hence, the value, of people across multiple borders. Thus, as a Jew committed to the existence and well-being of the State of Israel, I anguish over the suffering and senseless killing of both Jews and Palestinians in the ongoing Middle East conflict. I support organizations that work for peace, but also for constructive interaction among these two peoples who, after all, are descendants of a common mythic ancestor. As a practicing religious Jew, I choose to have close personal friendships with practicing Christians, and, perhaps less usual, with orthodox Muslims, with whom I engage across our religious and political differences.*

We have also seen that all of us, in the classroom and in our writing, are dedicated to working for the critical embrace of differences, for the recognition of those who are made into "others," and for the social transformation necessary to bring about a more inclusive world. In these ways, we have nurtured a "contrapuntal awareness" in ourselves and have attempted to encourage its development in our students and readers as well.

One of the lessons we take with us as we complete this work is a confirmation of our initial belief that real human beings need to be understood and connected to in concrete ways, in their embodied selves. We have explored at length in preceding chapters the complexities of our own identities and the hybridities that shape us; it has been insufficient for each of us to define herself simply as an abstraction, such as "human being," "individual," or "woman." We aspire, imaginatively, to return to this awareness again and again, recalling the ethnographic-like process that revealed, bit by bit, the fullness of our being to one another. We extend that memory into our daily encounters with family members, colleagues, students, strangers, and friends.

This kind of awareness, along with the reciprocity it assumes in our classrooms or everyday lives, entails hard work—especially if we hope to see it enacted on a more global scale as well. Especially in the wake of 9/11, on a very human level, we feel some urgency about this. We find it is particularly important at this point to keep in mind, as Beth tells her students, that education is not just about "stuff and self" (as we saw in chapter four); it must also be concerned with opening our eyes to how the rest of the world lives. Our vision of education suggests that circles of responsibility—from self and family to city, nation, and beyond—need to be continually assessed and widened. Linda models this perspective in her personal life, through her recognition that, given existing patterns of social privilege and inequality, she must always remember to "send something to Brooklyn" (chapter four). In the past three years, we each have made some educational efforts that advance an internationalizing agenda. For example, with the rise of incidents of harassment against Muslims in the United States, Frida has joined the many faculty members who are introducing units on Islam into their religious studies classes whenever possible. She has also directed a study abroad program in Spain, as Linda has done in South Africa and Beth in Scotland. All three of these programs, in unexpected synchronicity, focus on issues of multiculturalism *within* the internationalist context—something we did not discuss among ourselves before the fact. They look at a variety of constructions of civil society, democracy, religious experience, and culture and how these constructions intersect across cultural, national, and international boundaries.

Our interest in exposing students to those who live beyond their own worlds—physical and metaphoric—brings to mind the following story, recently aired on Chicago's National Public Radio affiliate:

> A woman has a problem with her knee; she cannot sit for very long without extending her leg, otherwise she experiences great discomfort. She finds herself sitting in a bus when, engaged in just such a procedure to relieve her pain, she inadvertently touches, with her toe, the heel of the man sitting in front of her. She notes that the man has flinched at the moment of contact but cannot be certain if this was the actual reason for his physical response. To play it safe, she whispers, "Excuse me." He turns around then and, fixing his gaze upon her, asks her to please pat him on the back three times. Puzzled, she nonetheless complies, even as he continues to look intently into her eyes. "Thank you," he tells her, relieved, relaxing his hold of her gaze before turning around. "I don't need no bad luck today. I don't want to end up in prison today." The woman's reflection on this brief but unusual exchange is unexpected but profound. Perhaps our obligation on meeting strangers, those populating other worlds, she suggests, is not necessarily to understand them; perhaps it is to respond to them, whether or not we understand them.[4]

For us, the storyteller's conclusion—extending respect for the man's personhood—is linked to our responsibility, as educators, of creating a hospitable environment in the classroom, not one that coddles students, but one that invites them into community and solidarity. We do not mean here the kind of "safe space" that encourages the avoidance of tough issues. Rather, we have in mind the kind of context that facilitates empathetic connection between ourselves and our students, among students, and between all of us and the subject matter.[5]

Parker Palmer believes that this kind of connectivity is central to the teaching mission, insofar as education is about "empowerment, liberation, transcendence, and renewing the vitality of life. It is about finding and claiming ourselves and our place in the world." For him, these efforts involve reclaiming the sacred from the kind of knowing that honors "a systematic disconnection of self from the world, self from others." As teachers devoted to our craft, we find his words both daunting and inspiring as a road map for our work: "By recovering the sacred, we might recover our sense of community with each other and with all of creation, the community that Thomas Merton named so wonderfully as the 'hidden wholeness.' I have become increasingly convinced that this recovery of community is at the heart of teaching."[6]

As the inheritors of the legacies and traditions discussed throughout this book—daughters of diaspora and the working class—who have steadfastly refused to give up on the ideal of community even as we have resisted the depredations of "identity politics" in our lives and work as college professors, we would extend Palmer's pedagogical vision. Our argument is, at once, simple and complex: the recovery of community is also at the heart of a feminist, cosmopolitan vision of a world in which human beings, in all their magnificent diversity, can claim their dignity and assert their fundamental right to just, humane, and equitable treatment. It is our hope that, in some small way, the stories and lessons that we have shared in this book can contribute to the realization of that vision.

NOTES

1. Gabriella Ibieta, "Fragmented Memories: An Exile's Return," in Herrera, ed., *ReMembering Cuba*, 78.

2. Beth's friend Kevin first used this phrase over twenty years ago to describe what she *thought* was a stylish new haircut.

3. Edward Said, "The Mind of Winter: Reflections on Life in Exile," *Harper's* (September 1984), 55.

4. This constitutes a loose paraphrase of Karen Christopher's story "Toe Touch," produced by "Hello, Beautiful!" and "Writer's Block," Chicago Public Radio, and broadcast August 8, 2004.

5. In interviews with college students, Palmer discovered that good teachers are seen to have the kind of connective capacity we have just described (Palmer, "The Grace of Great Things," 27).

6. Palmer, "The Grace of Great Things," 27. The reference to Thomas Merton is "Hagia Sophia," in *A Thomas Merton Reader*, Thomas P. McDonnell, ed. (New York: Doubleday, 1989), 506.

Bibliography

Adler, Mortimer J. *The Paideia Proposal: An Educational Manifesto* (New York: Macmillan Publishing, 1982).

Agosín, Marjorie. *Uncertain Travelers: Conversations with Jewish Women Immigrants to America* (Hanover, NH: University Press of New England, 1999).

Ahmad, Aijaz. "The Politics of Literary Postcoloniality." *Race & Class* 36, no. 3 (1995): 1–20.

Allison, Dorothy. *Two or Three Things I Know for Sure* (New York: Dutton, 1995).

Andolsen, Barbara Hilkert, C. E. Gudorf, and M. D. Pellauer, eds. *Women's Consciousness, Women's Conscience: A Reader in Feminist Ethics* (Minneapolis: Winston Press, 1985).

Annas, Pam. "Pass the Cake: The Politics of Gender, Class and Text in the Academic Workplace." In *Working-Class Women in the Academy: Laborers in the Knowledge Factory*, edited by Michelle M. Tokarczyk and Elizabeth A. Fay, 165–78. Amherst: University of Massachusetts Press, 1993.

Anthias, Floya. "New Hybridities, Old Concepts: The Limits of 'Culture.'" *Ethnic and Racial Studies* 24, no. 4 (July 2001): 619–41.

Anzaldúa, Gloria and Analouise Keating, eds. *This Bridge We Call Home: Radical Visions for Transformation* (New York: Routledge, 2002).

Anzaldúa, Gloria. *Borderlands/La Frontera: The New Mestiza* (San Francisco: Spinsters/Aunt Lute, 1987).

——."La conciencia de la mestiza: Toward a New Consciousness." In *Making Face, Making Soul: Haciendo Caras*, edited by Gloria Anzaldúa, 377–89. San Francisco: Aunt Lute Books, 1990.

——, ed. *Making Face, Making Soul: Haciendo Caras* (San Francisco: Aunt Lute Books, 1990).

Apple, Michael. *Teachers and Texts: A Political Economy of Class and Gender Relations in Education* (London: Routledge and Kegan Paul, 1986).

Arendt, Hannah. *The Human Condition* (Chicago: University of Chicago Press, 1958).

Azoulay, Katya Gibel. *Black, Jewish, and Interracial: It's Not the Color of Your Skin, but the Race of Your Kin, and Other Myths of Identity* (Durham, NC: Duke University Press, 1997).

Bakhtin, Mikhail M. *The Dialogic Imagination: Four Essays* (Austin: University of Texas Press, 1981).

Bannerji, Himani. *Thinking Through: Essays on Feminism, Marxism, and Anti-Racism* (Toronto: Women's Press, 1995).

Barvosa-Carter, Edwina. "Multiple Identity and Coalition Building: How Identity Differences within Us Enable Radical Alliances among Us." In *Forging Radical Alliances across Difference: Coalition Politics for the New Millennium*, edited by Jill M. Bystydzienski and Steven P. Schacht, 21–34. Lanham, MD: Rowman & Littlefield, 2001.

Bateson, Mary Catherine. *Composing a Life* (New York: Plume, 1990).

Behar, Ruth. *The Vulnerable Observer: Anthropology that Breaks Your Heart* (Boston: Beacon Press, 1996).

———. *Translated Woman: Crossing the Border with Esperanza's Story* (Boston: Beacon Press, 2003).

Belenky, Mary Field, B. Clinchy, N. Goldberger, and Jill Taruleet. *Women's Ways of Knowing: The Development of Self, Voice, and Mind* (New York: Basic Books, 1986).

Benjamin, Lois, ed. *Black Women in the Academy: Promises and Perils* (Gainesville: University of Florida Press, 1997).

Bérubé, Allan. *Coming Out under Fire: The History of Gay Men and Women in World War Two* (New York: Plume, 1991).

———. "Intellectual Desire." In *Queerly Classed: Gay Men and Lesbians Write about Class*, edited by Susan Raffo, 43–66. Boston: South End Press, 1997.

Bonvillain, Nancy. *Language, Culture and Communication: The Meaning of Messages* (Upper Saddle River, NJ: Prentice Hall, 2000).

Bordo, Susan. *Unbearable Weight: Feminism, Western Culture, and the Body* (Berkeley: University of California Press, 1993).

Bourdieu, Pierre. *Language and Symbolic Power.* Translated by Gino Raymond and Matthew Adamson (Cambridge: Harvard University Press, 1991).

Boyd, Nan Alamilla. *Wide Open Town: A History of Queer San Francisco to 1965* (Berkeley: University of California Press, 2003).

Brah, Avtar. *Cartographies of Diaspora: Contesting Identities* (New York: Routledge, 1996).

Braziel, Jana Evans and Anita Mannur. "Nation, Migration, Globalization: Points of Contention in Diaspora Studies." In *Theorizing Diaspora: A Reader*, edited by J. E. Braziel and A. Mannur, 1–22. Oxford: Blackwell Publishers, 2003.

———, eds. *Theorizing Diaspora: A Reader* (Oxford: Blackwell Publishers, 2003).

Bringle, Mary Louise. *The God of Thinness: Gluttony and Other Weighty Matters* (Nashville: Abingdon Press, 1992).

Brint, Steven and Jerome Karabel, eds. *The Diverted Dream: Community Colleges and the Promise of Educational Opportunity in America, 1980–1985* (New York: Oxford University Press, 1989).

Brock, Rita Nakashima and Susan Brooks Thistlethwaite. *Casting Stones: Prostitution and Liberation in Asia and the United States* (Minneapolis: Augsburg Fortress Press, 1996).

Bronner, Stephen Eric. *Socialism Unbound* (New York: Routledge, 1990).

Brown, Gillian and George Yule. *Discourse Analysis* (Cambridge: Cambridge University Press, 1983).

Brownworth, Victoria A. "Life in the Passing Lane: Exposing the Class Closet." In *Queerly Classed: Gay Men and Lesbians Write about Class*, edited by Susan Raffo, 67–78. Cambridge, MA: South End Press, 1997.

Buber, Martin. *I and Thou*. Translated by Ronald Gregor Smith (New York: Scribner, 2000).

Busman, Deb. "Representations of Working-Class 'Intelligence': Fiction by Jack London, Agnes Smedley, and Valerie Miner, and New Scholarship by Carol Whitehill and Janet Zandy." *Women's Studies Quarterly* 26, nos. 1 & 2 (Spring/Summer 1998), 75–92.

Butler, Judith. *Gender Trouble: Feminism and the Subversion of Identity* (New York: Routledge, 1990).

Card, Claudia, ed. *Feminist Ethics* (Lawrence: University of Kansas Press, 1991).

Cervero, Ronald M., A. L. Wilson, and Associates. *Power in Practice: Adult Education and the Struggle for Knowledge and Power in Society* (San Francisco: Jossey-Bass, 2001).

Chaliand, Gérard and Jean-Pierre Rageau. *The Penguin Atlas of Diaspora*. Translated by A. M. Berrett (New York: Viking, 1995).

Christopher, Karen. *Toe Touch*. Produced by "Hello, Beautiful!" and "Writer's Block." Chicago Public Radio, broadcast August 8, 2004.

Cliffs, Michelle. *Claiming an Identity They Taught Me to Despise* (Watertown, MA: Persephone Press, 1980).

Coates, Jennifer. *Women and Men and Language* (New York: Longman, 1986).

Coe, Richad. *When the Grass Was Taller: Autobiography and the Experience of Childhood* (New Haven, CT: Yale University Press, 1984).

Collins, Patricia Hill. *Black Feminist Thought: Knowledge, Consciousness, and the Politics of Empowerment* (New York: Routledge, 1991).

———. *Fighting Words: Black Women and the Search for Justice* (Minneapolis: University of Minnesota Press, 1998).

———. "Learning from the Outsider within: The Sociological Significance of Black Feminist Thought." *Social Problems* 33, no. 6 (1986): 14–32.

Connors, Jr., Russell B. and Patrick T. McCormick. *Character, Choices and Community: The Three Faces of Christian Ethics* (New York: Paulist Press, 1998).

Cooey, Paula M., Sharon A. Farmer, and Mary Ellen Ross. *Embodied Love: Sensuality and Relationship as Feminist Values* (New York: Harper & Row, 1987).

Cookson Jr., Peter W. and Caroline Hodges Persell. *Preparing for Power: America's Elite Boarding Schools* (New York: Basic Books, 1985).

Cruttenden, Alan. *Intonation* (Cambridge: Cambridge University Press, 1986).

Daloz, Laurent A., C. H. Keen, J. P. Keen, and S. D. Parks. *Common Fire: Leading Lives of Commitment in a Complex World* (Boston: Beacon Press, 1996).

Dews, C. L. Barney and Carolyn Leste Law. *This Fine Place so Far from Home: Voices of Academics from the Working Class* (Philadelphia: Temple University Press, 1995).

Dews, Peter. *Logics of Disintegration: Post-Structuralist Thought and the Claims of Critical Theory* (New York: Verso, 1987).

di Leonardo, Micaela. *The Varieties of Ethnic Experience* (Ithaca, NY: Cornell University Press, 1984).

Douglas, Jack D. "Deviance and Respectability: The Social Construction of Moral Meanings." In *Deviance and Respectability: The Social Construction of Moral Meanings*, edited by Jack D. Douglas, 3–30. New York: Basic Books, 1970.

Ehrenreich, Barbara. *Nickled & Dimed: On (Not) Getting by in America* (New York: Henry Holt and Company, 2001).

Enloe, Cynthia. *Maneuvers: The International Politics of Militarizing Women's Lives* (Berkeley: University of California Press, 2000).

Eskridge, Jr., William N. *Gaylaw: Challenging the Apartheid of the Closet* (Cambridge, MA: Harvard University Press, 1999).

Etter-Lewis, Gwendolyn and Michéle Foster, eds. *Unrelated Kin: Ethnic Identity and Gender in Women's Personal Narratives* (New York: Routledge, 1995).

Firmat, Gustavo Pérez. *Next Year in Cuba: A Cubano's Coming of Age in America* (New York: Anchor Books, 1995).

Freeman, Phyllis R. and Jan Zlotnick Schmidt, eds. *Wise Women: Reflections of Teachers at Midlife* (New York: Routledge, 2000).

Freeman-Moir, John and Alan Scott, eds. *Yesterday's Dreams: International and Critical Perspectives on Education and Social Class* (Canterbury, NZ: University of Canterbury Press, 2003).

Freire, Paulo and Donaldo P. Macedo. "A Dialogue: Culture, Language, and Race," *Harvard Education Review* 65, no. 3 (Fall 1995): 377–402.

Freire, Paulo, Donaldo P. Macedo, and Ann E. Berthoff. *Literacy: Reading the Word and the World* (Westport, CT: Bergin & Garvey, 1987).

Frost, Linda. "'Somewhere in Particular': Generations, Feminism, Class Conflict, and the Terms of Academic Success." In *Generations: Academic Feminists in Dialogue*, edited by Devoney Looser and E. Ann Kaplan, 219–36. Minneapolis: University of Minneapolis Press, 1997.

Furman, Frida Kerner. *Beyond Yiddishkeit: The Struggle for Jewish Identity in a Reform Synagogue* (Albany: State University of New York Press, 1987; reprinted by University Press of America, Lanham: MD, 1994).

———. *Facing the Mirror: Older Women and Beauty Shop Culture* (New York: Routledge, 1997).

———. "The Long Road Home: Migrant Experience and the Construction of the Self." In *Psychological, Political, and Cultural Meanings of Home*, edited by Miriam Ben-Yoseph and Mechthild Hart. Binghampton, NY: The Haworth Press, 2005. Forthcoming.

———. "There Are No Old Venuses: Older Women's Responses to Their Aging Bodies." In *Mother Time: Women, Aging, and Ethics*, edited by Margaret Urban Walker, 7–22. New York: Rowman & Littlefield, 1999.

——. "Women, Aging, and Ethics: Reflections on Bodily Experience." *The Annual of the Society of Christian Ethics* (1994): 229–54.

Gee, James Paul. *Social Linguistics and Literacies: Ideology in Discourses* (2nd edition, London: Taylor and Francis, 1996).

Gerth, Hans and C. Wright Mills, eds. *From Max Weber: Essays in Sociology* (New York: Oxford University Press, 1958).

——. "Introduction: The Man and His Work, I. A Biographical View." In *From Max Weber: Essays in Sociology*, edited by H. Gerth and C. W. Mills, 3–31. New York: Oxford University Press, 1958.

Gilligan, Carol. *In a Different Voice: Psychological Theory and Women's Development* (Cambridge: Harvard University Press, 1982).

Gilroy, Paul. "Diaspora and the Detours of Identity." In *Identity and Difference*, edited by Kathryn Woodward, 299–343. London: Sage, 1997.

——. *The Black Atlantis: Modernity and Double Consciousness* (Cambridge, MA: Harvard University Press, 1993).

Glazer, Steven, ed. *The Heart of Learning: Spirituality in Education* (New York: Putnam, 1999).

Goldberger, Nancy Rule, Mary Field Belenky, Jill Mattuck Tarule, and Blythe McVicker Clinchy. *Knowledge, Difference, and Power: Essays Inspired by Women's Ways of Knowing* (New York: Basic Books, 1996).

Goleman, Daniel. *Emotional Intelligence* (New York: Bantam Books, 1995).

Gort, Jerald D. "Liberative Ecumenism: Gateway to the Sharing of Religious Experience Today." In *On Sharing Religious Experience: Possibilities of Interfaith Mutuality*, edited by Jerald D. Gort, H. M. Vroom, R. Fernhout, and A. Wessels, 88–105. Grand Rapids, MI: Erdmans Publishing, 1992.

Grant, Gerald and David Riesman. *The Perpetual Dream: Reform and Experiment in the American College* (Chicago: University of Chicago Press, 1978).

Gross, Larry. *Contested Closets: The Politics and Ethics of Outing* (Minneapolis: University of Minnesota Press, 1993).

Grossberg, Lawrence. "Identity and Cultural Studies: Is that All There Is?" In *Questions of Cultural Identity*, edited by Stuart Hall and Paul du Gay, 85–107. London: Sage, 1996.

Gumperz, John J. *Discourse Strategies* (Cambridge: Cambridge University Press, 1982).

——, ed. *Language and Social Identity* (Cambridge: Cambridge University Press, 1982).

Habermas, Jürgen. *The Philosophical Discourse of Modernity: Twelve Lectures*. Translated by Frederick Lawrence (Cambridge, MA: The MIT Press, 1987).

Hall, Stuart. "Cultural Identity and Diaspora." In *Identity and Difference*, edited by Kathryn Woodward, 51–59. London: Sage, 1997.

Hallie, Philip P. "Camus's Hug." *American Scholar* 64, no. 3 (Summer 1995): 428–35.

——. *Lest Innocent Blood Be Shed: The Story of the Village of Le Chambon and How Goodness Happened There* (New York: Harper & Row, 1979).

——. "Scepticism, Narrative, and Holocaust Ethics." *The Philosophical Forum* 16, nos. 1–2 (Fall–Winter 1984–85): 45.

———. *Tales of Good and Evil, Help and Harm* (New York: HarperPerennial, 1998).

Hamel, Ronald P. and Kenneth R. Himes, eds. *Introduction to Christian Ethics: A Reader* (New York: Paulist Press, 1989).

Hamilton, Lise. "My Grandmother Died Last Night." In *Picturing Us*, edited by Deborah Willis, 3–30. New York: New Press, 1994.

Hanh, Thich Nhat. *Peace Is Every Step: The Path of Mindfulness in Everyday Life* (New York: Bantam, 1991).

Haraway, Donna Jeanne. *Simians, Cyborgs, and Women: The Reinvention of Nature* (New York: Routledge, 1991).

Hart, Mechthild. "Transforming Boundaries of Power in the Classroom: Learning from *La Mestiza*." In *Power in Practice: Adult Education and the Struggle for Knowledge and Power in Society*, edited by Ronald M. Cervero, A. L. Wilson, and Associates, 164–83. San Francisco: Jossey-Bass, 2001.

Hartman, Joan E. "Telling Stories: The Construction of Women's Agency." In *(En)Gendering Knowledge: Feminists in Academe*, edited by Joan E. Hartman and Ellen Messer-Davidow, 11–33. Knoxville: University of Tennessee Press, 1991.

Hartman, Joan E. and Ellen Messer-Davidow, eds. *(En)Gendering Knowledge: Feminists in Academe* (Knoxville: University of Tennessee Press, 1991).

Hauerwas, Stanley. "Towards an Ethics of Character." In *Introduction to Christian Ethics: A Reader*, edited by Ronald P. Hamel and Kenneth R. Himes, 151–61. (New York: Paulist Press, 1989).

Hennessy, Rosemary. "Desire as a Class Act: Lesbian in Late Capitalism." In *Profit and Pleasure: Sexual Identities in Late Capitalism*, edited by Rosemary Hennessy, 175–202. New York: Routledge, 2000.

Herrera, Andrea O'Reilly, ed. *ReMembering Cuba: Legacy of a Diaspora* (Austin: University of Texas Press, 2001).

Heschel, Abraham Joshua. *God in Search of Man* (Reprint edition, New York: Noonday Press, 1976).

———. *Man Is Not Alone* (Reprint edition, New York: Noonday Press, 1976).

Hoggart, Richard. *The Uses of Literacy* (London: Chatto and Windus, 1957).

Holler, Linda. *Erotic Morality: The Role of Touch in Moral Agency* (New Brunswick, NJ: Rutgers University Press, 2002).

hooks, bell. "Ecstasy: Teaching and Learning without Limits." In *Wise Women: Reflections of Teachers at Midlife*, edited by Phyllis R. Freeman and Jan Zlotnick Schmidt, 173–77. New York: Routledge, 2000.

———. "Embracing Freedom: Spirituality and Liberation." In *The Heart of Learning: Spirituality in Education*, edited by Steven Glazer and H. Smith, 113–29. New York: Putnam, 1998.

———. *Feminist Theory: From Margin to Center* (Boston: South End Press, 1984).

———. "Keeping Close to Home: Class and Education." In *Working-Class Women in the Academy: Laborers in the Knowledge Factory*, edited by Michelle M. Tokarczyk and Elizabeth A. Fay, 99–111. Amherst: University of Massachusetts Press, 1993.

———. *Talking Back: Thinking Feminist, Thinking Black* (Boston: South End Press, 1989).

———. *Teaching to Transgress: Education as the Practice of Freedom* (New York: Routledge, 1994).

Hymes, Dell. *Foundations in Sociolinguistics: An Ethnographic Approach* (Philadelphia: University of Pennsylvania Press, 1974).

Ibieta, Gabriella. "Fragmented Memories: An Exile's Return." In *ReMembering Cuba: Legacy of a Diaspora*, edited by Andrea O'Reilly Herrera, 69–78. Austin: University of Texas Press 2001.

Ignatiev, Noel. *How The Irish Became White* (New York: Routledge, 1996).

Isasi-Díaz, Ada María. "Toward an Understanding of Feminismo Hispano in the U.S.A." In *Women's Consciousness, Women's Conscience: A Reader in Feminist Ethics*, edited by Barbara Hilkert Andolsen, C. E. Gudorf, and M. D. Pellauer, 51–61. Minneapolis: Winston Press, 1985.

Jones, Charisse and Kumea Shorter-Gooden. *Shifting: The Double Lives of Black Women in America* (New York: Harper Collins, 2004).

Kadi, Joanna. "A Question of Belonging." In *Working-Class Women in the Academy: Laborers in the Knowledge Factory*, edited by Michelle M. Tokarczyk and Elizabeth A. Fay, 87–96. Amherst: University of Massachusetts Press, 1993.

Kalčik, Susan. "'. . . Like Ann's Gynecologist or the Time I Almost Got Raped': Personal Narratives in Women's Rap Groups." In *Women and Folklore*, edited by Claire R. Farrer, 3–11. Austin: University of Texas Press, 1975.

Kazanjian, Jr., Victor H. and Peter L. Laurence, eds. *Education as Transformation: Religious Pluralism, Spirituality, and a New Vision for Higher Education in America* (New York: Peter Lang, 2000).

Keen, James P. "Appreciative Engagement of Diversity: E Pluribus Unum and the EDUCATION as Transformation Project." In *Education as Transformation: Religious Pluralism, Spirituality, and a New Vision for Higher Education in America*, edited by Victor H. Kazanjian, Jr., and Peter L. Laurence, 205–12. New York: Peter Lang, 2000.

Kelly, Elizabeth A. *Education, Democracy, & Public Knowledge* (Boulder, CO: Westview Press, 1995).

———. "A House Made of Words: Class, Education, and Dissidence in Three Lives." In *Yesterday's Dreams: International and Critical Perspectives on Education and Social Class*, edited by John Freeman-Moir and Alan Scott, 248–80. Canterbury, NZ: University of Canterbury Press, 2003.

———. "You Could Throw Them Away Without Breaking Your Heart: My Life in Magazines." In *Talking Back and Acting Out: Women Negotiating the Media across Culture*, edited by Ann Russo and Sandra Jackson. New York: Peter Lang, 2002.

Kelly, Elizabeth A. and Kate Kane. "In Goldilocks' Footsteps: Exploring the Discursive Construction of Gay Masculinity in Bear Magazines." In *Opposite Sex: Lesbians and Gay Men Writing about Each Other's Sexuality*, edited by Eric Rofes and Sara Miles, 66–98. New York: New York University Press, 1998.

Kroeger, Brooke. *Passing: When People Can't Be Who They Are* (New York: Public Affairs, 2003).

Kuipers, Ronald A. "Violent Asymmetry: The Shape of Power in the Current Debate over the Morality of Homosexuality." In *Towards an Ethics of Community: Negotiations of Difference in a Pluralist Society*, edited by James H. Olthuis, 170–85.

Waterloo, Ontario, Canada: Wilfrid Laurier University Press, 2000.

Kumar, Amitava, ed. *Class Issues: Pedagogy, Cultural Studies, and the Public Sphere* (New York: New York University Press, 1997).

Kumar, Krishan. "'Englishness' and English National Identity." In *British Cultural Studies: Geography, Nationality, and Identity*, edited by David Morley and Kevin Robins, 41–55. Oxford: Oxford University Press, 2002.

Kupperman, Joel J. *Character* (New York: Oxford University Press, 1991).

Lavie, Smadar and Ted Swedenburg, eds. *Displacement, Diaspora, and Geographies of Identity* (Durham, NC: Duke University Press, 1996).

———. "Introduction: Displacement, Diaspora, and Geographies of Identity." In *Displacement, Diaspora, and Geographies of Identity*, edited by Smadar Lavie and Ted Swedenburg, 1–25. Durham, NC: Duke University Press, 1996.

Levinson, Stephen C. *Pragmatics* (Cambridge: Cambridge University Press, 1983).

Lifton, Robert Jay. *Boundaries: Psychological Man in Revolution* (New York: Vintage, 1970).

———. *The Protean Self: Human Resilience in an Age of Fragmentation* (New York: Basic Books, 1993).

Linde, Charlotte. *Life Stories: The Creation of Coherence* (New York: Oxford University Press, 1993).

Lipsitz, George. "Class Consciousness: Teaching about Social Class in Public Universities." In *Class Issues: Pedagogy, Cultural Studies, and the Public Sphere*, edited by Amitava Kumar, 9–21. New York: New York University Press, 1997.

Lorde, Audre. *Zami: A New Spelling of My Name* (New York: Persephone Press, 1982).

Lugones, María. "Playfulness, 'World'-Travelling, and Loving Perception." In *Making Face, Making Soul: Creative and Critical Perspectives by Feminists of Color*, edited by Gloria Anzaldúa, 390–402. San Francisco: Aunt Lute Books, 1990.

May, William F. "The Virtues and Vices of the Elderly." In *What Does It Mean to Grow Old? Reflections from the Humanities*, edited by Thomas R. Cole and S. A. Gadow, 43–61. Durham, NC: Duke University Press, 1986.

Mayberry, Katherine J. *Teaching What You're Not: Identity Politics in Higher Education* (New York: New York University Press, 1996).

McKenney, Mary. "Class Attitudes & Professionalism." In *Building Feminist Theory: Essays from Quest*, edited by Quest Book Committee, 139–48. New York: Longman, 1981.

Merton, Thomas. *A Thomas Merton Reader*. Edited by Thomas P. McDonnell (New York: Doubleday, 1989).

Meyer, Leisa D. *Creating G.I. Jane: Sexuality and Power in the Women's Army Corps during World War II* (New York: Columbia University Press, 1996).

Meyers, Diana Tietjens. *Feminists Rethink the Self* (Boulder, CO: Westview Press, 1997).

Miles, Margaret R. *Carnal Knowing: Female Nakedness and Religious Meaning in the Christian West* (New York: Vintage Books, 1989).

Miner, Valerie. "Writing and Teaching with Class." In *Working-Class Women in the Academy: Laborers in the Knowledge Factory*, edited by Michelle M. Tokarczyk and Elizabeth A. Fay, 73–86. Amherst: University of Massachusetts Press, 1993.

Mohanty, Chandra. "Cartographies of Struggle: Third World Women and the Politics of Feminism." In *Third World Women and the Politics of Feminism*, edited by Chandra Mohanty, Ann Russo, and Lourdes Torres, 1–47. Bloomington: Indiana University Press, 1991.

Mohanty, Chandra, Ann Russo, and Lourdes Torres, eds. *Third World Women and the Politics of Feminism* (Bloomington: Indiana University Press, 1991).

Montgomery, David. *The Fall of the House of Labor: The Workplace, the State, and American Labor Activism, 1865–1925* (Cambridge: Cambridge University Press, 1987).

Morrison, Toni. *Beloved* (New York: Signet/Penguin Books, 1991).

Narayan, Uma. "Essence of Culture and a Sense of History: A Feminist Critique of Cultural Essentialism." In *Decentering the Center: Philosophy for a Multicultural, Postcolonial, and Feminist World*, edited by Uma Narayan and Sandra Harding, 80–100. Bloomington: Indiana University Press, 2000.

Narayan, Uma and Sandra Harding, eds. *Decentering the Center: Philosophy for a Multicultural, Postcolonial, and Feminist World* (Bloomington: Indiana University Press, 2000).

Nelson, Linda Williamson. "A Co-constructed Narrative: Shared Memory, Recognition and the Reconstruction of Community in *Beloved*." Paper presented at the Second Biennial Conference of the Toni Morrison Society: Toni Morrison and the Meanings of Home, Lorain, OH, September 28–October 1, 2000.

———. "Begging the Question and Switching Codes: Insider and Outsider Discourse of African American Women." In *Black Women in the Academy: Promises and Perils*, edited by Lois Benjamin, 124–33. Gainesville: University of Florida Press, 1997.

———. "Codeswitching in the Oral Life Narratives of African American Women: Challenges to Linguistic Hegemony." Special issue, *Boston University Journal of Education*, no. 3 (1990): 142–55.

———. "Hands in the Chit'lins': Notes on Native Anthropological Research among African American Women." In *Unrelated Kin: Ethnic Identity and Gender in Women's Personal Narratives*, edited by Gwendolyn Etter-Lewis and Michele Foster, 183–99. New York: Routledge, 1995.

Noddings, Nel. *Caring: A Feminine Approach to Ethics and Moral Education* (Berkeley: University of California Press, 1984).

Nussbaum, Martha C. *Upheavals of Thought: The Intelligence of Emotions* (New York: Cambridge University Press, 2001).

Oakes, Jeannie. *Keeping Track: How Schools Structure Inequality* (New Haven, CT: Yale University Press, 1985).

Olthuis, James H., ed. *Towards an Ethics of Community: Negotiations of Difference in a Pluralist Society* (Waterloo, Ontario, Canada: Wilfrid Laurier University Press, 2000).

Palmer, Parker J. "Evoking the Spirit of Public Education." *Educational Leadership* 56, no. 4 (December 1998/January 1999): 6.

———. *The Courage to Teach: Exploring the Inner Landscape of a Teacher's Life* (San Francisco: Jossey-Bass Publishers, 1998).

———. "The Grace of Great Things: Reclaiming the Sacred in Knowing, Teaching, and Learning." In *The Heart of Learning: Spirituality in Education*, edited by Steven Glazer and H. Smith, 15–32. New York: Putnam, 1998.

Perry, Theresa and Lisa Delpit. *The Real Ebonics Debate: Power, Language, and the Education of African-American Children* (Boston: Beacon Press, 1998).

Phillips, Kevin. *Wealth and Democracy: A Political History of the American Rich* (New York: Broadway Books, 2002).

Pieterse, Jan Nederveen. "Hybridity, So What? The Anti-hybridity Backlash and the Riddles of Recognition." *Theory, Culture & Society* 18, no. 16 (2001): 219–45.

Quest Book Committee, ed. *Building Feminist Theory: Essays from Quest* (New York: Longman, 1981).

Raffo, Susan. "Introduction." In *Queerly Classed: Gay Men and Lesbians Write about Class*, edited by Susan Raffo, 1–8. Boston: South End Press, 1997.

——, ed. *Queerly Classed: Gay Men and Lesbians Write about Class* (Boston: South End Press, 1997).

Reagon, Bernice Johnson. "Coalition Politics: Turning the Century." In *Home Girls: A Black Feminist Anthology*, edited by Barbara Smith, 356–68. New York: Kitchen Table/Women of Color Press, 1983.

Remen, Rachel Naomi. "Educating for Mission, Meaning, and Compassion." In *The Heart of Learning: Spirituality in Education*, edited by Steven Glazer and H. Smith, 33–49. New York: Putnam, 1998.

Rich, Adrienne. *Poems: Selected and New 1950–1974* (New York: Norton, 1975).

——. *The Fact of a Doorframe: Poems Selected and New 1950–1984* (New York: Norton, 1984).

——. "When We Dead Awaken: Writing as Re-Vision." In *On Lies, Secrets, and Silence: Selected Prose 1966–1978*, edited by Adrienne Rich, 33–49. New York: W.W. Norton & Company, 1979.

Rodriguez, Richard. *Hunger of Memory: The Education of Richard Rodriguez* (Boston: David R. Godine, 1982).

Rofes, Eric and Sara Miles, eds. *Opposite Sex: Lesbians and Gay Men Writing about Each Other's Sexuality* (New York: New York University Press, 1998).

Roof, Wade Clark. "Religious Borderlands: Challenges for Future Study." *Journal for the Scientific Study of Religion* 37, no. 1 (1998): 1–14.

——. *Spiritual Marketplace: Baby Boomers and the Remaking of American Religion* (Princeton, NJ: Princeton University Press, 1999).

Rorty, Richard. *Contingency, Irony, and Solidarity* (Cambridge, MA: Cambridge University Press, 1989).

Rubin, Lillian A. *Worlds of Pain: Life in the Working-Class Family* (Reprint, New York: Basic Books, 1992).

Ruether, Rosemary Radford. *Gaia and God: An Ecofeminist Theology of Earth Healing* (New York: HarperCollins, 1992).

——. *Women Healing Earth: Third World Women on Ecology, Feminism, and Religion* (Maryknoll, NY: Orbis Books, 1996).

Rushdie, Salman. *Imaginary Homelands: Essays and Criticism 1981–1991* (London: Granta Books, 1991).

Russell, Kathy, Midge Wilson, and Ronald Hall. *The Color Complex* (New York: Doubleday, 1993).

Russo, Ann and Sandra Jackson, eds. *Talking Back and Acting Out: Women Negotiating the Media across Culture* (New York: Peter Lang, 2002).

Ryan, Jake and Charles Sackrey, eds. *Strangers in Paradise: Academics from the Working Class* (Lanham, MD: University Press of America, 1996).

Said, Edward. "The Mind of Winter: Reflections on Life in Exile." *Harper's* 55 (September 1984), 49–55.

Sandler, Kathe. "Finding a Space for Myself in My Film about Color Consciousness." In *Picturing Us*, edited by Deborah Willis, 3–30. New York: New Press, 1994.

Scales-Trent, Judy. *Notes of a White Black Woman: Race, Color, Community* (University Park: Pennsylvania State Press, 1995).

Sennett, Richard and Jonathan Cobb. *The Hidden Injuries of Class* (Reprint, New York: Norton, 1993).

Smith, Barbara, ed. *Home Girls: A Black Feminist Anthology* (New York: Kitchen Table/Women of Color Press, 1983).

Smith, Sidonie. "Performativity, Autobiographical Practice, Resistance." In *Women, Autobiography, Theory: A Reader*, edited by Sidonie Smith and Julia Watson, 108–15. Madison: University of Wisconsin Press, 1998.

Smith, Sidonie and Julia Watson, eds. *Women, Autobiography, Theory: A Reader* (Madison: University of Wisconsin Press, 1998).

Smitherman-Donaldson, Geneva. *Talkin and Testifyin: The Language of Black America* (Boston: Houghton Mifflin Company, 1977).

Sowinska, Suzanne. "Yer Own Motha Wouldna Reckanized Ya: Surviving an Apprenticeship in the 'Knowledge Factory.'" In *Working-Class Women in the Academy: Laborers in the Knowledge Factory*, edited by Michelle M. Tokarczyk and Elizabeth A. Fay, 148–61. Amherst: University of Massachusetts Press, 1993.

Steger, Manfred B. *Globalism: The New Market Ideology* (New York: Rowman & Littlefield, 2002).

Stein, Gertrude. *Everybody's Autobiography* (London: Virago Press, 1985).

Stivers, Camilla. "Reflections on the Role of Personal Narrative in Social Science." *Signs* 18, no. 2 (Winter 1993): 408–25.

Stone-Mediatore, Shari. "Chandra Mohanty and the Revaluing of 'Experience.'" In *Decentering the Center: Philosophy for a Multicultural, Postcolonial, and Feminist World*, edited by Uma Narayan and Sandra Harding, 110–27. Bloomington: Indiana University Press, 2000.

Sweet Honey in the Rock. *Feel Something Drawing Me On*. Flying Fish Records, 1989.

Tannen, Deborah. *Gender and Discourse* (New edition, New York: Oxford University Press, 1990).

Tatum, Beverly Daniel. "Changing Lives: Building a Capacity for Connection in a Pluralistic Context." In *Education as Transformation: Religious Pluralism, Spirituality, and a New Vision for Higher Education in America*, edited by Victor H. Kazanjian, Jr., and Peter L. Laurence, 79–88. New York: Peter Lang, 2000.

Tillich, Paul. *Dynamics of Faith* (New York: Harper & Row, 1957).

Tisdell, Elizabeth J. *Exploring Spirituality and Culture in Adult and Higher Education* (San Francisco: Jossey-Bass, 2003).

——. "Poststructural Feminist Pedagogies: The Possibilities and Limitations of Feminist Emancipatory Adult Learning Theory and Practice." *Adult Education Quarterly* 48, no. 3 (Spring 1998), 139–56.

Tokarczyk, Michelle M. and Elizabeth A. Fay, eds. *Working-Class Women in the Academy: Laborers in the Knowledge Factory* (Amherst: University of Massachusetts Press, 1993).

Turner, Victor. "Social Dramas and Stories about Them." In *On Narrative*, edited by W. J. T. Mitchell, 137–64. Chicago: University of Chicago Press, 1981.

Valdés, Gina. *Puentes y Fronteras: Coplas Chicanas* (Los Angeles: Castle Lithograph, 1982).

Van Gennep, Arnold. "Rukujo's Jealousy: Liminality and the Performative Genres." In *The Anthropology of Performance*, edited by Victor Turner, 99–122. New York: AJ Publishing, 1988.

Von Drehle, David. *Triangle: The Fire that Changed America* (New York: Grove Press, 2003).

Wade-Gayles, Gloria Jean, ed. *My Soul Is a Witness: African-American Women's Spirituality* (Boston: Beacon Press, 1995).

Walker, Christian. "Gazing Colored: A Family Album." In *Picturing Us*, edited by Deborah Willis, 65–70. New York: New Press, 1994.

Wendell, Susan. *The Rejected Body: Feminist Philosophical Reflections on Disability* (New York: Routledge, 1996).

Werbner, Pnina and Tariq Modood. *Debating Cultural Hybridity: Multi-Cultural Identities and the Politics of Anti-Racism* (London: Zed Books, 1997).

Williams, Patricia J. *The Alchemy of Race and Rights* (Reprint edition, Cambridge, MA: Harvard University Press, 1991).

——. *The Rooster's Egg: On the Persistence of Prejudice* (Cambridge: Harvard University Press, 1995).

Willis, Deborah. *Picturing Us* (New York: New Press, 1994).

Willis, Paul E. *Learning to Labor*. (New York: Columbia University Press, 1981).

——. *Learning to Labor: How Working-Class Kids Get Working-Class Jobs* (New York: Columbia University Press, 1977).

Woodward, Kathryn. "Concepts of Identity and Difference." In *Identity and Difference*, edited by Kathryn Woodward, 7–50. London: Sage, 1997.

——, ed. *Identity and Difference* (London: Sage, 1997).

Woolf, Virginia. *Three Guineas* (San Diego: Harcourt Trade Publishers, 1963).

Wuthnow, Robert. *After Heaven: Spirituality in America since the 1950s* (Berkeley: University of California Press, 1998).

——. *Creative Spirituality: The Way of the Artist* (Berkeley: University of California Press, 2001).

Zandy, Janet, ed. *Calling Home: Working-Class Women's Writings: An Anthology* (New Brunswick, NJ: Rutgers University Press, 1990).

——. *Liberating Memory: Our Work and Our Working-Class Consciousness* (New Brunswick, NJ: Rutgers University Press, 1995).

Index

About the Authors

Frida Kerner Furman is professor in the department of religious studies at DePaul University. Her research and teaching interests include social and feminist ethics, women and religion, and sociocultural understandings of the body. She is the author of *Beyond Yiddishkeit: The Struggle for Jewish Identity in a Reform Synagogue* and *Facing the Mirror: Older Women and Beauty Shop Culture*, which received the 1997 Elli Kongas-Maranda Prize of the American Folklore Society/Women's Section. She has also contributed her work to professional journals and edited collections. She lives in Chicago with her husband, Roy Furman, and is the proud mother of an adult daughter, Daniella Furman.

Elizabeth A. Kelly is associate professor in the women's and gender studies program at DePaul University. A political theorist by training and feminist by affinity, she has long been interested in issues of class, gender, education, and democracy. She was a founding member of the women's studies program at her undergraduate college and for six years served as director of DePaul's women's studies program. Her book *Education, Democracy, and Public Knowledge* received the Michael Harrington Award from the New Political Science Section of the American Political Science Association. She has also contributed chapters to several edited collections. She lives in Chicago.

Linda Williamson Nelson, a linguistic anthropologist, is an associate professor at the Richard Stockton College of New Jersey, where she recently joined the anthropology faculty after teaching in the writing program for many years. Her teaching and research are centered on constructions of gender and ethnic identities in written and spoken discourse, life history in ethnography, and narrative strategies in contemporary African American literature. Her essays have appeared in a number of edited works and journals. Her short story, "The Circle of White," was a 1995 prize winner in a competition sponsored by the Society for Humanistic Anthropology. She lives in Sicklerville, New Jersey. Her two adult children, of whom she is immensely proud, are Sean Randall Anthony, her son, and Robin Gair Nelson, her daughter.